150th 2017

To: Dr & Mrs:
Long term friends dating back to at least 40 years. A friendship that will last into eternity.

From: "Admiral" Joe, Dr Joe, Joe

**The incentive for this book was my family in the present and future generations so that they can know my concept of the philosophy of life. As the book was developed I have included my close friends.
Everyone should read Part Two**

Scriptures for Life

Rear Admiral Joseph Miller

Rear Admiral Joseph Miller

authorHOUSE®

AuthorHouse™
1663 Liberty Drive
Bloomington, IN 47403
www.authorhouse.com
Phone: 1-800-839-8640

© *2012 Rear Admiral Joseph Miller. All rights reserved.*

No part of this book may be reproduced, stored in a retrieval system, or transmitted by any means without the written permission of the author.

Published by AuthorHouse 9/19/2012

ISBN: 978-1-4772-7125-4 (sc)
ISBN: 978-1-4772-7124-7 (hc)
ISBN: 978-1-4772-7123-0 (e)

Library of Congress Control Number: 2012917362

Any people depicted in stock imagery provided by Thinkstock are models, and such images are being used for illustrative purposes only. Certain stock imagery © *Thinkstock.*

This book is printed on acid-free paper.

Because of the dynamic nature of the Internet, any web addresses or links contained in this book may have changed since publication and may no longer be valid. The views expressed in this work are solely those of the author and do not necessarily reflect the views of the publisher, and the publisher hereby disclaims any responsibility for them.

Rear Admiral Joseph and Cathy Miller

"Two are better than one; because they have a good reward for their labor."

Ecclesiastes 4: 9

Part I

Scripture That Has Inspired Me
And
Given Me Comfort

Part II

Some Criteria For The Development
Of
Character

Part I

Scripture That Has Inspired Me
And
Given Me Comfort

Dedication

This book is written for my family and my friends hoping they will be further inspired by these Scriptures as I am.

I am inspired by the magnanimity (The word with the highest description in the English language) of all the Scriptures, but these come to mind at this particular time.

Contents Part 1

Introduction	xv
Scriptures For Life As Selected In The Books Of The Bible.	
Old Testament	1
New Testament	39
How to Prolong Your Days	93
Prayer Does It All	98
The Review Of Prayers In The Old And New Testament	102
Praying in the Old Testament	102
Praying in the New Testament	114
A Review of Prayer of God's Chosen Biblical Leaders	145
Other Scriptural Notes on Prayer	157
All Men Need Prayer:	158
A Prayer for the Unsaved	158
A Soldiers Prayer Before Going into Battle	159
Our Prayer before Meals	161
Prayer for Our Souls	164
A Special Scripture of Comfort from God	165
The Last Verse In God's Word:	166

Introduction

This has been a hazardous review. Through the years I have picked out "my favorite scriptures". Each time after an interval when I read them again they were always inadequate and I had to add more scriptures.

All of God's Word is my favorite. I have had much Biblical experience since I made selections the first time.

Those of you who are critics or negatives, I ask you to do it yourself and let me be blessed by your work. Many people have done this.

I did this for my family and all my friends and other reviewers:

Since it is mostly selected scriptures I promise a blessing to all who read it.
If you are down, it will lift you.
If you feel weak it will strengthen you.
If you feel you are in the dark, it will give you light.
If you feel unloved, it will give you love.
If your courage seems weak it will give you valor.
If you lack truth, it will lead you to God.
If you feel alone, remember the Holy Spirit is within you.

Rear Admiral Joseph Miller

If you say, "Who am I?" read God's Word and learn that you are a little lower than the angels.
If you feel depressed, relax, that word is not in the Bible. It is man made since it is not from above.
If you feel lost in life, remember God is everywhere to lead you.
If you don't feel like a man or woman, don't insult God because you are.
If you feel isolated from the world, call any of my 24 grandchildren and great - grandchildren and you will be cured.

As a start make a list of your favorite Scriptures and then as you study and think about God's Word add to your list. All the Scriptures unless otherwise noted are from the Thompson Chain-Reference Bible, Fifth Improved Edition, King James Version, 2007 B.B. Kirkbride Bible Co.

The Bible: The Best Book Ever

The moon and the stars get their light from the sun. Our firmament of learning and light is from the Bible. (God's Word) It is the only Holy book for Christians. It is the only book filled with history of the lives of holy men. It is the only book where the author proves power over life or death. It is truth, free of falsehood. It is the only Divine Light. The Bible is the only blessed book and the only book that speaks. To have more we must go to the other side of the universe into Heaven. The concept of the time to be born and the time to die is established when we began to live; we began to die.

Scriptures For Life As Selected In The Books Of The Bible. Old Testament

Genesis

1:1 The Creation
The origin of the universe and the human race.

Exodus

The Deliverance
The deliverance and the beginning of Israel on the way to the Promised Land.

By God's power God's people emerged from slavery out of Egypt. Man's reconciliation with God was established through a mediator and covenant.

3:2,4   The Call of Moses
"And the angel of the LORD appeared unto him in a flame of fire out of the midst of a bush: and he looked, and, behold, the bush burned with fire, and the bush was not consumed…And when the LORD saw that he turned aside to see, God called unto him out of the midst of the bush, and said, Moses, Moses. And he said, Here am I."

3:14, 15 "I AM THAT I AM"
"And God said unto Moses, I AM THAT I AM: and he said, Thus shalt thou say unto the children of Israel, I AM hath sent me unto you. And God said moreover unto Moses, Thus shalt thou say unto the children of Israel, The LORD God of your fathers, the God of Abraham, the God of Isaac, and the God of Jacob, hath sent me unto you: **<u>this is my name for ever, and this is my memorial unto all generations</u>**."

The water from the Rock 17:6,
"Behold, I will stand before thee there upon the rock in Horeb; and thou shalt smite the rock, and there shall come water out of it, that the people may drink. And Moses did so in the sight of the elders of Israel." (The Rock was Christ; the Water was the Living Water.) "And did all drink the same spiritual drink: for they drank of that spiritual Rock that followed them: and that Rock was Christ." (I Corinthians 10:4)

31:3 The Workmen
"And I have filled him with the spirit of God, in wisdom, and

in understanding, and in knowledge, and in all manner of workmanship."

"For had ye believed Moses, ye would have believed me: for he wrote of me." (John 5:46)

NUMBERS

Unbelief and murmuring bars the entrance to abundant life. The 40 Years of wandering was in the wilderness. The whole generation was doomed due to disbelief!

14:29 "Your carcases shall fall in this wilderness; and all that were numbered of you, according to your whole number, from twenty years old and upward, which have murmured against me."

The book of Numbers is summarized in the Psalms, and in Hebrews.

"Forty years long was I grieved with this generation, and said, It is a people that do err in their heart, and they have not known my ways: Unto whom I sware in my wrath that they should not enter into my rest." (Psalms 95:10,11)

"Harden not your hearts, as in the provocation, in the day of temptation in the wilderness: When your fathers tempted me, proved me, and saw my works forty years. Wherefore I was grieved with that generation, and said, They do always err in their heart; and they have not known my ways. So I sware in my wrath, They shall not enter into my rest." (Hebrews 3:8-11)

"For had ye believed Moses, ye would have believed me: for he wrote of me." (John 5:46) **This was a warning from Jesus to believe Moses and also Him.**

Rear Admiral Joseph Miller

Deuteronomy

(Has been called the Fifth Book of Moses)

Deuteronomy 32:15-20

[15] But Jeshurun waxed fat, and kicked: thou art waxen fat, thou art grown thick, thou art covered with fatness; then he forsook God which made him, and lightly esteemed the Rock of his salvation.

[16] They provoked him to jealousy with strange gods, with abominations provoked they him to anger.

[17] They sacrificed unto devils, not to God; to gods whom they knew not, to new gods that came newly up, whom your fathers feared not.

[18] Of the Rock that begat thee thou art unmindful, and hast forgotten God that formed thee.

[19] And when the LORD saw it, he abhorred them, because of the provoking of his sons, and of his daughters.

[20] And he said, I will hide my face from them, I will see what their end shall be: for they are a very froward generation, children in whom is no faith.

Read ***Matthew Henry's Commentary*** the oldest and best Bible commentary since 1706. Spurgeon, Hobbs, Truett, etc recommended it. My copy was printed in April, 2002. This is a direct quote concerning Israel in **Deuteronomy 32:15-20. It describes us in 2012.**

This is a story of a dying nation when they became rich, prosperous, obese, and deserted God: (Matthew Henry)
"Security and sensuality, pride and insolence, and the other common abuses of plenty and prosperity, verse 15. These people were called Jeshurun-an upright people (so some), a seeing people, so others: but they soon lost the reputation of their knowledge and of their righteousness; for, being well-fed. They waxed fat, and grew thick, that is, they indulged themselves in all manner of luxury and **gratifications of their appetites**, as if they had nothing to do but to make provision for the flesh, to fulfil the lusts of it. They grew fat, that is, they grew big and unwieldy, unmindful of business, and **unfit for it; dull and stupid, careless and senseless**; and this was the effect of their plenty. (Thus the prosperity

of fools destroys them, Proverbs 1:32.) **Yet this was not the worst of it**. They kicked; they grew proud and insolent, and lifted up the heel even against God himself. If God rebuked them, either by his prophets or by his providence, they kicked against the goad, (A rod, used to stimulate them to move.) as an untamed heifer, or a bullock unaccustomed to the yoke, and in their rage persecuted the prophets, and flew in the face of providence itself. And thus he forsook God that made him (not paying due respect to his Creator, nor answering the ends of his creation), and **put an intolerable contempt upon the rock of his salvatio**n, as if he were not indebted to him for any past favours, nor had any dependence upon him for the future. **Those that make a god of themselves and a god of their bellies**, in pride and wantonness, and **cannot bear to be told of it**, certainly **thereby forsake God and show how lightly they esteem him**."

Deuteronomy is repetition of the laws given to Israel since the laws were given in Leviticus.
Key Thought: The divine requirement of obedience

10:12-13 "And now, Israel, **what doth the LORD thy God require of thee**, but to fear the LORD thy God, to walk in all his ways, and to love him, and to serve the LORD thy God with all thy heart and with all thy soul, To keep the commandments of the LORD, and his statutes, which I command thee this day for thy good?"
God's great requirement of obedience.

15:10 "Thou shalt surely give him, and thine heart shall not be grieved when thou givest unto him: because that for this thing the LORD thy God shall bless thee in all thy works, and in all that thou puttest thine hand unto."

4:5-8 "Behold, I have taught you statutes and judgments, even as the LORD my God commanded me, that ye should do so in the land whither ye go to possess it. Keep therefore and do them; for this is your wisdom and your understanding in the sight of the nations, which

shall hear all these statutes, and say, Surely this great nation is a wise and understanding people. For what nation is there so great, who hath God so nigh unto them, as the **LORD our God is in all things** that we call upon him for? And what nation is there so great, that hath statutes and judgments so righteous as all this law, which I set before you this day?"
God teaches us. Obedience

6:4-12 **Our to be testimony**
6:4-5 is the Shema. The most quoted verses in the Old Testament. It is also found in Deuteronomy 11:13-21 and Numbers: 15:37-41.

(Jesus quoted Deuteronomy 6:4-5 in Mark 12:28-30)
"Hear, O Israel: The LORD our God is one LORD:
And thou shalt love the LORD thy God with all thine heart, and with all thy soul, and with all thy might. And these words, which I command thee this day, shall be in thine heart: And thou shalt teach them diligently unto thy children, and shalt talk of them when thou sittest in thine house, and when thou walkest by the way, and when thou liest down, and when thou risest up. And thou shalt bind them for a sign upon thine hand, and they shall be as frontlets between thine eyes. And thou shalt write them upon the posts of thy house, and on thy gates."

"And it shall be, when the LORD thy God shall have brought thee into the land which he sware unto thy fathers, to Abraham, to Isaac, and to Jacob, to give thee great and goodly cities, which thou buildedst not, And houses full of all good things, which thou filledst not, and wells digged, which thou diggedst not, vineyards and olive trees, which thou plantedst not; when thou shalt have eaten and be full; **Then beware lest thou forget the LORD**, which brought thee forth out of the land of Egypt, from the house of bondage."

The Song of Moses (Deuteronomy 32:1-43)

The verse to remember in military combat:

33:27 "The eternal God is thy refuge, and underneath are the everlasting arms: and he shall thrust out the enemy from before thee; and shall say, Destroy them."

Joshua

(Shows good leadership with success.)
Joshua replaced Moses as leader. Moses led Israel out of Egypt; Joshua led Israel into Canaan, the Promised Land. Joshua is the Old Testament name for Jesus. Joshua means the **"*Lord is Salvation.*"** Joshua saved God's people from the Canaanites and Jesus saves them from their sins. Joshua was the general of the armies. His power is thought to have come from the Lord of Hosts. Joshua is also along with Christ (Hebrews 2:10) captain of our salvation and a commander of the people.

The conquest of Canaan under the leadership of Joshua in the battle of life.
1:8,9 "This book of the law shall not depart out of thy mouth; but thou shalt <u>**meditate therein day and night**</u>, that thou mayest observe to do according to all that is written therein: for then thou shalt make thy way prosperous, and then thou shalt have **good success**. Have not I commanded thee? <u>**Be strong and of a good courage; be not afraid, neither be thou dismayed: for the LORD thy God is with thee whithersoever thou goest**</u>."

23:14 **God never fails us.** (Joshua's farewell address: 23:1-16; 24:1-27)
"And, behold, this day <u>**I am going the way of all the earth**</u>: and ye know in all your hearts and in all your souls, that not one thing hath failed of all the good things which the LORD your God spake concerning you; all are come to pass unto you, and not one thing hath failed thereof."

24:15   **The Miller Motto:**
"And if it seem evil unto you to serve the LORD, choose you this day whom ye will serve; whether the gods which your fathers served that

were on the other side of the flood, or the gods of the Amorites, in whose land ye dwell: **but as for me and my house, we will serve the LORD.**"

Judges

One has to be inspired by Deborah the prophetess and judge.

Judges 4:4,8,9 "And Deborah, a prophetess, the wife of Lapidoth, she judged Israel at that time. And Barak said unto her, If thou wilt go with me, then I will go: but if thou wilt not go with me, then I will not go. And she said, I will surely go with thee: notwithstanding the journey that thou takest shall not be for thine honour; **for the LORD shall sell Sisera into the hand of a woman**. And Deborah arose, and went with Barak to Kedesh."

The song of Deborah in Chapter 5 is inspirational and concludes with 5:31 "So let all thine enemies perish, O LORD: but let them that love him be as the sun when he goeth forth in his might. And the land had rest forty years."

God Himself called Gideon, a military hero and spiritual leader, the "mighty man of valor". He delivered God's people from the Midianites. He was out numbered 13:1. **His spiritual life was sustained by his regular worship**. "The sword of the LORD and of Gideon." (Judges 7:20) I have noticed if I miss Sunday church I am not quite as good a person that week.

Samson was a hero of **great physical strength and moral weakness** who lived in the dark times of God's people. "In those days there was no king in Israel, but **every man did that which was right in his own eyes**."(Judges 17:6, and 21:25) His weakness was a pagan woman. He broke God's laws by intermarrying with one. (14:15) Returning from a prostitute he was almost captured by the Philistines. (16:1,3) One of the most amazing feats was when Samson caught 300 foxes, tied their tails together, set them on fire and sent them to the Philistines fields of corn and grapes as a revenge of Samson.

Out of his weakness he was made strong by the LORD. (Judges 16:29-30) (Hebrews 11:34) Delilah discovered his weakness. He was blinded. He prayed to the LORD and pulled down the pillar of the temple of Dagon killing himself and thousands of the enemy.

Ruth

A beautiful story for the spiritual guidance of a congregation in which Ruth appears as ancestress of David and Jesus Christ.
2:12   **Trust in the LORD**
"The LORD recompense thy work, and a full reward be given thee of the LORD God of Israel, under whose wings thou art come to trust."

II Chronicles

The record of David, Solomon and the Kings of Judah up to the time of the captivity

7:3 "And when all the children of Israel saw how the fire came down, and the glory of the LORD upon the house, they bowed themselves with their faces to the ground upon the pavement, and worshipped, and praised the LORD, saying, For he is good; for his mercy endureth for ever." (Also noted in 5:13 and I Chronicles 16:41)

7:14 "If my people, which are called by my name, shall humble themselves, and pray, and seek my face, and turn from their wicked ways; then will I hear from heaven, and will forgive their sin, and will heal their land." **(A Key verse)**

16:9 "For the eyes of the LORD run to and fro throughout the whole earth, **to shew himself strong in the behalf of them whose heart is perfect toward him**. Herein thou hast done foolishly: therefore from henceforth thou shalt have wars."

20:21 More Military verses
"And when he had consulted with the people, he appointed singers unto the LORD, and that should praise the beauty of holiness, as they went out before the army, and to say, Praise the LORD; for his mercy endureth for ever."

31:21 What we do, do it with all our heart and prosper:
"And in every work that he began in the service of the house of God, and in the law, and in the commandments, to seek his God, he did it with all his heart, and prospered."

Job

Where is wisdom?
The Book of Job is not connected with any other Biblical book and stands alone. **Job is a book of divine morals**, followed by the Psalms, a book of devotion, and Proverbs, a book of practical things. It is thought that Job lived before Moses. It is great primitive theology. It gives **the glorious attributes and perfection of God, His unsearchable wisdom, His irresistible power, inconceivable glory, inflexible justice, and His incontestable Creator of the world**. Job makes powerful the obligations upon us to serve, submit, and trust in the LORD and ruler of moral good and evil, virtue and vice showing the beauty of ones had of the other. Job shows the provocation and malice of Hell. The patience of Job is noted in James 5:11. The moral of the story seems to be that the **righteous has many afflictions**, but when the LORD delivers them out of the trial of faith they will be found to praise, honor, and glory. The patience of Job and the vanity of human philosophy with divine wisdom is revealed in the sufferer

28:7,8,13,17,19,20,28 **This reveals the source of wisdom and understanding.**
"There is a path which no fowl knoweth, and which the vulture's eye hath not seen:..The lion's whelps have not trodden it, nor the fierce lion passed by it…Man knoweth not the price thereof; neither is it found in the land of the living…The gold and the crystal cannot equal it: and the exchange of it shall not be for jewels of fine gold…The topaz of Ethiopia shall not equal it, neither shall it be valued with pure gold…Whence then cometh wisdom? and where is the place of understanding?..And unto man he said, **Behold, the fear of the Lord, that is wisdom; and to depart from evil is understanding**." (Job 28:28) (See also Deuteronomy 4:6 and Proverbs 1:7)

Psalms

1:2, 3 **Our son, Joe, III tombstone euology.** "But his delight is in the law of the LORD; and in his law doth he meditate day and night. And he shall be like a tree planted by the rivers of water, that bringeth forth his fruit in his season; his leaf also shall not wither; and whatsoever he doeth shall prosper."

The Psalms are a history of Israel and an abstract of both Testaments. It is filled with spiritual songs taught by the Holy Spirit. It kindles the soul of man. It conveys a divine life with power and holy warmth. What ever is working in us holy desire, hope, sorrow or joy we may find words for it in the Psalms. We can sing the Psalms with spirit and understanding.

A collection of 150 spiritual songs, poems, and prayers used through thousands of years by the church.

37:4 "Delight thyself also in the LORD; and he shall give thee the desires of thine heart."

37:25 "**I have been young, and now am old**; yet have I not seen the righteous forsaken, nor his seed begging bread."

46:1-2, 10 "God is our refuge and strength, a very present help in trouble…Therefore will not we fear, though the earth be removed, and though the mountains be carried into the midst of the sea…**Be still, and know that I am God:** I will be exalted among the heathen, I will be exalted in the earth. " In order to learn about God one must be "still and Listen". It is God speaking. His Word will not pass through loud drums, screaming ecstasy, jumping up and down, or riding a cowboy horse, etc. One must be quiet and listen to God to hear God.

119:143 "Trouble and anguish have taken hold on me: yet thy commandments are my delights."

121:7 "The LORD shall preserve thee from all evil: he shall preserve thy soul."

136:1-26 God's mercy is seen 26 times. Read it. God's mercy is also noted in 106:1, 118:1-4, 28.
[1] O give thanks unto the LORD; for he is good: **for his mercy endureth for ever.**
[2] O give thanks unto the God of gods: for **his mercy endureth for ever.**
[3] O give thanks to the Lord of lords: for **his mercy endureth for ever.**
[4] To him who alone doeth great wonders: **for his mercy endureth for ever.**
[5] To him that by wisdom made the heavens: **for his mercy endureth for ever.**
[6] To him that stretched out the earth above the waters: **for his mercy endureth for ever.**
[7] To him that made great lights: **for his mercy endureth for ever:**
[8] The sun to rule by day: **for his mercy endureth for ever:**

[9] The moon and stars to rule by night: **for his mercy endureth for ever**.
[10] To him that smote Egypt in their firstborn: **for his mercy endureth for ever:**
[11] And brought out Israel from among them: **for his mercy endureth for ever**:
[12] With a strong hand, and with a stretched out arm: **for his mercy endureth for ever.**
[13] To him which divided the Red sea into parts: **for his mercy endureth for ever:**
[14] And made Israel to pass through the midst of it: **for his mercy endureth for ever**:
[15] But overthrew Pharaoh and his host in the Red sea: **for his mercy endureth for ever.**
[16] To him which led his people through the wilderness: **for his mercy endureth for ever.**
[17] To him which smote great kings: **for his mercy endureth for ever:**
[18] And slew famous kings: **for his mercy endureth for ever:**
[19] Sihon king of the Amorites: **for his mercy endureth for ever:**
[20] And Og the king of Bashan: **for his mercy endureth for ever:**
[21] And gave their land for an heritage: **for his mercy endureth for ever**:
[22] Even an heritage unto Israel his servant: **for his mercy endureth for ever.**
[23] Who remembered us in our low estate: **for his mercy endureth for ever**:
[24] And hath redeemed us from our enemies: **for his mercy endureth for ever.**
[25] Who giveth food to all flesh: **for his mercy endureth for ever.**
[26] O give thanks unto the God of heaven: **for his mercy endureth for ever.**

139:7-10 (See Proverbs 15:3)
"Whither shall I go from thy spirit? or whither shall I flee from thy presence? If I ascend up into heaven, thou art there: if I make my bed in hell, behold, thou art there. If I take the wings of the morning, and

dwell in the uttermost parts of the sea; Even there shall thy hand lead me, and thy right hand shall hold me."

139:23 "Search me, O God, and know my heart: try me, and know my thoughts."

147:5 "Great is our Lord, and of great power: his understanding is infinite."

"Admiral" Joe's Treasures from the Psalms:

<u>(Revised July 2012)</u>

Psalms 3:8	"Salvation belongeth unto the LORD: thy blessing is upon thy people. Selah."
Psalms 27:1	"The LORD is my light and my salvation; whom shall I fear? the LORD is the strength of my life; of whom shall I be afraid?"
Psalms 51:14	"Deliver me from bloodguiltiness, O God, thou God of my salvation: and my tongue shall sing aloud of thy righteousness."
Psalms 98:2,3	"The LORD hath made known his salvation: his righteousness hath he openly shewed in the sight of the heathen. He hath remembered his mercy and his truth toward the house of Israel: <u>**all the ends of the earth have seen the salvation of our God**</u>."
Isaiah 45:17	"But Israel shall be saved in the LORD with an everlasting salvation: ye shall not be ashamed nor confounded world without end"
Isaiah 52:10	"Yet it pleased the LORD to bruise him; he hath put him to grief: when thou shalt make his soul an offering for sin, he shall see his seed, he shall prolong his days, and the pleasure of the LORD shall prosper in his hand."
John 2:9	"When the ruler of the feast had tasted the water

Scriptures for Life

	that was made wine, and knew not whence it was: (but the servants which drew the water knew;) the governor of the feast called the bridegroom."
Acts 16:17	"The same followed Paul and us, and cried, saying, These men are the servants of the most high God, which shew unto us the way of salvation."
Romans 10:20	"But Esaias is very bold, and saith, I was found of them that sought me not; I was made manifest unto them that asked not after me."
Ephesians 1:13	"In whom ye also trusted, after that ye heard the word of truth, the gospel of your salvation: in whom also after that ye believed, ye were sealed with that holy Spirit of promise."
Philippians 2:12	"Wherefore, my beloved, as ye have always obeyed, not as in my presence only, but now much more in my absence, **work out your own salvation with fear and trembling**."

This is one of our foundational beliefs. The teaching that we are predestined to Heaven or Hell is heresy by denying The Christ died and His death was sufficient for all.

Hebrews 2:3	"**How shall we escape, if we neglect so great salvation**; which at the first began to be spoken by the Lord, and was confirmed unto us by them that heard him."
Hebrews 2:10	"For it became him, for whom are all things, and by whom are all things, in bringing many sons unto glory, to make the **captain of their salvation** perfect through sufferings."
Hebrews 5:9	"And being made perfect, he became the author of eternal salvation unto all them **that obey him**."
I Peter 1:9	"**Receiving** the end of your faith, even the salvation of your souls."

Being sorry, depression, penitence

Psalms 25:2	"O, God I put my trust in thee."
38:4	"My sins are too heavy for me, in thee do I hope."
51:2,7,14	"Cleanse me from my sin, I shall be whiter than snow."
	"God of my salvation"
130:5	"My soul waits and In His word do I hope."

Forgiveness

Psalms 32:1,11	"Blessed is he whose sin is forgiven, shout for joy." (Also noted in Romans 4: 6,7)
Psalms 103:3	"Who forgiveth all thine iniquities; who healeth all thy diseases."
Psalm 130	"There is forgiveness with Thee."

Conversion, Saved

Psalms 40	"Blessed is that man that maketh the LORD his trust"
	"The LORD be magnified"

Devotion to God, Consecration

Psalms 116	"I love the LORD, He hath heard my voice. I call upon Him as long as I live."

Trust in God

Psalms 3:5	"I laid me down and slept; I awaked; for the LORD sustained me."
Psalms 7:1	"O Lord my God, in thee do I put my trust:"

Psalms 16:1, 25:2, 28:7; 31:1,6,14, 32:10, 34:8, 40:3,4; 52:8; 61:4; 84:12; 91:2; 118:8

"In Thee do I put my trust" Trust the Lord is repeated 18 times for us in the Psalms. "In Thy hand I commit my spirit"

Scriptures for Life

Psalms 18:2	"The LORD is my rock, and my fortress, and my deliverer; my God, my strength, in whom I will trust; my buckler, and the horn of my salvation, and my high tower.
Psalms 20:5; 27:1,9	"We will rejoice in Thy salvation"
Psalms 23:1	"The LORD is my shepherd, I shall not want."
Psalms 37:4	"Delight thyself also in the LORD; and he shall give thee the desires of thine heart."
Psalms 121:7,8	"The LORD shall preserve thee"

The LORD is our strength, our ROCK
Psalms 18, 19, 27, 28, 31, 40, 43, 46, 76, 81, 84, 94, 96, 118, 132,
18:1,2; 27:1,5; 28:1,7,8; 31:2,3; 40:2; 43:2; 46:1; 73:26; 76:3,7,12; 81:1; 84:5,7;
94:22; 95:1; 96:4; 118:14; 132:5,8.

Psalms 18:1,2	"I will love thee, O LORD, my strength. The LORD is my rock, and my fortress, and my deliverer; my God, my strength, in whom I will trust; my buckler, and the horn of my salvation, and my high tower."
Psalms 25:5,7	"Lead me in Thy truth, and teach me: for Thou art the **God of my salvation**; on Thee do I wait all the day…Remember not the sins of my youth, nor my transgressions: according to thy mercy remember thou me for thy goodness' sake, O LORD."
Psalms 27:11;	"Teach me Thy way O LORD…" To teach is also seen in: 51:13; 86:11; 90:12.

Give me ambition, a strong desire for thee

Psalms 73:25,26	"Whom have I in heaven but thee? and there is none upon earth that I desire beside thee. My flesh and my heart faileth: but **God is the strength of my heart**, and my portion for ever."
Psalms 145: 16,19	"Thou openest thine hand, and satisfiest the desire of every living thing. He will fulfil the

	desire of them that fear him: he also will hear their cry, and will save them."
Psalms 143:11	"Quicken me, LORD for thy name's sake: for thy righteousness' sake bring my soul out of trouble."

Prayer

Psalms 4:1; 17:1,6; 39:12	"Hear my prayers"
Psalms 55:17	"Evening and morning, and at noon will I pray." (The Apostles prayed the Lord's Prayer three times a day.)
Psalms 70:5	"O God: Thou art my help and deliver"
Psalms 77:14,18	"Thou art the God that doest wonders"
	"The voice of Thy thunder is in the heavens"
Psalms 85:4,7,9	"O God of our **salvation**, grant us **Thy salvation**, **Thy salvation** is nigh, that glory may dwell in our land."
Psalms 86:7,8	"In the day of my trouble I will call upon Thee. There is none like Thee."
Psalms 142:1,3,5	"I cried unto the LORD"
	"My spirit overwhelmed me"
	"Thou art my refuge"
Psalms 143:1, 10	"Hear my prayer, O LORD, teach me to do thy will, lead me into the land of righteousness"

Praise

Psalms 33:1,2;42:4,5,11;96:4;106:1,48;135:1,3;146:1,2,10;147:1,7,12;148:1,2,3,7,13,14; 149:1,6,9;150:1,2,3,4,5,6

"Praise ye the LORD"

Psalms 96:4	"The LORD is great, greatly to be praised"
Psalms 98:1,4,6	**This is the origin of "Joy to the World."** In verse 1, it says, "O sing unto the LORD a new song."
Psalm 100: 1,2,3,5	"Make a joyful noise unto the LORD, all ye lands. Serve

Scriptures for Life

the LORD with gladness: come before his presence with singing. Know ye that the LORD he is God: it is he that hath made us, and not we ourselves; we are his people, and the sheep of his pasture. For the LORD is good; **his mercy is everlasting; and his truth endureth to all generations"**.

Psalms 103:1,2   "Bless the LORD, O my soul: and all that is within me, bless His holy name. Bless the Lord, O my soul, and forget not all His benefits."

Psalms 107:6, 13, 19, 28   "Then they cried unto the LORD in their trouble, and He delivered them out of their distresses." (Repeated 4 times.)

Psalms 136   "**Give thanks unto the LORD.**" (This is repeated 26 times in Psalms 136 alone.)
"**O give thanks unto the LORD**; for He is good: for His mercy endureth for ever. **O give thanks unto the God of gods**: for His mercy endureth for ever. **O give thanks to the LORD of lords**: for His mercy endureth for ever.", etc. And in Psalms 106:1; 118:1, 28.

Worship

Psalms 29:2; 96:9   "Worship the LORD in the beauty of holiness"

Psalms 43:4   "I will go unto the altar of God"

Psalms 84:4   "**Blessed are they that dwell in Thy house.**"

Psalms 95:6   "O come, let us worship and bow down: let us kneel before the LORD our maker."

Psalms 100   "Make a joyful noise unto the LORD, all ye lands. Serve the LORD with gladness: come before his presence with singing. Know ye that the LORD he is God: it is he that hath made us, and not we ourselves; we are his people, and the sheep of his pasture. Enter into his gates with thanksgiving, and into his courts with praise: be thankful unto him, and bless his name. **For the LORD is good;**

	his **mercy is everlasting; and his truth endureth to all generations.**"
Psalms 122: 1	"**I Was glad** when they said unto me, Let us go into the house of the LORD." **All Christians love to worship!**
Psalms 132:7	"We will go into His tabernacles: we will worship at **His footstool.**" **(Repeated in 99:5; Isaiah 66:1; Acts 7:49; James 2:31)**

Jesus also related the earth was God's footstool. The Temple was a place of God's footstool. It was holy.

Pain, Distress, affliction, Depression, Suicidal

Psalms 6:4	"Return, O LORD, deliver my soul: oh save me for Thy mercies' sake."
Psalms 13: 3,5	"Consider and hear me, O LORD my God: lighten mine eyes, lest I sleep the sleep of death; But I have trusted in Thy mercy; **my heart shall rejoice in Thy salvation**."
Psalms 22	This has been called the "5th Gospel"
22:24,26	"For He hath not despised nor abhorred the affliction of the afflicted; neither hath He hid His face from him; but when he cried unto Him, He heard." (God hears us.)

"<u>Those that seek Him shall live foreve</u>r"

Psalms 69: 1,5,13	"Save me, O God; for the waters are come in unto my soul… O God, thou knowest my foolishness; and my sins are not hid from Thee…But as for me, my prayer is unto Thee, O LORD, in an acceptable time: O God, in the multitude of **Thy mercy hear me**, in the truth of Thy salvation."

Psalms 88:1,2,3,15 A prayer of David to the sons of Korah who survived being swallowed up. (I Chronicles 6:33)

"**O LORD God of my salvation**, I have cried day and night before Thee: Let my prayer come before Thee: incline Thine ear unto my cry; For my soul is full of troubles: and my life draweth nigh unto the grave…I am afflicted and ready to die from my youth up: while I suffer thy terrors I am distracted." Psalms 89 is the answer to David. 89:4 "Thy seed will I establish for ever, and build up thy throne to all generations. Selah." This is referred to in Luke 1:33.

Psalms 102: 1,7,12,28 (102: 25-28 quoted in Hebrews 1:10-12 "And, Thou, Lord, in the beginning hast laid the foundation of the earth; and the heavens are the works of thine hands: They shall perish; but thou remainest; and they all shall wax old as doth a garment; And as a vesture shalt thou fold them up, and they shall be changed: **but thou art the same, and thy years shall not fail**."

Old Age (This is my prayer.)
Psalms 71:18, 20, 21 "Now also when I am old and grayheaded, **O God, forsake me not; until I have shewed Thy strength unto this generation**, and **Thy power to every one that is to come**…Thou, which hast shewed me great and sore troubles, shalt quicken me again, and shalt bring me up again from the depths of the earth…Thou shalt increase my greatness, and comfort me on every side."

Speeding Life
Psalms 39:4, 7   "LORD, make me to know mine end, and the measure of my days, what it is: that I may know how frail I am…And now, LORD, what wait I for? my hope is in Thee."
Psalms 49: 15   "**But God will redeem my soul from the power of the grave**: for He shall receive me. Selah."
Psalms 90: 1, 4, 12, 14   "**LORD, Thou hast been our dwelling place in all generations**…For a thousand years in

Thy sight are but as yesterday when it is past, and as a watch in the night…So teach us to number our days, that we may apply our hearts unto wisdom…O satisfy us early with Thy mercy; **that we may rejoice and be glad all our days**."

Our Home
Psalms 127:1   "Except the LORD build the house, they labour in vain that build it: except the LORD keep the city, the watchman waketh but in vain."

In Florida, Homesick for Alabama, etc. (A Joke)
Psalms 137: 4   "How shall we sing the LORD's song in a strange land?"

Proverbs

A collection of religious and moral truths on wisdom temperance, and justice

To give moral instruction especially to young people. We must use the talents entrusted to us.
We are to know ourselves. **A concept from above.** "**Examine yourselves**, whether ye be in the faith; prove your own selves. Know ye not your own selves, how that Jesus Christ is in you, except ye be reprobates?" (II Corinthians 13:5)

1:4-10 "To give subtilty to the simple, to the young man knowledge and discretion. A wise man will hear, and will increase learning; and a man of understanding shall attain unto wise counsels: To understand a proverb, and the interpretation; the words of the wise, and their dark sayings. The fear of the LORD is the beginning of knowledge: **but fools despise wisdom and instruction**. My son, hear the instruction of thy father, and forsake not the law of thy mother: For they shall be an ornament of grace unto thy head, and chains about thy neck. My son, if sinners entice thee, consent thou not."

3:5 "Trust in the LORD with all thine heart; and lean not unto thine own understanding."

11:24-25 "There is that scattereth, and yet increaseth; and there is that withholdeth more than is meet, but it tendeth to poverty. The liberal soul shall be made fat: and **he that watereth shall be watered also himself.**"

12:14 "A man shall be satisfied with good by the fruit of his mouth: and the recompence of a man's hands shall be rendered unto him."

15:3 "The eyes of the LORD are in every place, beholding the evil and the good." (See psalms 139:7)

16:16 "How much better is it to get wisdom than gold! and to get understanding rather to be chosen than silver!" (All of my life I have sought knowledge and wisdom for my specialty, which I was a directed to by God. I learned early that the love of money and wisdom conflicted with each other. I turned my investments over to an expert in money management. He gave me a one-page report each month. A Samurai warrior knew that the thought of money interfered with the development of his spirit and body. He had an assistant that handled all his money matters. If one mentioned money in his presence he would be killed because the Samurai's spirit had been contaminated.)

16:32 "He that is slow to anger is better than the mighty; and he that ruleth his spirit than he that taketh a city."

18:15, 16 **Wise men learn**
"The heart of the **prudent getteth knowledge**; and **the ear of the wise**

seeketh knowledge. A man's gift maketh room for him, and bringeth him before great men."

18:21 "Death and life are in the power of the tongue: and they that love it shall eat the fruit thereof."

20:18 **Get good advice**
"Every purpose is established by counsel: and with good advice make war."

29:25 **Trust in God and be safe.**
"The fear of man bringeth a snare: but whoso putteth his trust in the LORD shall be safe."

Ecclesiastes

The choicest of all the dictates of his wisdom.
It is thought that Solomon wrote the Song of Solomon **while he was young**, Proverbs in **middle age**, and Ecclesiastes **when he was old**. (Matthew Henry)

Reflections on the vanity of life, and man's duty and obligations to God.

1:2,4 "Vanity of vanities, saith the Preacher, vanity of vanities; all is vanity. One generation passeth away, and another generation cometh: but the earth abideth for ever." (Also seen in 12:8 and Psalms 62:9)

2:1 "I said in mine heart, Go to now, I will prove thee with mirth, therefore enjoy pleasure: and, behold, this also is vanity."

3:14 "I know that, whatsoever God doeth, it shall be for ever: nothing can be put to it, nor any thing taken from it: and God doeth it, that men should fear before him."

4:9-10 "**Two are better than one**; because they have a good reward for their labour. For if they fall, the one will lift up his fellow: but woe to him that is alone when he falleth; for he hath not another to help him up."

The benefits of two versus one include the intimacy and sharing of life, that brings relief from loneliness and isolation. God said, "It is not good that man should be alone." (Genesis 2:18) "The man and wife…they shall be one flesh."(Genesis 2:18) "If the husband or wife is not a believer, the other will be sanctified by the believer. Their children are not unclean." (I Corinthians 7:12-16)

5:10-11 "He that loveth silver shall not be satisfied with silver; nor he that loveth abundance with increase: this is also **vanity**. When goods increase, they are increased that eat them: and what good is there to the owners thereof, saving the beholding of them with their eyes?"

The Summary of Ecclesiastes:
12:13,14 (Solomon here returns to God's grace.)
"Let us hear the conclusion of the whole matter: Fear God, and keep his commandments: for this is the whole duty of man. For **God shall bring every work into judgment**, with every secret thing, whether it be good, or whether it be evil."

Isaiah

The Evangelical Prophet, he preached many sermons. The great prophet of redemption He gave Infinite Wisdom to us on whom the ends of the world will come.

1:18 "Come now, and let us reason together, saith the LORD: though your sins be as scarlet, they shall be as white as snow; though they be red like crimson, they shall be as wool."

6:8 "Also I heard the voice of the Lord, saying, Whom shall I send, and who will go for us? Then said I, **Here am I; send me**."

9:6 "For unto us a child is born, unto us a son is given: and the government shall be upon his shoulder: and his name shall be called Wonderful, Counseller, The mighty God, The everlasting Father, The Prince of Peace."

12:2 (English Standard Version) "Lift ye up a banner upon the high mountain, exalt the voice unto them, shake the hand, that they may go into the gates of the nobles."

25:8 In *Handel's Messiah*
"He will swallow up death in victory; and the Lord GOD will wipe away tears from off all faces; and the rebuke of his people shall he take away from off all the earth: for the LORD hath spoken it."

"So when this corruptible shall have put on incorruption, and this mortal shall have put on immortality, then shall be brought to pass the saying that is written, Death is swallowed up in victory. O death, where is thy sting? O grave, where is thy victory? The sting of death is sin; and the strength of sin is the law. But thanks be to God, which giveth us the victory through our Lord Jesus Christ." (I Corinthians 15:54-57)

26:3 "Thou wilt keep him in perfect peace, whose mind is stayed on thee: because he trusteth in thee."

29:18,19 "**And in that day** shall the deaf hear the words of the book, and the eyes of the blind shall see out of obscurity, and out of darkness. The meek also shall increase their joy in the LORD, and the poor among men shall rejoice in the Holy One of Israel."

33:6 "And wisdom and knowledge shall be the stability of thy times, and strength of salvation: the fear of the LORD is his treasure."

35: 5,6,10 **A great promise for all of us.**
"Then the eyes of the blind shall be opened, and the ears of the deaf shall be unstopped. Then shall the lame man leap as an hart, and the tongue of the dumb sing: for in the wilderness shall waters break out, and streams in the desert. And the ransomed of the LORD shall return, and come to Zion with songs and everlasting joy upon their heads: they shall obtain joy and gladness, and sorrow and sighing shall flee away."

40:8-11 "The grass withereth, the flower fadeth: but the word of our God shall stand for ever. O Zion, that bringest good tidings, get thee up into the high mountain; O Jerusalem, that bringest good tidings, lift up thy voice with strength; lift it up, be not afraid; say unto the cities of Judah, Behold your God! Behold, the Lord GOD will come with strong hand, and his arm shall rule for him: behold, his reward is with him, and his work before him. He shall feed his flock like a shepherd: he shall gather the lambs with his arm, and carry them in his bosom, and shall gently lead those that are with young."

40:30,31 "Even the youths shall faint and be weary, and the young men shall utterly fall: But they that wait upon the LORD shall renew their strength; they shall mount up with wings as eagles; they shall run, and not be weary; and they shall walk, and not faint."

43:18,19 "Remember ye not the former things, neither consider the things of old. Behold, I will do a new thing; now it shall spring forth; shall ye not know it? I will even make a way in the wilderness, and rivers in the desert."

45:8,12,22 "Drop down, ye heavens, from above, and let the skies pour down righteousness: let the earth open, and let them bring forth salvation, and let righteousness spring up together; I the LORD have created it. I have made the earth, and created man upon it: I, even my hands, have stretched out the heavens, and all their host have I commanded. **Look unto me, and be ye saved, all the ends of the earth:**

for I am God, and there is none else." (Spurgeon was saved with this verse in a small church that he went into because of a storm.)

52:7 (See Nahum 1:15, Romans 10:15, Ephesians 6:15)
"How beautiful upon the mountains are the feet of him that bringeth good tidings, that publisheth peace; that bringeth good tidings of good, that publisheth salvation; that saith unto Zion, Thy God reigneth!"

Isaiah 53 This chapter improves our knowledge of Jesus Christ, Him crucified, glorified, dying for our sins, rising again for our justification before God.
[1] Who hath believed our report? and to whom is the arm of the LORD revealed?
[2] For he shall grow up before him as a tender plant, and as a root out of a dry ground: he hath no form nor comeliness; and when we shall see him, there is no beauty that we should desire him.
[3] He is despised and rejected of men; a man of sorrows, and acquainted with grief: and we hid as it were our faces from him; he was despised, and we esteemed him not.
[4] Surely he hath borne our griefs, and carried our sorrows: yet we did esteem him stricken, smitten of God, and afflicted.
[5] But he was wounded for our transgressions, he was bruised for our iniquities: the chastisement of our peace was upon him; and with his stripes we are healed.
[6] All we like sheep have gone astray; we have turned every one to his own way; and the LORD hath laid on him the iniquity of us all.
[7] He was oppressed, and he was afflicted, yet he opened not his mouth: he is brought as a lamb to the slaughter, and as a sheep before her shearers is dumb, so he openeth not his mouth.
[8] He was taken from prison and from judgment: and who shall declare his generation? for he was cut off out of the land of the living: for the transgression of my people was he stricken.
[9] And he made his grave with the wicked, and with the rich in his death; because he had done no violence, neither was any deceit in his mouth.

[10] Yet it pleased the LORD to bruise him; he hath put him to grief: when thou shalt make his soul an offering for sin, he shall see his seed, he shall prolong his days, and the pleasure of the LORD shall prosper in his hand.

[11] He shall see of the travail of his soul, and shall be satisfied: by his knowledge shall my righteous servant justify many; for he shall bear their iniquities.

[12] Therefore will I divide him a portion with the great, and he shall divide the spoil with the strong; because he hath poured out his soul unto death: and he was numbered with the transgressors; and he bare the sin of many, and made intercession for the transgressors.

The Spirit of Christ testified before the sufferings of Christ and the glory that followed. Isaiah is known as **the gospel of the evangelist Isaiah where the unsearchable riches of Christ are seen**. Christ was in His Fathers will. "Surely he hath borne our griefs, and carried our sorrows: yet we did esteem him stricken, smitten of God, and afflicted. All we like sheep have gone astray; we have turned every one to his own way; and the LORD hath laid on him the iniquity of us all."(53:4,6), an offering for our sins (53:10), bore our sufferings "He was oppressed, and he was afflicted, yet he opened not his mouth: he is brought as a lamb to the slaughter, and as a sheep before her shearers is dumb, so he openeth not his mouth." (53:7) It ended in honor. (53:10-12)

53:3-6 (In *Handel's Messiah*)

"He is despised and rejected of men; a man of sorrows, and acquainted with grief: and we hid as it were our faces from him; he was despised, and we esteemed him not. Surely he hath borne our griefs, and carried our sorrows: yet we did esteem him stricken, smitten of God, and afflicted. But he was wounded for our transgressions, he was bruised for our iniquities: the chastisement of our peace was upon him; and with his stripes we are healed. All we like sheep have gone astray; we have turned every one to his own way; and the LORD hath laid on him the iniquity of us all."

53:9 "And he made his grave with the wicked, and with the rich in his death; because he had done no violence, neither was any deceit in his mouth."

(I Peter 2:22,24) "Who did no sin, neither was guile found in his mouth: Who his own self bare our sins in his own body on the tree, that we, being dead to sins, should live unto righteousness: by whose stripes ye were healed."

53:10-12 "Yet it pleased the LORD to bruise him; he hath put him to grief: when thou shalt make his soul an offering for sin, he shall see his seed, he shall prolong his days, and the pleasure of the LORD shall prosper in his hand. He shall see of the travail of his soul, and shall be satisfied: by his knowledge shall my righteous servant justify many; for he shall bear their iniquities. Therefore will I divide him a portion with the great, and he shall divide the spoil with the strong; because he hath poured out his soul unto death: and he was numbered with the transgressors; and he bare the sin of many, and made intercession for the transgressors." (See Hebrews 9:28)

55:6-9 "**Seek ye the LORD while he may be found**, call ye upon him while he is near: Let the wicked forsake his way, and the unrighteous man his thoughts: and let him return unto the LORD, and he will have mercy upon him; and to our God, for he will abundantly pardon. For my thoughts are not your thoughts, neither are your ways my ways, saith the LORD. For as the heavens are higher than the earth, so are my ways higher than your ways, and my thoughts than your thoughts."

64:4 "**For since the beginning of the world men have not heard, nor perceived by the ear, neither hath the eye seen, O God, beside thee, what he hath prepared for him that waiteth for him.**"

Isaiah lists 11 **Results** of Salvation:

Scriptures for Life

1. "Can draw from the wells of (12:3) "Therefore with joy shall ye **draw water out of the wells of salvation**."
2. The joy of (25:9) "And it shall be said in that day, Lo, this is our God; we have waited for him, and he will save us: this is the LORD; we have waited for him, we will **be glad and rejoice** in his salvation."
3. The walls of (26:1) "In that day shall **this song be sung** in the land of Judah; We have a strong city; salvation will God appoint for walls and bulwarks."
4. The Everlasting of (45:17) "But Israel **shall be saved** in the LORD with an everlasting salvation: ye shall not be ashamed nor confounded world without end."
5. The days of (49:8) "Thus saith the LORD, In an acceptable time have I heard thee, and in a day of salvation have I helped thee: and **I will preserve thee**, and give thee for a covenant of the people, to establish the earth, to cause to inherit the desolate heritages."
6. The feet of the beauty of (52:7) "How beautiful upon the mountains are the feet of him that bringeth good tidings, that publisheth peace; that **bringeth good tidings of good**, that publisheth salvation; that saith unto Zion, Thy God reigneth!"
7. The spread of (52:10) "The LORD hath made bare his holy arm in the eyes of all the nations; and all **the ends of the earth shall see the salvation of our God**."
8. The arm of (59:16) "And he saw that there was no man, and wondered that there was no intercessor: therefore his arm brought salvation unto him; and his righteousness, it sustained him."
9. The helmet of (59:17) "For he put on righteousness as a breastplate, and an helmet of salvation upon his head; and he put on the garments of vengeance for clothing, and was clad with zeal as a cloke."
10. The garments of (61:10) "Go through, go through the gates; prepare ye the way of the people; cast up, cast up the highway; gather out the stones; lift up a standard for the people."
11. The light of peace, rest, and righteousness (62:1) "For Zion's sake will I not hold my peace, and for Jerusalem's sake I will

not rest, until the righteousness thereof go forth as brightness, and the salvation thereof as a lamp that burneth."

Salvation of everlasting things in Isaiah:
- God's strength (26:4) "Trust ye in the LORD for ever: for in the LORD JEHOVAH is everlasting strength:"
- Judgment of hypocrites (33:14) "The sinners in Zion are afraid; fearfulness hath surprised the hypocrites. Who among us shall dwell with the devouring fire? who among us shall dwell with everlasting burnings?"
- Joy without sorrow (35:10) "And the ransomed of the LORD shall return, and come to Zion with songs and everlasting joy upon their heads: they shall obtain joy and gladness, and sorrow and sighing shall flee away."
- Everlasting salvation without confusion (45:17) "But Israel shall be saved in the LORD with an everlasting salvation: ye shall not be ashamed nor confounded world without end." (Many of the Calvinists are confused.)
- The Soul shall live (55:3) "Incline your ear, and come unto me: hear, and your soul shall live; and I will make an everlasting covenant with you, even the sure mercies of David."
- The light and glory (60:19) "The sun shall be no more thy light by day; neither for brightness shall the moon give light unto thee: but the LORD shall be unto thee an everlasting light, and thy God thy glory."

Isaiah's prophecy concerning Christ 800 (760 B.C. ?) years before is one of the best proofs of Scripture. Prophecy supports and verifies itself.

The birth of Christ (7:14) Immanuel, God with us "Therefore the Lord himself shall give you a sign; Behold, a virgin shall conceive, and bear a son, and shall call his name Immanuel." Made clear the light (9:2), Mighty God and Everlasting Father, Prince of Peace, (9:6) "For unto us a child is born, unto us a son is given: and the government shall be upon his shoulder: and his name shall be called Wonderful, Counselor,

Scriptures for Life

The mighty God, The everlasting Father, The Prince of Peace." from the family of Jesse (11:1) "And there shall come forth a rod out of the stem of Jesse, and a Branch shall grow out of his roots:" wisdom anointing (11:2) "And the spirit of the LORD shall rest upon him, the spirit of wisdom and understanding, the spirit of counsel and might, the spirit of knowledge and of the fear of the LORD;" judge, spiritual discernment (11:3) "And shall make him of quick understanding in the fear of the LORD: and he shall not judge after the sight of his eyes, neither reprove after the hearing of his ears.", justice and reproof with equity (11:4), "But with righteousness shall he judge the poor, and reprove with equity for the meek of the earth: and he shall smite the earth with the rod of his mouth, and with the breath of his lips shall he slay the wicked." righteousness, faithfulness (11:5), "And righteousness shall be the girdle of his loins, and faithfulness the girdle of his reins." Righteous King (32:1) "Behold, a king shall reign in righteousness, and princes shall rule in judgment." Divine Servant, Judge (42:1) "Behold my servant, whom I uphold; mine elect, in whom my soul delighteth; I have put my spirit upon him: he shall bring forth judgment to the Gentiles." Silence (42:2 noted also in 53:7) "He shall not cry, nor lift up, nor cause his voice to be heard in the street." Judgment, truth (42.3) "A bruised reed shall he not break, and the smoking flax shall he not quench: he shall bring forth judgment unto truth." Perseverance (42:4) "He shall not fail nor be discouraged, till he have set judgment in the earth: and the isles shall wait for his law." Radiance (42:6 and seen in 9:2) "I the LORD have called thee in righteousness, and will hold thine hand, and will keep thee, and give thee for a covenant of the people, for a light of the Gentiles;" Arm of the Lord (53:1) "Who hath believed our report? and to whom is the arm of the LORD revealed?" Compassion, Burden bearer, sin bearer (53:4) "Surely he hath borne our griefs, and carried our sorrows: yet we did esteem him stricken, smitten of God, and afflicted." Meekness (53:7) "He was oppressed, and he was afflicted, yet he opened not his mouth: he is brought as a lamb to the slaughter, and as a sheep before her shearers is dumb, so he openeth not his mouth." Sinlessness (53:9) "And he made his grave with the wicked, and with the rich in his death; because he had done no violence, neither was any deceit in his mouth." Saving power (53:11) "He shall see of the travail of his soul, and shall be satisfied: by his knowledge shall my righteous servant justify many; for he shall bear their iniquities." Greatness, Intercessor (53:12) "Therefore will I divide him a portion with the great, and he shall divide the spoil with the strong; because he hath poured out his soul unto death: and he was numbered with the transgressors; and he bare the sin of many, and made intercession for the transgressors." anointed preacher (61:1) "The Spirit of the Lord GOD is upon me; because the LORD hath anointed me to preach good tidings unto the meek; he hath sent me to bind up the brokenhearted, to proclaim liberty to the captives, and the opening of the prison to them that are bound." Mighty traveler, great strength, speaks in righteousness, mighty to save (63:1) "Who is this that cometh from Edom, with dyed garments from Bozrah? this that is glorious in his apparel, travelling in the greatness of his strength? I that speak in righteousness, mighty to save." and our only Savior, his soul was an offering for our sins. (53:10) "Yet it pleased the LORD to bruise him; he hath put him to grief: when thou shalt make his soul an offering for sin, he shall see his seed, he shall prolong his days, and the pleasure of the LORD shall prosper in his hand."

Jeremiah

The backsliding, bondage, and restoration of the Jews.
God touched Isaiah's mouth with fire to purge away his iniquity, but when **God touched Jeremiah's mouth** it was to **put words in his mouth**. He was a weeping prophet because of the sins of the people.

When Alexander entered Egypt he dug up Jeremiah's bones and buried them in Alexandria. Jeremiah was persecuted by his own people more than any other prophet.

29:11-14 Seek God with all your heart and find Him.
"For I know the thoughts that I think toward you, saith the LORD, thoughts of peace, and not of evil, to give you an expected end. Then shall ye call upon me, and ye shall go and pray unto me, and I will hearken unto you. And ye shall seek me, and find me, when ye shall

search for me with all your heart. And I will be found of you, saith the LORD: and I will turn away your captivity, and I will gather you from all the nations, and from all the places whither I have driven you, saith the LORD; and I will bring you again into the place whence I caused you to be carried away captive."

Daniel

One of the great prophets of the Bible and the angel Gabriel called him a man greatly beloved. A personal biography of his visions of history.

12:3 <u>**Turn souls to righteousness and be wise**</u>**. This is one of the greatest wisdom verses in the Bible.** (Noah, Daniel, and Job had the greatest interest in Heaven.)
"And they that be wise shall shine as the brightness of the firmament; and they that turn many to righteousness as the stars for ever and ever." (Those who water others are watered themselves.) "The liberal soul shall be made fat: and he that watereth shall be watered also himself." (Proverbs 11:25)

Daniel's famous prayer for his people is in 9:1-19. Daniel did not understand, but he knew the wise later would understand. (12:8-10) Jesus referred to those who would later understand. "**And this gospel of the kingdom shall be preached in all the world for a witness unto all nations; and then shall the end come. When ye therefore shall see the abomination of desolation, spoken of by Daniel the prophet, stand in the holy place, (whoso readeth, let him understand:)**"(Matthew 24: 14,15)

Hosea

Who is wise? The first of the writing prophets.
The apostasy of Israel's spiritual adultery.
14:9 "Who is wise, and he <u>**shall understand**</u> these things? prudent,

and **he shall know them**? for the ways of the LORD are right, and the just shall walk in them: but the transgressors shall fall therein." (See proverbs 10:29)

Joel

The people were called to repentance. (2:12) The promises of the pouring of the Spirit in later days. (2:28,29)

Judah's enemies judged.
"Proclaim ye this among the Gentiles; Prepare war, wake up the mighty men, let all the men of war draw near; let them come up: **Beat your plowshares into swords, and your pruninghooks into spears**: let the weak say, I am strong. Let the heathen be wakened, and come up to the valley of Jehoshaphat: for there will I sit to judge all the heathen round about. Multitudes, multitudes in the valley of decision: for the day of the LORD is near in the valley of decision. So shall ye know that I am the LORD your God dwelling in Zion, my holy mountain: then shall Jerusalem be holy, and there shall no strangers pass through her any more." (3:9,10,12,14,17)

2:32   **Call upon the name of the LORD and be delivered.**
"And it shall come to pass, that whosoever shall call on the name of the LORD shall be delivered: for in mount Zion and in Jerusalem shall be deliverance, as the LORD hath said, and in the remnant whom the LORD shall call."

Micah

Foretells the Messianic Kingdom
Micah foretold the destruction of Jerusalem. (3:12) He also foretold the birth of Christ. (5:2)

6:8   **God shows what is required of us.**

Scriptures for Life

"He hath shewed thee, O man, what is good; and what doth the LORD require of thee, but to do justly, and to love mercy, and to walk humbly with thy God?"

7:19 **Our sins are thrown into the sea.**
"He will turn again, he will have compassion upon us; he will subdue our iniquities; and thou wilt cast all their sins into the depths of the sea."

Zechariah

Emphasizes in a vision the future glory of Israel
1:3 Turn to God and He will turn to us.
"Therefore say thou unto them, Thus saith the LORD of hosts; Turn ye unto me, saith the LORD of hosts, and I will turn unto you, saith the LORD of hosts."

Zechariah announces the coming of the Messiah. "Rejoice greatly, O daughter of Zion; shout, O daughter of Jerusalem: behold, thy King cometh unto thee: he is just, and having salvation; lowly, and riding upon an ass, and upon a colt the foal of an ass."(9:9) and establishes His Kingdom in this world. "And the LORD shall be king over all the earth: in that day shall there be one LORD, and his name one."(14:9)

Malachi

A picture of the ending of the Old Testament and the reforms needed before the coming of the Messiah.

3:8 **Do Not Rob God** "Will a man rob God? Yet ye have robbed me. But ye say, Wherein have we robbed thee? In tithes and offerings."

3:16-18 "Then they that feared the LORD spake often one to another: and the LORD hearkened, and heard it, and a book of remembrance was written before him for them that feared the LORD, and that thought upon his name. And they shall be mine, saith the LORD of hosts, in that day when I make up my jewels; and I will spare them, as a man spareth his own son that serveth him. Then shall ye return, and discern between the righteous and the wicked, between him that serveth God and him that serveth him not."

4:5,6 "Behold, I will send you Elijah the prophet before the coming of the great and dreadful day of the LORD: And he shall turn the heart of the fathers to the children, and the heart of the children to their fathers, lest I come and smite the earth with a curse."

Malachi was the last prophet and with him prophesy ceased. God wisely orders it so that divine inspiration should cease for some ages before the coming of the Messiah. Attention was directed to the coming of the Messiah. The people were to be in expectation to the gospel of Christ.

End of the Old Testament

New Testament

New Covenant

THERE ARE 400 SILENT YEARS BETWEEN THE OLD
AND
THE NEW TESTAMENT

Christ's Acts and Deeds become <u>a force after his death and resurrection</u>.
"For where a testament is, there must also of necessity be the death of the testator. For a testament is of force after men are dead: otherwise it is of no strength at all while the testator liveth."**(Hebrews 9:16,17)**

The will, the free will, the goodwill of Christ. All grace in the Bible is from Jesus Christ our Lord and Savior. <u>**It will always be new, will never be old, or grow out of date**</u>. The <u>**grace has appeared to all men**</u>. (Mark 13:10, Romans 10:18) It brings salvation. This is the last words and testament of <u>**Jesus that lives**</u> on with His love and unsearchable riches for us. It is the <u>**whole council of God**</u>. (Acts 20:27) It is the <u>**only Gospel**</u> (Galatians 1:6, 8) It is the <u>**Good News**</u>, glad tidings of the history of <u>**Christ's coming into the world to save sinners**</u>. "And the angel said unto them, Fear not: for, behold, I bring you good tidings of great joy, which **shall be to all people.**"(Luke 2:10)

It was foretold hundreds of years before. "How beautiful upon the mountains are the feet of him that bringeth good tidings, that publisheth peace; that bringeth good tidings of good, that publisheth salvation; that saith unto Zion, Thy God reigneth!"**(Isaiah 52:7)** "The Spirit of the Lord GOD is upon me; because the LORD hath anointed me to preach good tidings unto the meek; he hath sent me to bind up the brokenhearted, to proclaim liberty to the captives, and the opening of the prison to them that are bound." **(Isaiah 61:1)**

When we read it a "spell" or a **wise charmed sensation comes over us**. It is from **the book that speaks with power of its own**. It is the beauty and love of our Redeemer. Paul refers to the whole New Testament as "our gospel". **(I Thessalonians 1:5)** There is natural history, but the Old and New Testament are **a sacred history** and **sacred truth**.

Paul refers to the whole New Testament as "our gospel". (I Thessalonians 1:5) There is natural history, but the Old and New Testament are a sacred history and sacred truth.

"But these are written, that ye **might believe** that Jesus is the Christ, the Son of God; and **that believing** ye might have life through his name."**(John 20:31)**

"And there are also many other things which Jesus did, the which, if they should be written every one, I suppose that even the world itself could not contain the books that should be written. Amen." **(John 21:25)**

The Old Testament Prophesies were fulfilled in Christ! Old Testament-Christ-New Testament

The 27 Books in the New Testament Include:
- **4 Biographical**

Scriptures for Life

- 1 Historical
- 14 Pauline Epistles
- 7 General Epistles
- 1 Prophetic Book

Having knowledge of some of these related activities between the Old And the New Testament gives one a meaningful relationship between the two.

The Old and New Testament is full of great and wonderful quotes. I will relate only a few that have come to my mind. Every time I read this I think of something else, as I am sure each of you who read this will also!!!

1. Creator (Genesis 1:1)
2. First Things (Genesis 1:1)
3. Death Reigning (Genesis 3:1)
4. Satan's Victory (Genesis 3:6)
5. Sin's Curse (Genesis 3:6)
6. State of Bliss Lost (Genesis 3:23)
7. Animal Blood Sacrifice (Ex. 12:3-7)
8. Majestic God (Exodus 19:18)
9. The Law (Exodus 20:1-17)
10. Desire for the Unattainable (Job 23:3)
11. Spiritual Darkness (Psalms 82:4)
12. Bondage (Proverbs 5:22)
13. Prophesy (Isaiah 11:1,2)
14. God's Messenger (Malachi 3:1)

Our Father (Matthew 6:9)
Our Savior (Luke 2:11)
Life Eternal (John 1:29)
The Lamb–Christ (John 1:29)
Life Accomplished (John 1:45)
Sin's Remedy (John 3:16)
Rising Sun (John 8:12)
Fulfillment (Acts 3:18,19)
Gospel of Christ (Romans 1:6)
Liberty (Romans 8:2)
Redeemer (Galatians 3:13)
Last Things (II Peter 3:10)
Satan's Defeat (Revelation 20:10)
Tree of Life Regained (Rev. 22:14

(Adapted from the Thompson Chain Reference Bible, King James Version)

Matthew

Matthew was with Jesus all the time that the Lord went out which began at His baptism unto the day that He ascended. (Acts 1:21,22) He was a competent witness to record what he saw. He wrote in Hebrew for the Jews and in Greek for the Gentiles.

The key words in Matthew are "fulfilled", "kingdom" which occurs 50 times, and "Kingdom of Heaven" 30 times.

The purpose of Matthew is to show that Jesus is the Kingly Messiah of prophesy. It gives a genealogy of Christ.
Jesus began His ministry about the time of the death of John the Baptist.

The Teachings on the Mountain is the most condensed teachings of Jesus. (Matthew 5,6,7) A Must Read!

Matthew 5

[1] And seeing the multitudes, he went up into a mountain: and when he was set, his disciples came unto him:
[2] And he opened his mouth, and taught them, saying,
[3] **Blessed are the poor in spirit: for theirs is the kingdom of heaven.**
[4] Blessed are they that mourn: for they shall be comforted.
[5] Blessed are the meek: for they shall inherit the earth.
[6] Blessed are they which do hunger and thirst after righteousness: for they shall be filled.
[7] Blessed are the merciful: for they shall obtain mercy.
[8] Blessed are the pure in heart: for they shall see God.
[9] Blessed are the peacemakers: for they shall be called the children of God.
[10] Blessed are they which are persecuted for righteousness' sake: for theirs is the kingdom of heaven.
[11] Blessed are ye, when men shall revile you, and persecute you, and shall say all manner of evil against you falsely, for my sake.
[12] Rejoice, and be exceeding glad: for great is your reward in heaven: for so persecuted they the prophets which were before you.
[13] Ye are the salt of the earth: but if the salt have lost his savour, wherewith shall it be salted? it is thenceforth good for nothing, but to be cast out, and to be trodden under foot of men.

[14] Ye are the light of the world. A city that is set on an hill cannot be hid.

[15] Neither do men light a candle, and put it under a bushel, but on a candlestick; and it giveth light unto all that are in the house.

[16] Let your light so shine before men, that they may see your good works, and glorify your Father which is in heaven.

[17] Think not that I am come to destroy the law, or the prophets: I am not come to destroy, but to fulfil.

[18] For verily I say unto you, Till heaven and earth pass, one jot or one tittle shall in no wise pass from the law, till all be fulfilled.

[19] Whosoever therefore shall break one of these least commandments, and shall teach men so, he shall be called the least in the kingdom of heaven: but whosoever shall do and teach them, the same shall be called great in the kingdom of heaven.

[20] For I say unto you, That except your righteousness shall exceed the righteousness of the scribes and Pharisees, ye shall in no case enter into the kingdom of heaven.

[21] Ye have heard that it was said by them of old time, Thou shalt not kill; and whosoever shall kill shall be in danger of the judgment:

[22] But I say unto you, That whosoever is angry with his brother without a cause shall be in danger of the judgment: and whosoever shall say to his brother, Raca, shall be in danger of the council: but whosoever shall say, Thou fool, shall be in danger of hell fire

[23] Therefore if thou bring thy gift to the altar, and there rememberest that thy brother hath ought against thee;

[24] Leave there thy gift before the altar, and go thy way; first be reconciled to thy brother, and then come and offer thy gift.

[25] Agree with thine adversary quickly, whiles thou art in the way with him; lest at any time the adversary deliver thee to the judge, and the judge deliver thee to the officer, and thou be cast into prison.

[26] Verily I say unto thee, Thou shalt by no means come out thence, till thou hast paid the uttermost farthing

[27] Ye have heard that it was said by them of old time, Thou shalt not commit adultery:

[28] But I say unto you, That whosoever looketh on a woman to lust after her hath committed adultery with her already in his heart.

[29] And if thy right eye offend thee, pluck it out, and cast it from thee: for it is profitable for thee that one of thy members should perish, and not that thy whole body should be cast into hell.

[30] And if thy right hand offend thee, cut if off, and cast it from thee: for it is profitable for thee that one of thy members should perish, and not that thy whole body should be cast into hell.

[31] It hath been said, Whosoever shall put away his wife, let him give her a writing of divorcement:

[32] But I say unto you, That whosoever shall put away his wife, saving for the cause of fornication, causeth her to commit adultery: and whosoever shall marry her that is divorced committeth adultery.

[33] Again, ye have heard that it hath been said by them of old time, Thou shalt not forswear thyself, but shalt perform unto the Lord thine oaths:

[34] But I say unto you, Swear not at all; neither by heaven; for it is God's throne:

[35] Nor by the earth; for it is his footstool: neither by Jerusalem; for it is the city of the great King.

[36] Neither shalt thou swear by thy head, because thou canst not make one hair white or black.

[37] But let your communication be, Yea, yea; Nay, nay: for whatsoever is more than these cometh of evil.

[38] Ye have heard that it hath been said, An eye for an eye, and a tooth for a tooth:

[39] But I say unto you, That ye resist not evil: but whosoever shall smite thee on thy right cheek, turn to him the other also.

[40] And if any man will sue thee at the law, and take away thy coat, let him have thy cloke also.

[41] And whosoever shall compel thee to go a mile, go with him twain.

[42] Give to him that asketh thee, and from him that would borrow of thee turn not thou away.

[43] Ye have heard that it hath been said, Thou shalt love thy neighbour, and hate thine enemy.

[44] But I say unto you, Love your enemies, bless them that curse you,

do good to them that hate you, and pray for them which despitefully use you, and persecute you;
[45] That ye may be the children of your Father which is in heaven: for he maketh his sun to rise on the evil and on the good, and sendeth rain on the just and on the unjust.
[46] For if ye love them which love you, what reward have ye? do not even the publicans the same?
[47] And if ye salute your brethren only, what do ye more than others? do not even the publicans so?
[48] Be ye therefore perfect, even as your Father which is in heaven is perfect.

Matthew 6

[1] Take heed that ye do not your alms before men, to be seen of them: otherwise ye have no reward of your Father which is in heaven.
[2] Therefore when thou doest thine alms, do not sound a trumpet before thee, as the hypocrites do in the synagogues and in the streets, that they may have glory of men. Verily I say unto you, They have their reward.
[3] But when thou doest alms, let not thy left hand know what thy right hand doeth:
[4] That thine alms may be in secret: and thy Father which seeth in secret himself shall reward thee openly.
[5] And when thou prayest, thou shalt not be as the hypocrites are: for they love to pray standing in the synagogues and in the corners of the streets, that they may be seen of men. Verily I say unto you, They have their reward.
[6] But thou, when thou prayest, enter into thy closet, and when thou hast shut thy door, pray to thy Father which is in secret; and thy Father which seeth in secret shall reward thee openly.
[7] But when ye pray, use not vain repetitions, as the heathen do: for they think that they shall be heard for their much speaking.
[8] Be not ye therefore like unto them: for your Father knoweth what things ye have need of, before ye ask him.

[9] After this manner therefore pray ye: Our Father which art in heaven, Hallowed be thy name.
[10] Thy kingdom come. Thy will be done in earth, as it is in heaven.
[11] Give us this day our daily bread.
[12] And forgive us our debts, as we forgive our debtors.
[13] And lead us not into temptation, but deliver us from evil: For thine is the kingdom, and the power, and the glory, for ever. Amen.
[14] For if ye forgive men their trespasses, your heavenly Father will also forgive you.
[15] But if ye forgive not men their trespasses, neither will your Father forgive your trespasses.
[16] Moreover when ye fast, be not, as the hypocrites, of a sad countenance: for they disfigure their faces, that they may appear unto men to fast. Verily I say unto you, They have their reward.
[17] But thou, when thou fastest, anoint thine head, and wash thy face;
[18] That thou appear not unto men to fast, but unto thy Father which is in secret: and thy Father, which seeth in secret, shall reward thee openly.
[19] Lay not up for yourselves treasures upon earth, where moth and rust doth corrupt, and where thieves break through and steal:
[20] But lay up for yourselves treasures in heaven, where neither moth nor rust doth corrupt, and where thieves do not break through nor steal:
[21] For where your treasure is, there will your heart be also.
[22] The light of the body is the eye: if therefore thine eye be single, thy whole body shall be full of light.
[23] But if thine eye be evil, thy whole body shall be full of darkness. If therefore the light that is in thee be darkness, how great is that darkness!
[24] No man can serve two masters: for either he will hate the one, and love the other; or else he will hold to the one, and despise the other. Ye cannot serve God and mammon.
[25] Therefore I say unto you, Take no thought for your life, what ye shall eat, or what ye shall drink; nor yet for your body, what ye shall put on. Is not the life more than meat, and the body than raiment?

[26] Behold the fowls of the air: for they sow not, neither do they reap, nor gather into barns; yet your heavenly Father feedeth them. Are ye not much better than they?
[27] Which of you by taking thought can add one cubit unto his stature?
[28] And why take ye thought for raiment? Consider the lilies of the field, how they grow; they toil not, neither do they spin:
[29] And yet I say unto you, That even Solomon in all his glory was not arrayed like one of these.
[30] Wherefore, if God so clothe the grass of the field, which to day is, and to morrow is cast into the oven, shall he not much more clothe you, O ye of little faith?
[31] Therefore take no thought, saying, What shall we eat? or, What shall we drink? or, Wherewithal shall we be clothed?
[32] (For after all these things do the Gentiles seek:) for your heavenly Father knoweth that ye have need of all these things.
[33] But seek ye first the kingdom of God, and his righteousness; and all these things shall be added unto you.
[34] Take therefore no thought for the morrow: for the morrow shall take thought for the things of itself. Sufficient unto the day is the evil thereof.

Matthew 7

[1] Judge not, that ye be not judged.
[2] For with what judgment ye judge, ye shall be judged: and with what measure ye mete, it shall be measured to you again.
[3] And why beholdest thou the mote that is in thy brother's eye, but considerest not the beam that is in thine own eye?
[4] Or how wilt thou say to thy brother, Let me pull out the mote out of thine eye; and, behold, a beam is in thine own eye?
[5] Thou hypocrite, first cast out the beam out of thine own eye; and then shalt thou see clearly to cast out the mote out of thy brother's eye.
[6] Give not that which is holy unto the dogs, neither cast ye your

pearls before swine, lest they trample them under their feet, and turn again and rend you.

[7] Ask, and it shall be given you; seek, and ye shall find; knock, and it shall be opened unto you:

[8] For every one that asketh receiveth; and he that seeketh findeth; and to him that knocketh it shall be opened.

[9] Or what man is there of you, whom if his son ask bread, will he give him a stone?

[10] Or if he ask a fish, will he give him a serpent?

[11] If ye then, being evil, know how to give good gifts unto your children, how much more shall your Father which is in heaven give good things to them that ask him?

[12] Therefore all things whatsoever ye would that men should do to you, do ye even so to them: for this is the law and the prophets.

[13] Enter ye in at the strait gate: for wide is the gate, and broad is the way, that leadeth to destruction, and many there be which go in thereat:

[14] Because strait is the gate, and narrow is the way, which leadeth unto life, and few there be that find it.

[15] Beware of false prophets, which come to you in sheep's clothing, but inwardly they are ravening wolves.

[16] Ye shall know them by their fruits. Do men gather grapes of thorns, or figs of thistles?

[17] Even so every good tree bringeth forth good fruit; but a corrupt tree bringeth forth evil fruit.

[18] A good tree cannot bring forth evil fruit, neither can a corrupt tree bring forth good fruit.

[19] Every tree that bringeth not forth good fruit is hewn down, and cast into the fire.

[20] Wherefore by their fruits ye shall know them.

[21] Not every one that saith unto me, Lord, Lord, shall enter into the kingdom of heaven; but he that doeth the will of my Father which is in heaven.

[22] Many will say to me in that day, Lord, Lord, have we not prophesied in thy name? and in thy name have cast out devils? and in thy name done many wonderful works?

[23] And then will I profess unto them, I never knew you: depart from me, ye that work iniquity.

[24] Therefore whosoever heareth these sayings of mine, and doeth them, I will liken him unto a wise man, which built his house upon a rock:

[25] And the rain descended, and the floods came, and the winds blew, and beat upon that house; and it fell not: for it was founded upon a rock.

[26] And every one that heareth these sayings of mine, and doeth them not, shall be likened unto a foolish man, which built his house upon the sand:

[27] And the rain descended, and the floods came, and the winds blew, and beat upon that house; and it fell: and great was the fall of it.

[28] And it came to pass, when Jesus had ended these sayings, the people were astonished at his doctrine:

[29] For he taught them as one having authority, and not as the scribes.

Matthew 6:5 The prayer of hypocrites. "And when thou prayest, thou shalt not be as the hypocrites are: for they love to pray standing in the synagogues and in the corners of the streets, that they may be seen of men. Verily I say unto you, They have their reward."

Matthew 6:8-13 "Be not ye therefore like unto them: for your Father knoweth what things ye have need of, before ye ask him. <u>After this manner therefore pray ye</u>: Our Father which art in heaven, Hallowed be thy name. Thy kingdom come. Thy will be done in earth, as it is in heaven. Give us this day our daily bread. And forgive us our debts, as we forgive our debtors. And lead us not into temptation, but deliver us from evil: For thine is the kingdom, and the power, and the glory, forever. Amen." (The Apostles prayed this prayer 3 times every day.)

Matthew 6:24 "No man can serve two masters: for either he will hate the one, and love the other; or else he will hold to the one, and despise the other. Ye cannot serve God and mammon."

Matthew 6:33 "But seek ye first the kingdom of God, and his righteousness; and all these things shall be added unto you."

Matthew 11:28-29 "Take my yoke upon you, and learn of me; for I am meek and lowly in heart: and ye shall find rest unto your souls. <u>For my yoke is easy, and my burden is light</u>."

Matthew made two strong statements about the church.
"And I say also unto thee, That thou art Peter, and upon this rock I will build my church; and the gates of hell shall not prevail against it."(Matthew 16:18)
"And if he shall neglect to hear them, tell it unto the church: but if he neglect to hear the church, let him be unto thee as an heathen man and a publican."(Mathew 18:17)

Matthew was a tax collector. (The famous verse on money)
"He unto them, **Render therefore unto Caesar the things which are Caesar's; and unto God the things that are God's.**"(Matthew 22:21)

Matthew 28:18-20 And Jesus came and spake unto them, saying, "**All power is given unto me in heaven and in earth. Go ye therefore, and teach all nations, baptizing them in the name of the Father, and of the Son, and of the Holy Ghost: Teaching them to <u>observe all things whatsoever I have commanded you</u>: and, lo, I am with you alway, even unto the end of the world. Amen.**"

Mark

Since it is only recorded in Mark he was probably the young man who followed Jesus when all the others left Him when Jesus was arrested. (14:51,52)

Mark had a lasting impact on the church. He was the first to develop the literary form known as the "Gospel" and was highly regarded as a literary artist. He wrote the book of Mark under the direction of Peter. Mark was not one of the 12 Apostles, but he was one of the 70 disciples who companioned with the Apostles all along. He was commissioned like one of the seventy. (Luke 10:19) He founded a church in Alexandria. His example influenced all the followers of Christ.

Christ is the Servant of God and man. Mark reveals the power of Christ over nature.

Mark 7:7 "Howbeit in vain do they worship me, teaching <u>for doctines the commandments of men</u>."
(Such as the man made doctrines of Calvinism, Islam, and many cults.)

"Neither pray I for these alone, but for them also which shall believe on me through their word; That they all may be one; as thou, Father, art in me, and I in thee, that they also may be one in us: that the world may believe that thou hast sent me. And the glory which thou gavest me I have given them; that they may be one, even as we are one: <u>I in them, and thou in me</u>, that they may be made perfect in one; and that the world may know that thou hast sent me, and hast loved them, as thou hast loved me."
(John 17:20,21,22,23)

Mark 9:35 "And he sat down, and called the twelve, and saith unto them, **If any man desire to be first, the same shall be last of all, and servant of all.**" The desire to be first makes one be last and the servant of all.

Mark 12:30, 31 **"And thou shalt love the Lord thy God with all thy heart, and with all thy soul, and with all thy mind, and with all thy strength: <u>this is the first commandment</u>. And <u>the second is</u> like, namely this, Thou shalt love thy neighbour as thyself. There is none other commandment greater than these."** The first and second commandments.

Mark records Jesus' Words, **"Go ye into all the world, and preach the gospel to every creature."**(16:15)
Mark saw Jesus received up into Heaven. (16:19)

Luke

Luke never met Jesus, but he chose to follow Him. (1:2)

Half of the material in Luke is not in the other gospels. Luke is the only non-Jewish author of a New Testament Book. Luke gives a unique review of the birth, death, and Resurrection of Jesus. Examples: The fish broke their nets 5:16, the widow's son raised from the dead 7:11-15, ten lepers healed 17:12-14, and the high priest's servant's right ear replaced 22:51.

Luke was the **"beloved physician"**. (Colossians 4:14)
Luke reveals the life of Christ as seen by eyewitnesses, and the universal Grace of God. Luke is the longest of the four Gospels. Only Luke describes the Ascension of Jesus in detail and gives the most detailed description of Jesus' ministry. Luke emphasizes that God's Grace was available to the Gentiles.

The Christian Hymns Taken from Luke:
"The Ave Maria" (1:28-33) The words of the angel to Mary
"The Magnificant" (1:46-55) Mary's Song
"The Benedictus" (1:68-79) of Zacharias
"The Gloria in Excelesis", (2:13-14) Heavenly angels
"The Nuno Dimittis", (2:29-32) The rejoicing of Simeon.
The Passion Week and Crucifixion (19:29-23:55)
The Resurrection and Ascension (24:1-51)

Women Are Honored:
Mary and Elizabeth (Chapter 1)
Mary and Martha (Chapter 10)

Daughters of Jerusalem (23:27)
Lukewidows (2:37; 4:26; 7:12-15; 18:3; 21:2)
Luke has the most complete biography of Christ.

Luke 1:38 "And Mary said, Behold the handmaid of the Lord; be it unto me according to thy word. And the angel departed from her." **Nothing is impossible with God.**

Luke 4:18,19 "The Spirit of the Lord is upon me, because he hath anointed me to preach the gospel to the poor; he hath sent me to heal the brokenhearted, to preach deliverance to the captives, and recovering of sight to the blind, to set at liberty them that are bruised, To preach the acceptable year of the Lord." **This is a quote from Isaiah 61:1.**

6:31 "And as ye would that men should do to you, do ye also to them likewise." (The Golden Rule)

12:8 **Confess Jesus** "Also I say unto you, Whosoever shall confess me before men, him shall the Son of man also confess before the angels of God:"

12:15 "And he said unto them, Take heed, and beware of covetousness: for a man's life consisteth not in the abundance of the things which he possesseth." **Take heed of covetousness.**

Luke is continued in the Book of Acts that he also wrote. It is the only New Testament book that has a sequel. (The Book of Acts)

John

He lived longer than any of the 12 Apostles and was the only one that died a natural death. He wrote about the spiritual things of the Gospel, the life and soul of it. This Gospel is a key to the evangelist as it <u>opens the door to Heaven</u>.

The beloved disciple. John is thought by many to be the **most spiritual book of the Bible**. Christ speaks of God as "The Father" over 100 times.

"But these are written, that ye might believe that Jesus is the Christ, the Son of God; and that believing ye might have life through his name." (John 20:31) **The key verse of John that we might believe.** This tells us how to find eternal life.

John 1:12 "But as many as received him, to them gave he power to become the sons of God, even to them that believe on his name." **We can be sons of God.** (Also noted in Deuteronomy 14:1; Galatians 3:26; 4:5,6,7; Romans 8:14, 16, 17; I John 3:1,2,10; Ephesians 5:1; Luke 20:36; Mark 10:14)

John 1:14 "And the Word was made flesh, and dwelt among us, (and we beheld his glory, the glory as of the only begotten of the Father,) full of grace and truth."

John 1:29 "The next day John seeth Jesus coming unto him, and saith, Behold the Lamb of God, **which taketh away the sin of the world**."

This famous verse tells of the beginning of eternal life.
John 3:15-17 "That whosoever believeth in him should not perish, but have eternal life. For God so loved the world, that he gave his only begotten Son, that whosoever believeth in him should not perish, but have everlasting life. For God sent not his Son into the world to condemn the world; but that the world through him might be saved." **A must know! (Or you are Biblically illiterate?)**

John 8:31-32 "Then said Jesus to those Jews which believed on him, "If ye continue in my word, then are ye my disciples indeed; And ye shall know the truth, and the truth shall make you free." Truth makes you free.

Scriptures for Life

John 13:34,35 "A new commandment I give unto you, That ye love one another; as I have loved you, that ye also love one another. By this shall all men know that ye are my disciples, if ye have love one to another." The new Commandment.

John 14:9 Jesus saith unto him, "Have I been so long time with you, and yet hast thou not known me, Philip? he that hath seen me hath seen the Father; and how sayest thou then, Shew us the Father?"

John 14:16 "And I will pray the Father, and he shall give you another Comforter, that he may abide with you for ever."

John 14:27 "Peace I leave with you, my peace I give unto you: not as the world giveth, give I unto you. Let not your heart be troubled, neither let it be afraid." His peace He leaves with us.

John 15:8 "Herein is my Father glorified, that <u>ye bear much fruit</u>; so shall ye be my disciples." With Jesus we can bring forth much fruit.

John 15:15 "Henceforth I call you <u>not servants</u>; for the <u>servant knoweth</u> not what his lord doeth: but I have called you friends; <u>for all things that I have heard of my Father I have made known unto you</u>." "Wherefore thou art **no more a servant, but a so**n; and if a son, then an heir of God through Christ."(Galatians 4:7) We are not legal property as slaves are, but we are the sons of God. (Mark 10:14; Luke 20:30) (Deuteronomy 14:1; John 1:12; Romans 8:14; Ephesians 5:1; I John 3:1,2)

Jesus was the last prophet. He has told us all we need to know, "**<u>for all things that I have heard of my Father I have made known unto you</u>.**" **John 15:15**) Therefore, there are no prophets after Jesus.

John is referred to as the "one Jesus loved" in 13:23; 19:26; 20:2; 21:7,20.

John 21:22 Jesus saith unto him, **"If I will that he tarry till I come, <u>what is that to thee</u>? follow thou me."**

Summary of John
He clearly notes the deity of Jesus:
- **Jesus is the Word and**
- **God (1:1) and**
- **He became a Man (1:14)**

Jesus called Himself - I Am:
- The Bread of Life (6:35,41,48,51),
- The Light of the world (8:12; 9:5;),
- The Door for the sheep (10:7,9)
- The Good Shepherd (10:11, 14)
- The Resurrection and the Life (11:25),
- The Way The Truth and The Life (14:6)
- The True Vine (15:1,5)

In John miracles are called signs, which can only be done by God. There are seven such signs:

1. Jesus turned water into wine (2:9)
2. Jesus healed the nobleman's son (4:51)
3. Healed on the Sabbath (5:4, 9)
4. Fed five thousand (John 6:11,13,14)
5. Jesus walks on the sea (6:19)
6. He healed a man born blind (9:1,7)
7. Jesus raises Lazarus from the dead (11:43,44)

John Chapter 17
This has been termed "The Holy of Holies of the New Covenant." Jesus is praying in the shadow of the Cross. He prays for His own life and work, for us given Him by God, and for the multitudes who down through the age who will believe. This is us!

This is longest recorded prayer of Jesus. Read all of it for a great blessing from Christ Himself. I have also outlined it for a rapid reading of the main message:

John 17:1-26
1. These words spake Jesus, and lifted up his eyes to heaven, and said, Father, the hour is come; glorify thy Son, that thy Son also may glorify thee:
2. As thou hast given him power over all flesh, that he should give eternal life to as many as thou hast given him.
3. And this is life eternal, that they might know thee the only true God, and Jesus Christ, whom thou hast sent.
4. I have glorified thee on the earth: I have finished the work which thou gavest me to do.
5. And now, O Father, glorify thou me with thine own self with the glory which I had with thee before the world was.
6. I have manifested thy name unto the men which thou gavest me out of the world: thine they were, and thou gavest them me; and they have kept thy word.
7. Now they have known that all things whatsoever thou hast given me are of thee.
8. For I have given unto them the words which thou gavest me; and they have received them, and have known surely that I came out from thee, and they have believed that thou didst send me.
9. I pray for them: I pray not for the world, but for them which thou hast given me; for they are thine.
10. And all mine are thine, and thine are mine; and I am glorified in them.
11. And now I am no more in the world, but these are in the world, and I come to thee. Holy Father, keep through thine own name those whom thou hast given me, that they may be one, as we are.
12. While I was with them in the world, I kept them in thy name: those that thou gavest me I have kept, and none of them is lost, but the son of perdition; that the scripture might be fulfilled.
13. And now come I to thee; and these things I speak in the world, that they might have my joy fulfilled in themselves.
14. I have given them thy word; and the world hath hated them, because they are not of the world, even as I am not of the world.
15. I pray not that thou shouldest take them out of the world, but that thou shouldest keep them from the evil.

16. They are not of the world, even as I am not of the world.

17. Sanctify them through thy truth: thy word is truth.

18. As thou hast sent me into the world, even so have I also sent them into the world.

19. And for their sakes I sanctify myself, that they also might be sanctified through the truth.

20. Neither pray I for these alone, but for them also which shall believe on me through their word;

21. That they all may be one; as thou, Father, art in me, and I in thee, that <u>they also may be one in us</u>: that the world may believe that thou hast sent me.

22. And the glory which thou gavest me I have given them; <u>that they may be one, even as we are one</u>:

23. I in them, and thou in me, that they may be made perfect in one; and that the world may know that thou hast sent me, and hast loved them, as thou hast loved me.

24. Father, I will that they also, whom thou hast given me, be with me where I am; that they may behold my glory, which thou hast given me: for thou lovedst me before the foundation of the world.

25. O righteous Father, the world hath not known thee: but I have known thee, and these have known that thou hast sent me.

26. And I have declared unto them thy name, and will declare it: that the love wherewith thou hast loved me may be in them, and I in them.

Outline:
Verse 1:	"the hour is come"
Verse 2:	"given him power over all flesh, and eternal life"
Verse 3:	"that they might know thee the only true God, and Jesus Christ"
Verse 4:	"I have glorified thee"
	"I have finished the work"
Verse 5:	"glorify me with that glory that I had with thee before the world was."
Verse 6:	"I have manifested thy name to men:
	"thou gavest them me"

	"they have kept thy word." (Obedient)
Verse 7:	"they know all things are of thee thou hast given me."
Verse 8:	"I have given them Your words"
Verse 9:	"I pray for them: they are mine."
Verse 10:	"all mine are thine, and thine are mine"
Verse 11:	"I come to thee Holy Father"
Verse 12:	"I have kept them none are lost, the scripture is fulfilled.
Verse 13:	"my joy is fulfilled in themselves"
Verse 14:	"I have given them thy word"
Verse 15:	"I pray that thou keep them from the evil"
Verse 16:	"They are not of this world, as I am not"
Verse 17:	"Sanctify them through thy truth"
Verse 18:	"As thou hast sent me I send them"
Verse 19:	"I sanctify myself, that they might be"
Verse 20:	"I pray for these and all those who will believe"
Verse 21:	" That they all may be one"
Verse 22:	" I give them the glory you gave Me."
Verse 23:	"I in them, and thou in me, that they may be made perfect in one; and that the world may know that thou hast sent me, and hast loved them, as thou hast loved me."
Verse 24:	"behold my glory, from before the foundation of the world"
Verse 25:	"I have known them, these have known thee, the world has not"
Verse 26:	"wherewith thou hast loved me may be in them, and I in them."

The prayers of Christ were for all kinds of people and over everything. He emphasized:
- **Sincerity**
- **Humility**
- **Repentance**
- **Obedience**

- Faith
- Forgiveness
- Fasting
- Persistence
- Privacy
- Divine Will
- Divine Name and the Holy Spirit

Acts

It shows the fulfillment of Jesus' Name and of Jesus" Words. **"And I say also unto thee, That thou art Peter, and upon this rock I will build my church; and the gates of hell shall not prevail against it."** (Matthew 16:18) **"And said unto them, Thus it is written, and thus it behoved Christ to suffer, and to rise from the dead the third day: And that repentance and remission of sins should be preached in his name among all nations, beginning at Jerusalem. And ye are witnesses of these things. And, behold, I send the promise of my Father upon you: but tarry ye in the city of Jerusalem, until ye be endued with power from on high."** (Luke 24:46-49)

The Acts of the Apostles, of the holy Apostles (The History of the Apostles.)
By Dr. Luke, the "beloved physician" (Colossians 4:14) Luke was the only one that did not desert Paul at his death. (II Timothy 4:11) Acts is the only historical book. The Acts are the history of the development of the early church. They were to be filled with the Holy Spirit. (Ephesians 5:18) and to be witnesses in all the earth. "That thou mightest know the certainty of those things, wherein thou hast been instructed." **(Luke 1:4)** and "To whom also he shewed himself alive after his passion by many infallible proofs, being seen of them forty days, and speaking of the things pertaining to the kingdom of God." **(Acts 1:3)**

The infallible proofs of Jesus and things related to the Kingdom of God. The history is filled with the Apostles sermons, sufferings, and

Scriptures for Life

labor in preaching and exposed themselves to sufferings with their achievements.

Acts Features Paul's Missionary Journeys:
First Journey (13:4-14:25)
Second Journey (15:36-18:22)
Third Journey (18:23-21:15)

Acts includes the "Council of Jerusalem". (15:5-30)
Acts 20:24 "But none of these things move me, neither count I my life dear unto myself, so that I might finish my course with joy, and the ministry, which I have received of the Lord Jesus, to testify the gospel of the grace of God." **Dr. Luke testifies to the gospel of the grace of God.**

Romans

Romans is one of the longest and fullest of Paul's fourteen Epistles and is listed first.
Romans is the mighty leveler.
"For all have sinned, and come short of the glory of God."(3:23)

The Good News,
"But God commendeth his love toward us, in that, while we were yet sinners, Christ died for us."(5:8)

The book of Romans is addressed to Roman Christians. It reveals the need and the plan of salvation. The book of Romans give the most systematic presentation of theology found any where in Scriptures and is the most doctrinal book in the Bible. It can be used as and in-depth study or a short introduction to the Christian faith.

Key Verses:
Romans 1:16 "<u>**For I am not ashamed**</u> of the gospel of Christ: <u>**for it is**</u>

the power of God unto salvation to every one that believeth; to the Jew first, and also to the Greek."

Romans 1:17 "For therein is the righteousness of God revealed from faith to faith: as it is written, The just shall live by faith."

Romans 1:20 "For the invisible things of him from the creation of the world are clearly seen, being understood by the things that are made, even his eternal power and Godhead; so that they are without excuse."

Early in Romans God, through Paul, deals with some of the worst sins, which are also prevalent today.

Chapter one lays the foundation for justification. (See also 3:23)
Nelson's Bible Commentary p. 789:
Romans 1:26 "For this cause God gave them up unto vile affections: for even their women did change the natural use into that which is against nature:" **Lesbianism is against nature; it is contrary to the intention of the Creator**.

Romans 1:27 "And likewise also the men, leaving the natural use of the woman, burned in their lust one toward another; men with men working that which is unseemly, and receiving in themselves that recompence of their error which was meet." **Homosexuality is sin**. "Thou shalt not lie with mankind, as with womankind: it is abomination. " (Leviticus 18:23)

Romans 1:28-32 "And even as they did not like to retain God in their knowledge, God gave them over to a reprobate mind, to do those things which are not convenient; Being filled with all unrighteousness, fornication, wickedness, covetousness, maliciousness; full of envy, murder, debate, deceit, malignity; whisperers, Backbiters, haters of God, despiteful, proud, boasters, inventors of evil things, disobedient to parents, Without understanding, covenantbreakers, without natural affection, implacable, unmerciful: **Who knowing the judgment of God,** that they which commit such things are worthy of death, not only do the same, but have pleasure in them that do them." One of the most extensive lists of sins in all Scripture.

Matthew Henry's Commentary, pp. 2195-2196
Man refusing to understand the God that made him, thus becomes worse than the beasts that perish, Psalms 49:20. Man becomes worse that the beasts of the fields, thus one, by the divine permission, becomes the punishment of another; but it is through the lust of their own hearts. (1:24) "God gave them up." (1:24,26,28).

Those who dishonoured God were given up to dishonour themselves. A man cannot be delivered up to a greater slavery than to be given up to his own lusts. The sins of Sodom and Gomorrah are famous and referred to throughout the Bible.

"Then the LORD rained upon Sodom and upon Gomorrah brimstone and fire from the LORD out of heaven; And he overthrew those cities, and all the plain, and all the inhabitants of the cities, and that which grew upon the ground." (Genesis 19:24,25)

Isaiah 1:9,10 "Except the LORD of hosts had left unto us a very small remnant, we should have been as Sodom, and we should have been like unto Gomorrah. Hear the word of the LORD, ye rulers of Sodom; give ear unto the law of our God, ye people of Gomorrah." (It is also described in Ezekiel 16:46-49, Amos 4:11, and Romans 9:29.)

One reference with 23 sorts of sins is listed here.
"Being filled with all unrighteousness, fornication, wickedness, covetousness, maliciousness; full of envy, murder, debate, deceit, malignity; whisperers, Backbiters, haters of God, despiteful, proud, boasters, inventors of evil things, disobedient to parents, Without understanding, covenant breakers, without natural affection, implacable, unmerciful: **Who knowing the judgment of God, that they which**

commit such things are worthy of death, not only do the same, but have pleasure in them that do them."(Romans 1:29-32)

These sins are listed as Haters of God. The Devil in his own colors, sin appearing as sin. The second charge of sin is the unrighteousness noted in all sin. Sinners invent new sins.

Romans 5:1 "Therefore being **justified by faith**, we have peace with God through our Lord Jesus Christ."

Chapter 8 is a great spiritual chapter. The Holy Spirit is referred to 19 times.

8:11 "But if the Spirit of him that raised up Jesus from the dead dwell in you, he that raised up Christ from the dead shall also quicken your mortal bodies by his **Spirit that dwelleth in you**." **We shall live if the Holy Spirit is in us.**

8:19-25 "For the earnest expectation of the **creature** waiteth for the manifestation of the sons of God. For the **creature** was made subject to vanity, not willingly, but by reason of him who hath subjected the same in hope, Because the **creature** itself also shall be delivered from the bondage of corruption into the glorious liberty of the children of God. For we know that the whole **creation groaneth** and travaileth in pain together until now. And not only they, but ourselves also, which have the firstfruits of the Spirit, even we ourselves groan within ourselves, waiting for the adoption, to wit, the redemption of our body. For we are saved by hope: but hope that is seen is not hope: for what a man seeth, why doth he yet hope for? But if we hope for that we see not, then do we with patience wait for it." **To get the true meaning of this Scripture one must know that the creature refers to the Gentiles. Nothing else fits these verses as you read them.**

8:28 "And we know that all things work together for good to them that

Scriptures for Life

love God, to them who are the called according to his purpose." **A famous verse.**

8:38,39 "For I am persuaded, that neither death, nor life, nor angels, nor principalities, nor powers, nor things present, nor things to come, Nor height, nor depth, nor any other creature, shall be able to separate us from the love of God, which is in Christ Jesus our Lord." **Nothing can take us away from Jesus.**

The Plan of Salvation by Faith: 10:4-18

"For Christ is the end of the law for righteousness to every one that believeth. For Moses describeth the righteousness which is of the law, That the man which doeth those things shall live by them. But the righteousness which is of faith speaketh on this wise, Say not in thine heart, Who shall ascend into heaven? (that is, to bring Christ down from above:) Or, Who shall descend into the deep? (that is, to bring up Christ again from the dead.) But what saith it? The word is nigh thee, even in thy mouth, and in thy heart: that is, the word of faith, which we preach; **That if thou shalt confess with thy mouth the Lord Jesus, and shalt believe in thine heart that God hath raised him from the dead, thou shalt be saved**. For with the heart man believeth unto righteousness; and with the mouth confession is made unto salvation. For the scripture saith, Whosoever believeth on him shall not be ashamed. For there is no difference between the Jew and the Greek: for the same Lord over all is rich unto all that call upon him. For **whosoever shall call upon the name of the Lord shall be saved**. How then shall they call on him in whom they have not believed? and how shall they believe in him of whom they have not heard? and how shall they hear without a preacher? And how shall they preach, except they be sent? as it is written, How beautiful are the feet of them that preach the gospel of peace, and bring glad tidings of good things! But they have not all obeyed the gospel. For Esaias saith, Lord, who hath believed our report? So then faith cometh by hearing, and hearing by the word of God. But I say, Have they not heard? Yes verily, their sound went into all the earth, and their words unto the ends of the world."

The Duties of a Christian
Romans 12:1-21
[1] I beseech you therefore, brethren, by the mercies of God, that **ye present your bodies a living sacrifice**, holy, acceptable unto God, which is your reasonable service.
[2] And be not conformed to this world: but be **ye transformed by the renewing of your mind**, that ye may prove what is that good, and acceptable, and perfect, will of God.
[3] For I say, through the grace given unto me, to every man that is among you, not to think of himself more highly than he ought to think; but to **think soberly**, according as God hath dealt to every man the measure of faith.
[4] For as we have many members in one body, and **all members have not the same offic**e:
[5] So we, being many, are **one body in Christ**, and **every one members one of another**.
[6] **Having then gifts differing according to the grace** that is given to us, whether prophecy, let us prophesy according to the proportion of faith;
[7] Or **ministr**y, let us wait on our ministering: or he that **teacheth**, on teaching;
[8] Or he that **exhorteth**, on exhortation: he that **giveth**, let him do it with simplicity; he that **ruleth**, with diligence; he that **sheweth mercy**, with cheerfulness.
[9] **Let love be without dissimulation**. Abhor that which is evil; cleave to that which is good.
[10] Be kindly affectioned one to another with brotherly love; **in honour preferring one another**;
[11] **Not slothful in business**; fervent in spirit; serving the Lord;
[12] Rejoicing in **hope**; patient in **tribulation**; continuing instant in **prayer**;
[13] **Distributing to the necessity of saints**; given to hospitality.
[14] **Bless them which persecute you**: bless, and curse not.

[15] **Rejoice** with them that do rejoice, and **weep** with them that weep.
[16] Be of the **same mind one toward another**. Mind not high things, but condescend to men of low estate. Be not wise in your own conceits.
[17] Recompense to **no man evil for evil**. Provide things honest in the sight of all men.
[18] **If it be possible**, as much as lieth in you, **live peaceably with all men**.
[19] Dearly beloved, **avenge not yourselves**, but rather give place unto wrath: for it is written, Vengeance is mine; I will repay, saith the Lord.
[20] Therefore if thine enemy hunger, **feed him**; if he thirst, **give him drink**: for in so doing thou shalt heap coals of fire on his head.
[21] Be not overcome of evil, but overcome evil with good.

Romans 1:12 "That is, that I may be **comforted together with you by the mutual faith** both of you and me." **Comfort for us.**

3:23-24 "For all have sinned, and come short of the glory of God; Being justified freely by his grace through the redemption that is in Christ Jesus." **We have all sinned.**

8:1 "There is therefore now no condemnation to them, which are in Christ Jesus, who walk not after the flesh, but after the Spirit." **No condemnation if we are in Christ.**

Paul's final words in Romans warn us about those who cause division by doctrine. I believe this in our age refers to evolutionists, homosexuality, drug addiction, alcoholism, Calvinism, gluttony ("God is their belly. They eat in excess and are poor representatives of Christ") and other immoralities.

I Corinthians
The cleansing of the church with doctrine instructions.
Factions, immorality, and abuse of the spiritual gifts split the Corinthian

church. This is another example of a nation being destroyed by decadence and prosperity. Paul stayed there eighteen months. The church was mostly gentile, but some were some converted Jews.

Corinthians is the love chapter. The preeminence of Love!
2:9 "But as it is written, Eye hath not seen, nor ear heard, neither have entered into the heart of man, the things which God hath prepared for them that love him."
Our victory promise.

6:19-20 "What? know ye not that your body is the temple of the Holy Ghost which is in you, which ye have of God, and ye are not your own? For ye are bought with a price: therefore glorify God in your body, and in your spirit, which are God's."
Your life does not belong to you. It belongs to God; therefore, suicide is murder of God's created life.

9:24 "Know ye not that they which run in a race run all, but one receiveth the prize? So run, that ye may obtain." **Run to win.**

Chapter 13:1-13 (Memorize this chapter.) The Love Chapter.
(English Standard Version translates *"Charity"* as *"Love"*, which seem best to me.)
[1] Though I speak with the tongues of men and of angels, and have not love, I am become as **sounding brass, or a tinkling cymbal**.
[2] And though I have the gift of prophecy, and understand all mysteries, and all knowledge; and though I have all faith, so that I could remove mountains, and have not love, **I am nothing**.
[3] And though I bestow all my goods to feed the poor, and though I give my body to be burned, and have not clove, it **profiteth me nothing**.
[4] Love suffereth long, and is kind; love envieth not; love vaunteth not itself, is not puffed up,
[5] Doth not behave itself unseemly, seeketh not her own, is not easily provoked, thinketh no evil;
[6] Rejoiceth not in iniquity, but rejoiceth in the truth;

[7] Beareth all things, believeth all things, hopeth all things, endureth all things.
[8] Love never faileth: but whether there be prophecies, they shall fail; whether there be tongues, they shall cease; whether there be knowledge, it shall vanish away.
[9] For we know in part, and we prophesy in part.
[10] But when that which is perfect is come, then that which is in part shall be done away.
[11] When I was a child, I spake as a child, I understood as a child, I thought as a child: but when I became a man, I put away childish things.
[12] For now we see through a glass, darkly; but then **face to face**: now I know in part; but then shall I know even as also I am known.
[13] And now abideth faith, hope, love, these three; but the greatest of these is love.

Romans 15:1-8 **Summary of the Gospel and a plan for Salvation**
This is the most detailed explanation of the Resurrection of Christ and Christians.
[1] Moreover, brethren, I declare unto you the gospel which I preached unto you, which also ye have received, and wherein ye stand;
[2] By which also ye are saved, if ye keep in memory what I preached unto you, unless ye have believed in vain.
[3] For I delivered unto you first of all that which I also received, how that **Christ died for our sins according to the scriptures**;
[4] And that **he was buried, and that he rose again the third day according to the scriptures**:
[5] And that he was **seen of Cephas**, then of the twelve:
[6] After that, **he was seen** of above five hundred brethren at once; of whom the greater part remain unto this present, but some are fallen asleep.
[7] After that, **he was seen** of James; then of all the apostles.
[8] And last of all **he was seen** of me also, as of one born out of due time.

15:33 "Be not deceived: evil communications corrupt good manners."

Rear Admiral Joseph Miller

Bad friends, bad habits.

15:42-44 "So also is the resurrection of the dead. It is sown in corruption; it is raised in incorruption: It is sown in dishonour; it is raised in glory: it is sown in weakness; it is raised in power: It is sown a natural body; it is raised a spiritual body. There is a natural body, and there is a spiritual body." **There is a natural body and a spiritual body.**

15:55-57 **The victory over death**: "O death, where is thy sting? O grave, where is thy victory? The sting of death is sin; and the strength of sin is the law. But thanks be to God, which giveth us the victory through our Lord Jesus Christ."

16:13, 14 "Watch ye, stand fast in the faith, quit you like men, be strong. Let all your things be done with love." **Be a man!**

II Corinthians

This is the most autobiographical of Paul's letters. He defended his character and his apostolic authority. The characteristics of an apostolic ministry show the labor and success of preaching. **Caution is given to the Corinthians against mingling with unbelievers**. (6:14)

1:3-4 "Blessed be God, even the Father of our Lord Jesus Christ, the Father of mercies, and the God of all comfort; Who comforteth us in all our tribulation, that we may be able to comfort them which are in any trouble, by the comfort wherewith we ourselves are comforted of God."
This is the best comfort verse in the Bible. I have used these verses in hundreds of letters to the bereaved. (The death of a loved one.)

3:1 "Do we begin again to commend ourselves? or need we, as some others, epistles of commendation to you, or letters of commendation from you?" **Communicate with others.**

Scriptures for Life

3:12 "Seeing then that we have such hope, we use great plainness of speech." **With hope nothing holds us back.**

4:18 "While we look not at the things which are seen, but at the things which are not seen: for the things which are seen are temporal; but the things which are not seen are eternal." **Christians <u>see</u> the unseen.**

5:7, 8 "(For we walk by faith, not by sight:) We are confident, I say, and willing rather to be absent from the body, and to be present with the Lord." **Also** "Grace be unto you, and peace, from God our Father, and from the Lord Jesus Christ. I thank my God upon every remembrance of you." (Also in Philippians 1:2,3)

5:12 "For we commend not ourselves again unto you, but give you occasion to glory on our behalf, that ye may have somewhat to answer them which glory in appearance, and not in heart." **Have answers for the weak in mind.**

6:2 ("For he saith, I have heard thee in a time accepted, and in the day of salvation have I succoured thee: behold, now is the accepted time; behold, now is the day of salvation.") **Now is the day of salvation.**

6:14 "Be ye not unequally yoked together with unbelievers: for what fellowship hath righteousness with unrighteousness? and what communion hath light with darkness?"

11:13 Paul confronted the "false apostles". They were like some today playing God.

12:9 "And he said unto me, **My grace is sufficient for thee: for my strength is made perfect in weakness.** Most gladly therefore will I rather glory in my infirmities, that the power of Christ may rest upon me." **When we are weak God's power is better seen.**

Galatians

The repeated phrase is "**The Truth of the Gospel**".
Salvation is through faith in Christ alone. There is no other path to salvation.

Doctrine of <u>**justification by faith**</u> and warning of false teachers.
This has been called "The Magna Charta of the Church." Justification by faith is noted in Romans 5:1.
Galatians 2:16, 3:24: <u>**James makes the point that faith is always associated with works**</u>! (<u>**James 2:24**</u>) Jesus said man can be justified by his words or condemned by is words. (Matthew 12:37)
2:16 "Knowing that a man is not justified by the works of the law, but by the faith of Jesus Christ, even we have believed in Jesus Christ, that we might be justified by the faith of Christ, and not by the works of the law: for by the works of the law shall no flesh be justified." **A must know verse! No sinful person has ever been granted eternal life based on his works and no man could ever fulfill all of the Law.**
3:28,29 "There is neither <u>**Jew nor Greek**</u>, there is neither <u>**bond nor free**</u>, there is neither <u>**male nor female**</u>: for ye are all one in Christ Jesus. And if ye be Christ's, then are ye Abraham's seed, and heirs according to the promise." **We have God's promise as heirs.**

5:1 "Stand fast therefore in the liberty wherewith Christ hath made us free, and be not entangled again with the yoke of bondage." We **are free, free!**

5:22,23,25 "But the <u>**fruit of the Spirit**</u> is love, joy, peace, longsuffering, gentleness, goodness, faith, Meekness, temperance: against such there is no law. If we live in the Spirit, let us also walk in the Spirit...Walk in the footprints of the Holy Spirit." **Walk in the footprints of the Holy Spirit**

6:2 "Bear ye one another's burdens, and so fulfil the law of Christ." **Fulfill the law of Christ.**

6:4 "But let every man prove his own work, and then shall he have rejoicing in himself alone, and not in another." **Prove yourself.**

Ephesians

On Paul's missionary journey he spent three years in Ephesus.
All the barriers between the Jews and the Gentiles are broken down.

The Theme of Ephesians is: Unity in the Church.
Faith plays a great part in the unity of believers. All believers are united in Christ because the Church is the one body of Christ.

The Key Verse:
4:13 "But all things that are reproved are made manifest by the light: for whatsoever doth make manifest is light."

4:4-6 "There is one body, and one Spirit, even as ye are called in one hope of your calling; One Lord, one faith, one baptism, One God and Father of all, **who is above all, and through all, and in you all**."

Verses 4-6 reveal the 7 Unities of Our Faith.

1. **"One body**
2. **One Spirit**
3. **One hope**
4. **One Lord**
5. **One faith**
6. **One baptism,**
7. **One God and Father of all, who is above all, and through all, and <u>in you all</u>."**

This is until the end of time:
4:13 "Till we all come in the unity of the faith, and of the knowledge of the Son of God, unto a perfect man, unto the measure of the stature of the fullness of Christ:"

The Whole Armor of God:
6:11-13 "Put on the whole armour of God, that ye may be able to stand against the wiles of the devil. For we wrestle not against flesh and blood, but against principalities, against powers, against the rulers of the darkness of this world, against spiritual wickedness in high places. Wherefore take unto you the whole armour of God, that ye may be able to withstand in the evil day, and having done all, to stand."
Whole Armor:
The Helmet of Salvation (Verse 6:17)
The Shield of Faith (Verse 6:16)
The Breastplate of Righteousness (Verse 14)
The Belt of Truth (Verse 6:14)
The Sandals of Peace (Verse 6:15)
The Sword of the Spirit (Verse 17)
The Word of God (Verse 17)
Praying always (6:18)
We open our mouths boldly to make known the mystery of the gospel. (Verse 6:19)

6:24 "Grace be with all them that love our Lord Jesus Christ in sincerity. Amen." **One must love the Lord to get His grace!**

Paul led many people to Christ in Ephesus, so many that the makers of idols due to a decrease in business rioted. (Acts 19:27) The temple of Diana was one of the seven wonders of the ancient world. It would hold 25,000 people.

Philippians
The church of Philippi was the first church in Europe. (Acts 16:12)
Paul wrote Philippians when he was a prisoner in Rome. It is a speech of spiritual love of the Church. The theme of Philippians is joy, specifically the joy of serving Christ.

1:11 "Being filled with the fruits of righteousness, which are by Jesus

Christ, unto the glory and praise of God." **The source of spiritual power is from Christ.**

1:6 "Being confident of this very thing, that he which hath begun a good work in you will perform it until the day of Jesus Christ". **A great verse. Those who began will continue to perform.**

1:18,21 "What then? notwithstanding, every way, whether in pretence, or in truth, Christ is preached; and I therein do rejoice, yea, and will rejoice. For to me to live is Christ, and to die is gain." **Preaching is the highest spiritual motive of life.**

The knowledge of Christ is the supreme prize in life.
3:8, 4:19 "Yea doubtless, and I count all things but loss for the excellency of the knowledge of Christ Jesus my Lord: for whom I have suffered the loss of all things, and do count them but dung, that I may win Christ. But my God shall supply all your need according to his riches in glory by Christ Jesus."

4:7 "And the peace of God, which passeth all understanding, shall keep your hearts and minds through Christ Jesus." **Do not worry.**

Paul and Silas were freed from prison by an earthquake. The jailor made the famous statement. " Sirs, what must I do to be saved?"(Acts 16:30)

Colossians

The Glory of Christ or Head of the Church
The church was in great conflict. Paul warned against false prophets. Paul had to deal with a doctrinal heresy in the church, which was a mixture of Judaism and Gnosticism.

Ephesians and Colossians together present a true understanding of who

Christ is and about His life, death and resurrection and what it meant to believers.

3:12-14 "Put on therefore, as the elect of God, holy and beloved, bowels of mercies, kindness, humbleness of mind, meekness, longsuffering; Forbearing one another, and forgiving one another, if any man have a quarrel against any: even as Christ forgave you, so also do ye. And above all these things put on love, which is the bond of perfectness."

3:23 "And whatsoever ye do, do it heartily, as to the Lord, and not unto men."

2:2,3,4,8.9,10 "That their hearts might be comforted, being knit together in love, and unto all riches of the full assurance of understanding, to the acknowledgement of the mystery of God, and of the Father, and of Christ; In whom are hid all the treasures of wisdom and knowledge. And this I say, lest any man should beguile you with enticing words. Beware lest any man spoil you through philosophy and vain deceit, **after the tradition of men**, after the rudiments of the world, and not after Christ. For in him dwelleth all the fulness of the Godhead bodily. **And ye are complete in him**, which is the head of all principality and power."

The Calvinists and the Muslims believe in predestination. Calvinists believe that Christ died for only those He selected before they were born. These verses warn that Christ is sufficient for the salvation of all and all are complete in Christ, which refutes Calvinism. (Islam is now the 4th largest religion.)

3:16,17 "Let the word of Christ dwell in you richly in all wisdom; teaching and admonishing one another in psalms and hymns and spiritual songs, singing with grace in your hearts to the Lord. And whatsoever ye do in word or deed, do all in the name of the Lord Jesus, giving thanks to God and the Father by him"

3:23 "And whatsoever ye do, do it heartily, as to the Lord, and not unto men."

Recently a former Southern Baptist preacher said we had to resort to a "contemporary form of worship". The word "***Contemporary***" is not in the Bible, but contempt and contemptible are in the Scriptures.

Worship in the Bible is clearly described:
Psalms 29:2 "Give unto the LORD the glory due unto his name; worship the LORD in the beauty of holiness."

Psalms 95:6,7 "O come, let us worship and **bow down**: **let us kneel** before the LORD our maker. For he is our God; and we are the people of his pasture, and the sheep of his hand. **To day if ye will hear his voice**."

Psalms 96:9 "O worship the LORD in the beauty of holiness: fear before him, all the earth."

In Matthew 4:10 Jesus said, "**Thou shalt worship the Lord thy God, and him only shalt thou serve.**"

In John 4:23,24 "**But the hour cometh, and now is, when the true worshippers shall worship the Father in spirit and in truth: for the Father seeketh such to worship him. God is a Spirit: and they that worship him must worship him in spirit and in truth.**"

Acts 17:25 "Neither is worshipped with men's hands, as though he needed any thing, seeing he giveth to all life, and breath, and all things." **We do not worship with our hands.**

We worship God by keeping the words in His Book (Bible.)

Revelation 22:9 "Then saith he unto me, See thou do it not: for I am thy fellowservant, and of thy brethren the prophets, and of them which keep the sayings of this book: worship God." **So Be It!**

I Thessalonians

The emphasis is on Comfort and Hope of the Second Coming of Christ.
Paul was deep in his love for souls. He had good success in his preaching, he established them in faith, and persuaded them to have holy conversation. Paul established the church there and sent Timothy back to reinforce the Gospel message with practical applications of the spiritual truths. It was the hub for a very successful evangelism. (1:8)

2:4 "But as we were allowed of God to be put in trust with the gospel, even so we speak; not as pleasing men, but God, which trieth our hearts."

2:8 "So being affectionately desirous of you, we were willing to have imparted unto you, not the gospel of God only, but also our own souls, because ye were dear unto us."

Every Sunday I see our pastor's heart going out to the unsaved. It is broken when no one comes forward to be saved.

Matthew 11:22 **"But I say unto you, It shall be more tolerable for Tyre and Sidon at the day of judgment, than for you."**

Revelation 9:21 "Neither repented they of their murders, nor of their sorceries, nor of their fornication, nor of their thefts."

I Thessalonians 5:21-24 "Prove all things; hold fast that which is good. Abstain from all appearance of evil. And the very God of peace sanctify you wholly; and I pray God your whole spirit and soul and body be preserved blameless unto the coming of our Lord Jesus Christ. Faithful is he that calleth you, who also will do it."

II Thessalonians
The theme is the Second Coming of Christ

3:5 "And the Lord direct your hearts into the love of God, and into the patient waiting for Christ." **We must work.**

3:10 "For even when we were with you, this we commanded you, that if any would not work, neither should he eat." The "busybodies" do not work. (3:11)

I Timothy
The theme is advice to a young minister about personal conduct and ministerial work.

6:6 "But godliness with contentment is great gain."
1:15 "For some are already turned aside after Satan."

3:5 "(For if a man know not how to rule his own house, how shall he take care of the church of God?)"

3:15 "But if I tarry long, that thou mayest know how thou oughtest to behave thyself in the house of God, which is the church of the living God, the pillar and ground of the truth."

4:4-6 "For every creature of God is good, and nothing to be refused, if it be received with thanksgiving: For it is sanctified by the word of God and prayer. If thou put the brethren in remembrance of these things, thou shalt be a good minister of Jesus Christ, nourished up in the words of faith and of good doctrine, whereunto thou hast attained."

4:10-11 "For therefore we both labour and suffer reproach, because we trust in the living God, who is the Saviour of all men, specially of those that believe. These things command and teach." **For those who believe.**

4:12 "Let no man despise thy youth; but be thou an example of the believers, in word, in conversation, in love, in spirit, in faith, in purity." **(Be an example in word, conversation, love, in spirit, in faith, in purity.)**

4:16 "Take heed unto thyself, and unto the doctrine; continue in them: for in doing this thou shalt both save thyself, and them that hear thee." **Save yourself and others.**

For the rich men:
6:17-19 "Charge them that are rich in this world, that they be not highminded, nor trust in uncertain riches, but in the living God, who giveth us richly all things to enjoy; That they do good, that they be rich in good works, ready to distribute, willing to communicate; Laying up in store for themselves a good foundation against the time to come, that they may lay hold on eternal life." **Lay up treasures that hold to eternal life.**

6:12 "Fight the good fight of faith, lay hold on eternal life, whereunto thou art also called, and hast professed a good profession before many witnesses."

6:6,7 "But godliness with contentment is great gain. For we brought nothing into this world, and it is certain we can carry nothing out."

II Timothy

Paul's last words to Timothy with final instructions about the Christian life.

1:7 "But godliness with contentment is great gain. For we brought nothing into this world, and it is certain we can carry nothing out." **God gave us a sound mind.**

2:2 "And the things that thou hast heard of me among many witnesses, the same commit thou to faithful men, who shall be able to teach others also." **Teach others.**

2:3 "Thou therefore endure hardness, as a good soldier of Jesus Christ. **Be a good soldier.**

2:16 "But shun profane and vain babblings: for they will increase unto more ungodliness." **Shun false prophets. These words are a canker, which is a spreading sore that eats tissues.**

4:6 "For I am now ready to be offered, and the time of my departure is at hand."

4:16-18 "At my first answer no man stood with me, but all men forsook me: I pray God that it may not be laid to their charge. Notwithstanding the Lord stood with me, and strengthened me; that by me the preaching might be fully known, and that all the Gentiles might hear: and I was delivered out of the mouth of the lion. And the Lord shall deliver me from every evil work, and will preserve me unto his heavenly kingdom: to whom be glory for ever and ever. Amen". **All men forsook Paul, but God gave his strength.**

I have met several spiritual missionaries who were hurt because in their mind they were not a success. Look what happened to the greatest missionary who ever lived, Paul!

Titus

Titus was a Gentile helper of Paul whom he converted. He helped build the church on Crete and tradition says he spent the last days of his life there. (Cathy and I visited one of our military bases on Crete.)

All teachers were to use sound doctrine, learn and teach their duties, set forth the free grace of God in man's salvation by Christ and show good works of those who believed in God and had hope for eternal life from Him. Titus taught church leadership and organization.

2:7,14 "In all things shewing thyself a pattern of good works: in doctrine shewing uncorruptness, gravity, sincerity, who gave himself for us, that he might redeem us from all iniquity, and purify unto himself a peculiar people, zealous of good works." **No corrupt doctrine.**

2:13 "Looking for that blessed hope, and the glorious appearing of the great God and our Saviour Jesus Christ."
All Christians look for the "Blessed Hope".

3:8 "This is a faithful saying, and these things I will that thou affirm constantly, that they which have believed in God might be careful to maintain good works. These things are good and profitable unto men."
To believers, there is emphasis on good works, but there is no conflict of doctrine with it.

1:16 "They profess that they know God; but in works they deny him, being abominable, and disobedient, and unto every good work reprobate."

3:1,14 "Put them in mind to be subject to principalities and powers, to obey magistrates, to be ready to every good work, And let ours also learn to maintain good works for necessary uses, that they be not unfruitful."

Hebrews

Hebrews establishes the supremacy and sufficiency of Christ. (1:2,3; 9:14) Hebrews was written to conform minds and confirm judgment. It was also written to Jewish Christians and was correcting doubts about the conversion to Christianity. The Gospel was above the Law. There is no Gospel replenished with more divine, and heavenly matters than Hebrews.

The 11 words of advice:

1. "Fear"(4:1)
2. "Labor" (4:11)
3. Come boldly to Grace "Let us therefore come boldly unto the throne of grace, that we may obtain mercy, and find grace to help in time of need." (4:16)
4. "Go on", "Therefore leaving the principles of the doctrine of Christ, let us go on unto perfection; not laying again the foundation of repentance from dead works, and of faith toward God,"(6:1)
5. "Draw near" (10:22)
6. "Hold fast" (10:23)
7. "Consider one another" (10:24)
8. "Run with patience" (12:1)
9. "Have grace" (12:28)
10. "Go forth" (13:13)
11. "Offer praise" "By him therefore let us offer the sacrifice of praise to God continually, that is, the fruit of our lips giving thanks to his name."(13:15)

The Faith Chapter: Read all of Chapter 11 and note the call of heroes.

11:1,3 "Now faith is the substance of things hoped for, the evidence of things not seen. Through faith we understand that the worlds were framed by the word of God, so that things which are seen were not made of things which do appear."

11:6 "But without faith it is impossible to please him: for he that cometh to God must believe that he is, and that he is a rewarder of them that diligently seek him."

11:16 "But now they desire a better country, that is, an heavenly: wherefore God is not ashamed to be called their God: for he hath prepared for them a city."

4:12 "For the word of God is quick, and powerful, and sharper than any twoedged sword, piercing even to the dividing asunder of soul and spirit, and of the joints and marrow, and is a discerner of the thoughts and intents of the heart."

10:24, 25 "And let us consider one another to provoke unto love and to good works: **Not forsaking the assembling of ourselves together**, as the manner of some is; but exhorting one another: and so much the more, as ye see the day approaching." **One must go to a Christian church.**

12:1 "Wherefore seeing we also are compassed about with so great a cloud of witnesses, let us lay aside every weight, and the sin which doth so easily beset us, and let us run with patience the race that is set before us."
Run with patience.

4:12 "For when for the time ye ought to be teachers, ye have need that one teach you again which be the first principles of the oracles of God; and are become such as have need of milk, and not of strong meat."

James

The book of James is instruction and encouragement to Christians experiencing problems. The truths laid down for practical religion manifesting itself in good works. They are still relevant in our times.

The main theme is a Practical Religion that manifests itself in good works.

Key Verses
1:27 "Pure religion and undefiled before God and the Father is this, To visit the fatherless and widows in their affliction, and to keep himself unspotted from the world."

2:26 "For as the body without the spirit is dead, so faith without works is dead also." **For James works were a natural result of faith.**

1:19,20 "Wherefore, my beloved brethren, let every man be swift to hear, slow to speak, slow to wrath: For the wrath of man worketh not the righteousness of God." **Hear fast, speak slowly.**

3:17,18 "But the wisdom that is from above is first pure, then peaceable, gentle, and easy to be intreated, full of mercy and good fruits, without partiality, and without hypocrisy. And the fruit of righteousness is sown in peace of them that make peace." **Gently, pure wisdom with mercy and good result (fruits)**

4:7 "Submit yourselves therefore to God. Resist the devil, and he will flee from you." **Submit to God and be safe.**

5:8 "Be ye also patient; stablish your hearts: for the coming of the Lord draweth nigh." **Be patient and stable.**

5:15-16 "And the prayer of faith shall save the sick, and the Lord shall raise him up; and if he have committed sins, they shall be forgiven him. Confess your faults one to another, and pray one for another, that ye may be healed. The effectual fervent prayer of a righteous man availeth much." **Confess and pray and be fervent (glowing with intensity)**

"A righteous man availeth much!!"

I Peter

The Privileges of Believers and the central truth of the Gospel.

The 8 Features of Christ:
Christ is the:

1. Source of lively hope (1:3)
2. The Sacrificial Lamb (1:19)
3. The Living and Chief Cornerstone (Christ Himself) (2:4,6)
4. Perfect example (2:6)
5. Sufferer (2:23)
6. Sin-bearer (2:24)
7. Shepherd of Souls (2:25)
8. Exalted Lord on the right hand of God. (3:22)

Christ's' sinless life, great endurance of suffering, and His commitment to truth should be our model for life.

Peter 3:4 "But let it be the hidden man of the heart, in that which is not corruptible, even the ornament of a meek and quiet spirit, which is in the sight of God of great price."

Peter 5:5 "<u>**Likewise, ye younger, submit yourselves unto the elder. Yea, all of you be subject one to another, and be clothed with humility: for God resisteth the proud, and giveth grace to the humble**</u>."

Peter 5:7 "Casting all your care upon him; for he careth for you."

II Peter

To grow in faith, knowledge with righteousness (Divine nature) was a matter of eternal life and death. **A warning against false teachers.** The emphasis was on holy living to refute false teachers.

1:4 "Whereby are given unto us exceeding great and precious promises:

that by these ye might be partakers of the divine nature, having escaped the corruption that is in the world through lust."

1:5-8
[5] And beside this, giving all diligence, add to your faith virtue; and to virtue knowledge;
[6] And to knowledge temperance; and to temperance patience; and to patience godliness;
[7] And to godliness brotherly kindness; and to brotherly kindness charity.
[8] For if these things be in you, and abound, they make you that ye shall neither be barren nor unfruitful in the knowledge of our Lord Jesus Christ.

The 7 Steps of True Knowledge:

1. Virtue
2. Knowledge
3. Temperance
4. Patience
5. Godliness
6. Brotherly kindness
7. Love

Our final destiny is the everlasting kingdom of our Lord and Savior, Jesus Christ.
1:11 "For so an entrance shall be ministered unto you abundantly into the everlasting kingdom of our Lord and Saviour Jesus Christ."
3:9 "The Lord is not slack concerning his promise, as some men count slackness; but is longsuffering to us-ward, not willing that any should perish, but that all should come to repentance." **The Lord is not willing that any should perish. There is no predestination of some for Heaven and some for Hell!**
3:18 "But grow in grace, and in the knowledge of our Lord and Savior Jesus Christ. To him be glory both now and forever. Amen." The key theological concepts include eternal life, knowing God, and abiding in

faith. John taught by contrasts: Walking in light or darkness, children of God or the Devil, life or death, and love or hate.

I John

A deep spiritual message
The word *"know"* occurs about 30 times in I John.
The problem of false teachers was countered by the eyewitness accounts of the Apostles. Gnosticism was a threat to the church.

1:9 "If we confess our sins, he is faithful and just to forgive us our sins, and to cleanse us from all unrighteousness." **Our doctrine can be seen by our righteous life and love**.

2:5 "But whoso keepeth his word, in him verily is the love of God perfected: hereby know we that we are in him."

A righteous life indicates a person has been reborn.
2:29 "If ye know that he is righteous, ye know that every one that doeth righteousness is born of him."

5:18 "We **know** that whosoever is born of God sinneth not; but he that is begotten of God keepeth himself, and that wicked one toucheth him not."

3:5 "And ye **know** that he was manifested to take away our sins; and in him is no sin." **Christ came to take away our sins.**

3:14 "We **know** that we have passed from death unto life, because we love the brethren. He that loveth not his brother abideth in death." **Pass from death to life.**

5:13 "These things have I written unto you that believe on the name of the Son of God; that ye may **know** that ye have eternal life, and that ye may believe on the name of the Son of God." **Believe and have eternal life.**

Scriptures for Life

5:15 "And if we **know** that he hear us, whatsoever we ask, we **know** that we have the petitions that we desired of him." **God hears us.**

3:2 "Beloved, now are we the sons of God, and it doth not yet appear what we shall be: but we **know** that, when he shall appear, we shall be like him; for we shall see him as he is." **We will be like Christ.**

II John

The question here is "Who is Jesus?" (Divine Truth or human error) **Warns against heresy and false teachers called Docetism who said Jesus did not come in the flesh.** Believers were to cling to the truth. Truth is referred to five times in the first four verses of II John. We are not to support doctrines of un-truth. (Verse 10) I have been asked by some ministers and missionaries for support, which was refused when they could not answer questions concerning the truth.

II John 9-11
"Whosoever transgresseth, and abideth not in the doctrine of Christ, hath not God. He that abideth in the doctrine of Christ, he hath both the Father and the Son. If there come any unto you, and bring not this doctrine, **receive him not into your house**, neither bid him God speed: For he that biddeth him God speed is partaker of his evil deeds." **There are many false teachers today.**

III John

This book concerned a struggle in the church by a member that violated Christ's command to love one another.

I have written many times III John 2 in my letters.
2. "Beloved, I wish above all things that thou mayest prosper and be in health, even as thy soul prospereth."

Jude

Jude was probably the half brother of Jesus.
The book of Jude is the history of apostasy and divine judgments. Jude's main defense of troublemakers was not to have confronted them, but to ignore them.
The **famous words,** "<u>**The faith which was once delivered unto the saints**</u>" is our objective to know and believe. (Jude 3)

Another warning:
Jude 4,5 "For there are certain men crept in unawares, who were before of old ordained to this condemnation, ungodly men, turning the grace of our God into lasciviousness, and denying the only Lord God, and our Lord Jesus Christ. I will therefore put you in remembrance, though ye once knew this, how that the Lord, having saved the people out of the land of Egypt, <u>**afterward destroyed them that believed not**</u>." **(We must believe to reach the Promised Land. (Heaven)**

Revelation

We had a several months' course on Revelation in our church. I have also taught and written about it extensively. These are the briefest of comments.
This is the only prophetical book.

The Theme is the Moral and Spiritual conflict of the ages. The Revelation is from Christ to John. (1:1) (It is not John's revelation, but is Christ's Revelation to us.)

The early church struggled with suffering, spiritual warfare, heretical doctrine, and practice, and spiritual apathy. Nothing has changed even though we know that the battle with the deceiver of the world has already been won by the blood of the Lamb. "And the great dragon was cast out, that old serpent, called the Devil, and Satan, which deceiveth the whole world: he was cast out into the earth, and his angels were cast out with him. And I heard a loud voice saying in heaven, Now is come salvation, and strength, and the kingdom of our God, and the power of his Christ: for the accuser of our brethren is cast down, which accused them before our God day and night. And they overcame him by the blood of the Lamb, and by the word of their testimony; and they loved not their lives unto the death." (Revelation 12:9-11)

1:3 "Blessed is he that readeth, and they that hear the words of this prophecy, and keep those things which are written therein: for the time is at hand."

The Conclusion:

7:9-10 "After this I beheld, and, lo, a great multitude, which no man could number, of all nations, and kindreds, and people, and tongues, stood before the throne, and before the Lamb, clothed with white robes, and palms in their hands; And cried with a loud voice, saying, Salvation to our God which sitteth upon the throne, and unto the Lamb." **The tree of life for the healing of nations:**

22:2 "In the midst of the street of it, and on either side of the river, <u>**was there the tree of life**</u>, which bare twelve manner of fruits, and yielded her fruit every month: and the leaves of the tree were for the healing of the nations."

No more curse:
22:3 "And there shall be no more curse: but the throne of God and of the Lamb shall be in it; and his servants shall serve him:"

We will see His face:
22:4 "And they shall see his face; and his name shall be in their foreheads."

In the Epilogue:
22:12 "And, behold, I come quickly; and my reward is with me, to give every man according as his work shall be."

How to Prolong Your Days

I am inspired to learn how to prolong my days:

Learn this while you are young, but there is no age limit in the Scriptures.

The Promises of God that will prolong your days:

a. **"Keep my commandments."**
Exodus 20:12 "Honour thy father and thy mother: **that thy days may be long** upon the land which the LORD thy God giveth thee."

Deuteronomy 5:33 "Ye shall walk in all the ways which the LORD your God hath commanded you, that ye may live, and that it may be well with you, and that **ye may prolong your days** in the land which ye shall possess."

Deuteronomy 6:2 "That thou mightest fear the LORD thy God, to keep all his statutes and his commandments, which I command thee, thou, and thy son, and thy son's son, all the days of thy life; and **that thy days may be prolonged**."

Proverbs 3:1,2 "My son, forget not my law; but let thine heart keep my commandments: **For length of days, and long life, and peace, shall they add to thee**."

Proverbs 4:4,6,8,10 "He taught me also, and said unto me, Let thine heart retain my words: keep my commandments, and live. Forsake her not, and she shall preserve thee: love her, and she shall keep thee. Exalt her, and she shall promote thee: she shall bring thee to honour, when thou dost embrace her. Hear, O my son, and receive my sayings; and the **years of thy life shall be many**."

Isaiah 53:10 "Yet it pleased the LORD to bruise him; he hath put him to grief: when thou shalt make his soul an offering for sin, he shall see his seed, **he shall prolong his days**, and the pleasure of the LORD shall prosper in his hand."

b. "Learn My Sayings"
Proverbs 4:10 (Noted above)

c. "Get Understanding and Wisdom"
Proverbs 3:13,16 "Happy is the man that findeth wisdom, and the man that getteth understanding. **Length of days is in her right hand**; and in her left hand riches and honour."

II. What will bring happiness, honor, glory?

a. Happiness (A merry heart)
Proverbs 3:13, 15:15 "Happy is the man that findeth wisdom, and the

man that getteth understanding. All the days of the afflicted are evil: but he that is of a merry heart hath a continual feast."
I Peter 3:10 "For he that will love life, and see good days, let him refrain his tongue from evil, and his lips that they speak no guile."

b. Honor
Proverbs 4:8 "Exalt her, and she shall promote thee: she shall bring thee to honour, when thou dost embrace her."

c. Glory
Proverbs 4:9 "She shall give to thine head an ornament of grace: a crown of glory shall she deliver to thee."

III. Summary
Abraham
Genesis 35:29
"And Isaac gave up the ghost, and died, and was gathered unto his people, being **old and full of days**: and his sons Esau and Jacob buried him."

Job 42:17 "So Job died, **being old and full of days**."

Psalms 37:18 "The LORD knoweth the **days of the upright**: and their inheritance shall be for ever."

Psalms 90:10,12,14 "The days of our years are threescore years and ten; and if **by reason of strength they be fourscore years**, yet is their strength labour and sorrow; for it is soon cut off, and we fly away. **So teach us to number our days**, that we may apply our hearts unto wisdom. O satisfy us early with thy mercy; that we may rejoice and be **glad all our days**."

Psalms 102: 3,11 "For my **days are consumed like smoke**, and my bones are burned as an hearth. **My days are like a shadow** that declineth; and I am withered like grass."

Psalms 103:15-18 "As for man, his days are as grass: as a flower of the field, so he flourisheth. **For the wind passeth over it, and it is gone**; and the place thereof shall know it no more. But the mercy of the LORD is from everlasting to everlasting upon them that fear him, and his righteousness unto children's children; To such as keep his covenant, and to those that remember his commandments **to do them**."

Psalms 55:23 "But thou, O God, shalt bring them down into the pit of destruction: **bloody and deceitful men shall not live out half their days**; but I will trust in thee."

Lamentations 5:21 "Turn thou us unto thee, O LORD, and we shall be turned; **renew our days as of old**."

Romans 13:12-14 "The night is far spent, the **day is at hand**: let us therefore cast off the works of darkness, and let us put on the armour of light. Let us walk honestly, **as in the day**; not in rioting and drunkenness, not in chambering and wantonness, not in strife and envying. But put ye on the Lord Jesus Christ, and make not provision for the flesh, to fulfil the lusts thereof."

Romans 14:5-8 "One man esteemeth one day above another: another esteemeth every day alike. Let every man be fully persuaded in his own mind. **He that regardeth the day, regardeth it unto the Lord**; and he that regardeth not the day, to the Lord he doth not regard it. He that eateth, eateth to the Lord, for he giveth God thanks; and he that eateth not, to the Lord he eateth not, and giveth God thanks. **For none of us liveth to himself, and no man dieth to himself. For whether we live, we live unto the Lord; and whether we die, we die unto the Lord: whether we live therefore, or die, we are the Lord's**."

II Corinthians 6:2-4 "(For he saith, I have heard thee in a time accepted, and in the day of salvation have I succoured thee: behold, now is the accepted time; behold, **now is the day of salvation**.) Giving no offence in any thing, that the ministry be not blamed: But in all things approving ourselves as the ministers of God, in much patience, in afflictions, in necessities, in distresses."

Hebrews 10:25 "Not forsaking the assembling of ourselves together, as the manner of some is; but exhorting one another: and so much the more, **as ye see the day approaching**."

James 5:3 "Your gold and silver is cankered; and the rust of them shall be a witness against you, and shall eat your flesh as it were fire. **Ye have heaped treasure together for the last days**."

II Peter 3:1-9 "This second epistle, beloved, I now write unto you; in both which I **stir up your pure minds by way of remembrance**: That ye may be mindful of the words which were spoken before by the holy prophets, and of the commandment of us the apostles of the Lord and Saviour: Knowing this first, **that there shall come in the last days** scoffers, walking after their own lusts, And saying, **Where is the promise of his coming**? for since the fathers fell asleep, all things continue as they were from the beginning of the creation.For this they willingly are ignorant of, that by the word of God the heavens were of old, and the earth standing out of the water and in the water: Whereby the world that then was, **being overflowed with water, perished**: But the heavens and the earth, which are now, by the same word are kept in store, **reserved unto fire against the day of judgment** and perdition of ungodly men. But, beloved, be not ignorant of this one thing, that one day is with the Lord as a thousand years, and a thousand years as one day. The Lord is not slack concerning his promise, as some men count slackness; but is longsuffering to us-ward, **not willing that any should perish**, but that all should come to repentance."

Revelation 22:12 "And, behold, I come quickly; and my reward is with me, to give every man according as his work shall be."

Prayer Does It All
("Through Prayer We See Eternity")

Outline

I.	Praying in the Old Testament
II.	Praying in the New Testament
III.	A Review of the Prayers of God's Chosen Leaders
IV.	Other Scriptural Notes on Prayer
V.	A Prayer for the Unsaved
VI.	A Soldiers Prayer Before Going into Battle (It is also called a traveler's prayer.)
VII.	Our Prayer Before Meals
	A. The Vocal or Mental Short Prayer
	B. The Mental Complete prayer
	1. Short Prayer Repeated
	2. The Word "Many" is Used Three Times
	C. Many Blessings
	1. Salvation
	2. Christian Family
	3. Successful Career
VIII.	Prayer for Our Souls
IX.	A Special Prayer for Comfort From God.

Prayer Does It All
("Through Prayer we see Eternity")

He Prayeth Well Who Loveth Well. He Prayeth Best who Loveth Best. ***The Ancient Mariner*** (1798): ***Laborare est Orare*** (To Labor is to Pray)

An action begins with a thought, to Pray is to Act!

There are 650 prayers in the Bible, 450 have recorded answers. These numbers do not include the Psalms since it is full of prayers. (**Lockyer**)

Prayer is the outpouring of our hearts. When there is no way to look "but up", we lift our eyes and hearts to see God. Prayer is talking to God. Man is the only "praying animal." However, the first blessing in the Bible is when "God blessed" animals. (Genesis 1:22) The second blessing was to man and woman. (Genesis 1:28) The third blessing was God blessing and sanctifying the seventh day. (Genesis 2:3) You are as likely to find a "living man without breath as you are to find a Christian without prayer."

I previously published a 45-page handout on my review of all the prayers in the Bible. I also included it in my book, ***"Explore the Brain for the Soul and Overcome the World."*** (It is interesting to me that except for one hospital nurse the only request I have had for this book was from academic Biblical scholars.)

I am again including it here because these prayers inspire me. Listen to the prayers of the great men of the Bible and I promise you will be inspired.

Listen to the Prayers of:
Abraham - (Genesis 13:4; 18:23)

Rear Admiral Joseph Miller

Jacob - (Genesis 32:24-30)
Moses - (Exodus 15:25)
Joshua - (Joshua 5:14, 15; 7:6-9)
Gideon - (Judges 6:36,37,39,40)
Deborah - (Judges 5:4-6)
Samson - (Judges 16:28)
Hannah - (I Samuel 1:27)
Elijah - (I Kings 18:37, 38)
Samuel - (I Samuel 7:9.10)
Solomon - (I Kings 9:3)
Jabez - (I Chronicles 4:10)
Hezekiah - (II Kings 19:19,20)
Jehosphet - (II Chronicles 18:31)
David - (II Samuel 15:30,31; Psalms 3:3, God was David's shield, glory, encourager. (Palm 51 –David's prayer for the sin of adultery with Bathsheba.)
Asa - (II Chronicles 14:11)
Man of Ethan - (I Chronicles 15:19; 16:41; Psalms 89:1)
Nehemiah - (Nehemiah 1:4-11)
Jeremiah - (Jeremiah 1:6; 20:7)
Isaiah - (Isaiah 6:5,11; 25:1-4)
Daniel - (Daniel 9:1-19) For the people
Joel - In emergency (1:19, 20) For the people (2:17)
Amos -For forgiveness (7:1-9)
Micah -No prayers in Micah, but evidence of prayer in 3:8 and the famous verse 6:8.
Habakkuk - (3:1-19) 3:18,19 are famous.
Paul - Too many prayers to list, but one stands out to me. (Romans 8:26)
Mary - (Zachariah, Luke 1:13)
The Apostles

JESUS The longest prayer of all in Chapter 17.
After I sent the Summary of the prayers in the Bible an elderly wonderful man who is always in church said to me as he was passing by me, "No one has to tell me how to pray!" He obviously had not read my report on

prayer and certainly did not know that Jesus' own disciples asked Him to teach them how to pray. "And it came to pass, that, as he was praying in a certain place, when he ceased, one of his disciples said unto him, Lord, teach us to pray, as John also taught his disciples. And he said unto them, When ye pray, say, Our Father which art in heaven, Hallowed be thy name. Thy kingdom come. Thy will be done, as in heaven, so in earth. Give us day by day our daily bread. And forgive us our sins; for we also forgive every one that is indebted to us. And lead us not into temptation; but deliver us from evil." (Luke 11:1-4) If Jesus' own disciples needed help with praying who among us is one that needs no help in prayer. All men need prayer and will come to it. "O thou that hearest prayer, unto thee shall all flesh come." (Psalms 65:2)

Romans 8:26 "Likewise the Spirit also helpeth our infirmities: for we know not what we should pray for as we ought: but the Spirit itself maketh intercession for us with groanings which cannot be uttered."

A study of prayer brings the subject of "self-transcendence" which is described as "transcending material existence" or the "primacy of the spiritual over the material."

Romans 8:26,27 "Likewise the Spirit also helpeth our infirmities: for we know not what we should pray for as we ought: but the Spirit itself maketh intercession for us with groanings which cannot be uttered. And he that searcheth the hearts knoweth what is the mind of the Spirit, because he maketh intercession for the saints according to the will of God." To believe this when one prays is a "self-transcendence" with the Holy Spirit. With this in mind, sometimes when I feel the need for prayer and I am not sure how I should pray; I simply say, "O God, O God, O God, O God." He always knows what I need and I feel answered. Our heart must be receptive and trust for this. Matthew 7:7 "**Ask**, and it shall be given you; **seek**, and ye shall find; **knock**, and it shall be opened unto you." Try it yourself. John 16:24 "But these things have I told you, that when the time shall come, ye may remember that I told you of them. And these things I said not unto you at the beginning, because I was with you."

Every Christian who has been filled by the Holy Spirit knows this. Science has shown that love is "vital to brain development" and "emotions" play a "gigantic role in all forms of thinking".

The Review Of Prayers In The Old And New Testament

Praying in the Old Testament

Genesis: Since prayer is talking to God, the first recorded word of Adam was his statement to God when God brought him a woman, whom He had created from one of Adam's ribs. Adam said his first words, "This is now bone of my bones, and flesh of my flesh; she shall be called **Woman** because she was taken out of Man." (Genesis 2:23) Adam had already named the beast of the field and the fowl of the air. "Whatsoever Adam called every living creature, that was the name thereof." (Genesis 2:19) Correspondence was established with heaven when woman arrived. (God found man hidden and naked and man's first words to God were, "The woman whom thou gavest to be with me, she gave me of the tree, and I did eat." (Genesis 3:12) "Then man began to call upon the name of the LORD." (Genesis 4:26) **Before *Woman*, God was talking to Man, now Man was talking to God.**

Enoch and Noah walked with God. (Genesis 5:22 and 6:9) This is constant communion with God even though there are no recorded prayers between them.

Abraham is described as the friend of God. (2 Chronicles 20:7, James 2:23) God said to Abraham, "Walk before Me, and be thou perfect." (Genesis 17:1). The first recorded prayer of a father for his son was Abraham to God, " O that Ishmael might live before thee." (Genesis

17:18) God answered, "And as for Ishmael, I have heard thee; Behold I have blessed him, and will make him fruitful." (Genesis 17:20)

Abram was the first tither, "and he gave tithes of all." (Genesis 14:20, Numbers 18:26, Hebrews 7: 9). Jacob was the second professed tither, "Of all that thou shalt give me, I will surely give the tenth unto thee." (Genesis 28:22) In this prayer, Jacob was also the first to make a vow with God. "Jacob vowed a vow that the LORD would be his God." (Genesis 28:20, 21)

Exodus: In Exodus Moses said unto God, "Who am I, that I should go to Pharaoh." God said, "Certainly I will be with thee." (Exodus 3:11,12). Moses said to God when the children of Israel ask me the name of the God of our fathers what will I tell them? God said, "I AM THAT I AM, say to them, I AM hath sent me to you. And God said moreover unto Moses, Thus shalt thou say unto the children of Israel, The LORD God of your fathers, the God of Abraham, the God of Isaac, and the God of Jacob, hath sent me unto you: this is my name forever, and this is my memorial unto all generations." (Exodus 3:13,14,15) Yahweh is LORD (always capital letters) and also means "I Am" and is seen 5,311 times in the Old Testament. Jesus is also "I Am" (John 8:58) LORD God is Yahweh Elohim. (Elohim is Creator) This combination is noted **582** times in the Old Testament. Yah is an abbreviation for Yahweh and is found 50 times in the Old Testament. Alleluia is Hebrew for "Praise the LORD" or "Praise ye Yah". Hallelujah should be Hallelayah, but they are the same. (This is seen in Psalm 33, 104, 106, 111-113, 117, 146-150 and Revelation 19:1, 3, 4, 6.) Note: Yahweh was changed by some in 1100 A.D to Jehovah, but it is not as close to the original scriptures as Yahweh. They however, are both the same. Moses then said I am slow of speech. God then said I make men deaf or dumb, blind or see, and make men's mouth. "I will be with thy mouth, and teach thee what thou shalt say." And Moses said, " O my LORD, send someone else I pray thee." (Exodus 4: 10-13) This made God angry, but He made Moses and Aaron His spokesman. God would talk to Moses and Moses would talk to Aaron and Aaron would talk to the people. (Exodus 4:14-16)

Moses and the children of Israel were delivered and they sang unto the LORD. "I will sing unto the LORD." (Exodus 15:11)

God answers prayers of widows or fatherless children in a strong way. "If thou afflict any widow or fatherless child and they cry unto me... **I will kill you** with the sword; and your wives shall be widows, and your children fatherless." (Exodus 22:22-24)

Leviticus: Leviticus deals with the way we approach God, but it does not mention prayer. We can assume that prayer was a part of the services in the Tabernacle.

Numbers: In Numbers we find the **famous prayer of benediction**. "The LORD bless thee, and keep thee, The LORD make his face to shine upon thee, and be gracious unto thee; the LORD lift up his countenance upon thee, and give thee peace." (Numbers 6: 24-26)

Deuteronomy: Deuteronomy gives a great prayer of thanksgiving. "We cried unto the LORD God of our fathers, the LORD heard our voice... and gave a land that floweth with milk and honey." (Deuteronomy 26: 7, 9)

Joshua: Prayer produced a miracle for Joshua. Joshua needed more light to completely defeat the five kings of the enemies of Israel. Joshua proceeded with "The mighty men of valour." (Joshua 10:7) More men died from hailstones from heaven than from the swords of the Israelites. (Joshua 10:11) Joshua said, "Sun and Moon stand still, and the sun and moon stood still until the people avenged themselves upon their enemies." (Joshua 10:12, 13) Joshua slew the five kings and hanged them on five trees. (Joshua 10: 26)

Judges: In Judges the people continued to sin and constantly repented and called on the LORD, "Israel cried unto the LORD." (Judges 3: 9, 4:3, 6:7, 10: 10)

Scriptures for Life

God heard the cry of the Israelites and raised up Gideon. An angel of the LORD appeared to Gideon and said, "**The LORD is with thee**, thou mighty man of valour." (Judges 6: 12)

Samson's father, Manoah, prayed for him before he was born and asked God for instructions in the manner of raising Samson. (Judges 13:12) Samson prayed in the face of death, "God, remember me, strengthen me only this once." God heard his prayer. Samson pulled the pillars of the house down and it fell upon the Lords and all the people inside. He slew more at his death than he did in all his life. (Judges 16:28-30)

Ruth: There are no recorded prayers in Ruth.

I Samuel: In Hannah's prayer she related, "**I rejoice in my salvation**." (I Samuel 2:1)

The LORD does not always answer prayer. "When Saul prayed to the LORD, the LORD answered him not." (I Samuel 28: 6,15) The LORD had departed from Saul and his doom was sealed. (See also Zechariah 7:13, "God would not hear.")

The last days of Saul as recorded in I Samuel brings up several points for discussion for followers of God who sin and become unrepentant. The LORD had departed from Saul because of his disobedience. Saul later repented but it was too late. God would not take him back. "Saul was afraid, He was afraid and his heart greatly trembled." (I Samuel 28:5). **His sins were before his eyes**. He had spared the guilty blood of the Amalekites. God had ordered Saul to, "Go and smite Amalek and utterly destroy all that they have, and spare them not, but slay both man and woman, infant and suckling, ox and sheep, camel and ass." (I Samuel 15:3) A very clear order from God, don't you agree? Saul disobeyed, "Saul spared Agag (king of the Amalekites) and the best of the sheep, oxen, fatlings, lambs, and all that was good." (I Samuel 15:9) **Saul spilled the innocent blood of the LORD's priests.** Saul said to his footmen, "Slay the priests of the LORD." (I Samuel 22:17) The LORD said to Samuel, "It repenteth me that I have set up Saul to be king; for he has turned away from following me; and hath not performed my commandments." (I Samuel 15:11) When Samuel confronted Saul he argued with Samuel. (I Samuel 15: 20-23) Saul then admitted that he had sinned and wanted to worship the LORD again. (I Samuel 15:24-25) **This is another example of God not showing mercy**. King Agag was brought to Samuel and the king said, "Surely the bitterness of death is past." Samuel said, "As thy sword hath made women childless, so shall thy mother be childless. And Samuel hewed Agag to pieces before the LORD." (I Samuel 15: 32, 33)

Samuel did not see Saul again before Samuel died and the LORD repented that he had made Saul king over Israel. (I Samuel 15: 35) It was too late. The LORD had departed from Saul. Samuel died. (I Samuel 25: 11) "**Seek ye the LORD while He may be found**". (Isaiah 55:6) Saul went to a witch and she raised up an evil spirit, (Some think the devil) disguised as Samuel. "Wherefore dost thou ask of me, seeing the LORD departed from thee, and has become thine enemy? Because thou obeyedst not the voice of the LORD…the LORD will deliver thee unto the hands of the Philistines; and tomorrow thou and thy sons shall be with me." (I Samuel 28: 16-19) This was an evil spirit and some think it was the devil speaking. This certainly meant death, which did happen to Saul and his sons. Did it mean they went to hell? Is it possible Saul appointed by God to be king and because of his disobedience he died and went to hell? Let me know what you think!

In the battle with the Philistines Saul's sons were killed and the archers hit Saul. (I Samuel 31: 2,3) Saul asked his armor-bearer to kill him, but he refused. (I Samuel 31: 4) This was the first request for a mercy killing (Euthanasia) and it was refused. Saul committed suicide by falling on his own sword and so did his armor–bearer. (Jews are not likely to commit suicide. They feel it is murder since one's life does not belong to him, but to God.) (What loyalty, most "armor-bearers" I know would run under those circumstance and so would I!) There is a second report of Saul's death, which sounds more feasible since a young man brought in Saul's crown and bracelet. David had him killed because he killed Saul, God's anointed. (2 Samuel 1: 6-16)

They cut off Saul's head and tied his body to the wall of Beth-shan along with his sons. (I Samuel 31: 9, 10)

The story of Saul disobeying God certainly gives us a lot to think about.

2 Samuel: David sinned with Bathsheba and she became with child. Nathan told David that because of his sin their child would die. (II Samuel 12:14) God struck the child and the child died on the seventh day. (2 Samuel 12:18) **God said no** to David's prayer to save the child conceived in sin. David was mourning the death of his son and made a profound statement. "…I shall go to him, but he shall not return to me." (II Samuel 12:23) This is the first statement in the Bible that indicates the belief that we will be with our families in heaven.

I Kings: Elijah became distressed at the wrath of Jezebel and **asked God to let him die**. (I Kings 19:4) God refused and later Elijah was taken by a whirlwind up to heaven. (2 Kings 2:11) Sometimes God refuses our requests for our own good. (Other great Biblical men who asked God to let them die include: Moses in Numbers 11:15; Job in Job 6:9; Jeremiah in Jeremiah 20:16; Jonah in Jonah 4:3; and Samson in Judges 16:30.

Solomon prayed for wisdom. "O LORD thou has made me king; and I am but as a little child; I know not how to go out or come in …give me understanding and wisdom."
(I Kings 3:7-9; 4:29; 2 Chronicles 1: 10). Solomon prayed for the people's dedication. (I Kings 8:22-61)

II Kings: God answers prayer for a longer life. King Hezekiah was very ill. Isaiah told him he would die, "for thou shall die and not live." (2 Kings 20:1) Hezekiah prayed and God answered, **"I have heard thy prayer and I will add fifteen years to thy days**." (II Kings 20:5-6)

During that fifteen years Hezekiah had a son Manasseh, who became an abomination unto the LORD. This is an example where it may have been better if Hezekiah had died earlier.

I Chronicles: The now familiar prayer of Jabez "Oh that thou wouldest bless me indeed, and enlarge my coast, and that thine hand might be with me, and that thou wouldest keep me from evil, that it may not grieve me." (I Chronicles 4:10) **God granted his request**.

We pray when we are afraid. David knew how to pray as well as play. "And David was afraid of God that day…" (I Chronicles 13:12)

David's most beautiful prayer of thanksgiving and giving **should be read by all.**
(I Chronicles 29: 10-20) Only a small part of the prayer is noted here. "For all that is in heaven and in earth is thine…both riches and honor come from thee… therefore, our God, we thank thee, and praise thy glorious name. But who are we that we should be able to offer so willingly …of thine own have we given thee…our days on earth are as a shadow…I have willingly offered…thy people have willingly offered… keep this forever in the hearts of thy people…and prepare their hearts unto thee." Gifts or prayer unless from a generous heart are to no avail. **Both the gifts and the giver must be placed on the altar.**

2 Chronicles: The effect of a pure and generous heart is given in God's answer to Solomon's request for wisdom. "And God said to Solomon, because this was in thine heart, and thou hast not asked for riches, wealth, or honor, nor the life of thine enemies, neither yet hast asked for long life, **but hast asked for wisdom**…that thou may judge my people…**wisdom and knowledge is granted unto you**; and I will give thee riches, and wealth, honor and such as none of the kings have that have been before thee, and neither shall there any after thee have the like." (2 Chronicles 1: 10-12)

Ezra: Ezra gives a prayer of thanksgiving and later a prayer of confession.

"Blessed be the LORD God of our fathers which hath put such a thing in the king's heart, **to beautify the house of the LORD."** (Ezra 7:27) **This reminds me of our pastor's call for our church's continued beautification and enlargement**. Ezra's prayer of confession reminds me of us. "O my God, I am ashamed and blush to lift up my face to thee, my God; for our iniquities are increased over our head and our trespass is grown up into the heavens." (Ezra 9:6)

Nehemiah: **Nehemiah prayed day and night.** (Nehemiah 1:6) God put in Nehemiah's heart to build at Jerusalem. (Nehemiah 2:12) Jerusalem was in "waste". The destroyed wall was a "reproach." (Nehemiah 2:17) The hand of God was upon Nehemiah and the people said, **"Let us rise up and build.** So they strengthened their hands for this good work." (Nehemiah 2:18) Nehemiah describes worship and prayer led by Ezra before all the people, "and Ezra opened the book…and all the people stood up. And Ezra blessed the LORD, the great God. And all the people answered, Amen, Amen, with lifting up their hands; and they bowed their heads, and worshipped the LORD with their faces to the ground." (Nehemiah 8:6)

Esther: There are no prayers in Esther.

Job: Job was a man of prayer. "Then Job arose and rent his mantle, and shaved his head, and fell down upon the ground, and worshipped, and said, Naked came I out of my mother's womb and naked shall I return thither. **The LORD gave, and the LORD hath taken away; blessed be the name of the LORD**. In all this Job sinned not, and did not charge God foolishly." (Job 1:20-22)

<u>**Psalms**</u>: The Psalms are the prayer-praise book of the Bible.
A few include prayer as an:
- <u>Ascent to God</u>: "Unto thee, O LORD, do I lift up my soul, O my God. I trust in thee, let me not be ashamed." (Psalms 25:1-2).
- <u>Accomplishment</u>: "I waited patiently for the LORD; and he inclined unto me and heard my cry. He brought me up

out of a horrible pit, out of miry clay, and set my feet upon a rock, and established my goings." (Psalms 40: 1-2).
- <u>Refuge</u>: "God is our refuge and strength, a very present help in trouble. Therefore we fear not…" (Psalms 46:1-2).
- <u>Broken heart</u>: "Have mercy upon me O God. According to thy lovingkindness, according unto the multitude of thy tender mercies blot out my transgressions." (Psalms 51:1)
- <u>Trust</u>: "For thou art my hope, O LORD God, thou are my trust from my youth." (Psalms 71:5)
- <u>Safe Passage at Sea</u>: "They that go down to the sea in ships, that do business in great waters;These see the works of the LORD, and his wonders in the deep. For he commandeth, and raiseth the stormy wind, which lifteth up the waves thereof. They mount up to the heaven, they go down again to the depths: their soul is melted because of trouble. They reel to and fro, and stagger like a drunken man, and are at their wit's end. Then they cry unto the LORD in their trouble, and he bringeth them out of their distresses. He maketh the storm a calm, so that the waves thereof are still." (Psalms 107: 23-29).
- <u>Soul Satisfier</u>: "For <u>he satisfieth the longing soul</u> and filleth the hungry soul with goodness." (Psalms 107:9)
- <u>Searching Heart</u>: "O LORD, thou hast searched me, and known me…If I take the wings of the morning, and dwell in the uttermost parts of the sea, even there shall thy hand lead me, and thy right hand shall hold me…I will praise thee; for I am fearfully and wonderfully made… if there be any wicked way in me, and lead me in the way everlasting." (Psalms 139:1, 9, 10, 14, 24)

Proverbs: Proverbs is the book of wisdom but there are no recorded prayers. There are some references to prayers. One of these include: <u>**Prayer, when uttered by unholy lips, is an abomination in God's sight**</u>. (Proverbs 28: 9)

Ecclesiastes: There are no prayers in Ecclesiastes even though Ecclesiastes means *"preacher".*

Some words of note include:
"To everything there is a season and a time to every purpose under the heaven," (Ecclesiastes. 3:1). "Dead flies cause the ointment of the apothecary to stink; as **doth a little folly** that is in him with reputation for wisdom and honor." (Ecclesiastes 10:1), **"Let us hear the conclusion, fear God, and keep his commandments, for this is the whole duty of man."** (Ecclesiastes 12: 13)

Song of Solomon: Contains no prayer or reference to God or any spiritual truth.

Isaiah: Isaiah stands out as **the prophet who knew how to pray**. God does not hear the prayers of the wicked. "When ye make many prayers, I will not hear; your hands are full of blood." (Isaiah 1:15) **Peace is for one who prays**. "Thou wilt keep him in perfect peace, whose mind is stayed on thee". (Isaiah 26:3) **God also answers prayer before they are given**. "Before they call, I will answer, I will answer while they are yet speaking." (Isaiah 65:24)

Jeremiah: **Jeremiah knew how to pray** as well as weep. Jeremiah confessed his weakness, "LORD God behold, I cannot speak, for I am a child." (Jeremiah 1:6). God said, "Whatsoever I command, thou shall speak." (Jeremiah 1:7) Jeremiah mourned for lack of support, "The priest said not, where is the LORD? And they that handle the law knew me not, the pastors also transgressed against me, and the prophets prophesied by Baal, and walked after things that do not profit." (Jeremiah 2:8) "O LORD, I know that the way of man is not in himself: it is not in man that walketh to direct his steps. O LORD, correct me, but with judgment; not in thine anger, lest thou bring me to nothing." (Jeremiah 10: 23,24) Through prayer God's way becomes known. "The LORD thy God may show us the way wherever we may walk, and the thing that we may do." (Jeremiah 42:3)

Lamentations: Lamentations is a follow-up of Jeremiah. There are prayers of:
- **Pain:** "O LORD, for I am in distress, my bowels are troubled, mine heart is turned within me…there is none to comfort me." (Lamentations 1:20,21)
- **Pity:** "The young and old lie on the ground in the streets, my virgins and my young men have fallen by the sword… in the day of the LORD's anger that hast killed and not pitied." (Lamentations 2:21)

Jeremiah concludes "Thou, O LORD remainest forever; **thy throne from generation to generation**." (Lamentations 5:19)

Ezekiel: In Ezekiel (He was a captive in Babylon, which is now modern day Iraq) we learn that **blessings must be sought after** and God provides a sanctuary. "Then fell I upon my face, and cried with a loud voice…yet will I be to them as a little sanctuary in the countries where they shall come." (Ezekiel 11: 13,16)

Daniel: Daniel prayed that they would know the secret of the King's dream. (Daniel 2:18) (**Note:** Daniel had a death sentence on him and his friends. **What did he do?** **He prayed** and **went to bed** and **fell asleep**. God gave him the answer to save their lives in a deep sleep dream. Check that out for faith in prayer and God. Daniel 2:19) Daniel interpreted Nebuchadnezzar's dream and he replied, "Of a truth it is, that your God is a God of gods, and a LORD of kings, and a revealer of secrets." (Daniel 2:47) Then the king made Daniel great.

The famous model prayer of Daniel: (Read the whole prayer in Daniel 9:3-20.) "O, our God, hear the prayers of thy servants, and his supplications and cause thy face to shine upon thy sanctuary that is desolate, for the LORD's sake. O my God incline thine ear, and hear; open thine eyes, and behold our desolations, and the city which is called by thy name, for we do not present our supplications before thee for our righteousness, but for thy great mercies, O LORD **hear**, O LORD **forgive**, O LORD **hearken** and do, **defer not**, for thine own sake, O my

God, for thy city and **thy people are called by thy Name**." (Daniel 9: 17-19)

Daniel's prayer produced instant results from God and freedom from fear, "Fear not Daniel, for from the first day that thou didst set thy heart to understand, and to chasten thyself before thy God, **thy word's were heard**." (Daniel 10: 12)

And Daniel received **wisdom**, "Now I come to make thee understand," (Daniel 10:14), and strength, "and he **strengthened** me." (Daniel 10:18)

Hosea: There are no recorded prayers in Hosea.

Joel: Joel gives an example of prayer in an emergency. "**O LORD To thee will I cry,** for the fire had devoured the pastures of the wilderness, and the flame hath burned all the trees." (Joel: 1:9)

Amos: In Amos we learn that Jehovah is the God of the world not just the Jewish race. "You only have I known of all the families of the earth." (Amos 3:2)

Obadiah: There are no recorded prayers in Obadiah, the shortest book of the Old Testament.

Jonah: Jonah prayed and repented because he had no other choice, "Jonah prayed unto the LORD his God out of the fish's belly, "**I cried by reason of mine affliction.**" (Jonah 2: 1,2) "When my soul fainted within me I remembered the LORD, and my prayer came in unto thee." (Jonah 2: 7)

Micah: There are no recorded prayers in Micah.

Nahum: There are no recorded prayers in Nahum.

Rear Admiral Joseph Miller

Habakkuk: In an answer to Habakkuk's prayer God included a statement central to the Christian faith, "**The just shall live by his faith.**" (Habakkuk 2:4) In Habakkuk's prayer again it is noted that, "the sun and moon stood still." (Habakkuk 3:11) Habakkuk concludes with the famous, "**I will joy in the God of my salvation. The LORD is my strength, and he will make my feet like hinds feet, and he will make me to walk upon mine high places.**" (Habakkuk 3:18,19)

Zephaniah: There are no recorded prayers in Zephaniah.

Haggai: There are no recorded prayers in Haggai.

Zechariah: The LORD spoke to Zechariah through angels. There is no reference of Zechariah speaking directly to God. "I spoke to the angel that talked to me." (Zechariah 4:4 and 6:4) Another example of God not answering prayer from wicked men, "So they cried, and I would not hear, saith the LORD of hosts." (Zechariah 7 13) (See I Samuel 28:6,15. God would not hear Saul.)

Malachi: Malachi has six protest prayers all with the word Wherein:

1. Hast thou loved us (1: 2)
2. Have we despised thy name (1:61)
3. Have we polluted thee (the priests gave God their cast –offs) (1:7)
4. Have we wearied Him (tried God's patience) (2:17)
5. Shall we return (They did not return and rejected God.) (3:7)
6. Have we robbed thee (In tithes and offerings) (3:8)

Praying in the New Testament

The prayers of the Old Testament are more earthly. In the New Testament they are more spiritual.

The prayers of Christ were for all kinds of people and over everything. He emphasized: sincerity, humility, repentance, obedience, faith, forgiveness, fasting, persistence, privacy, according to divine will, in the Divine Name, and in the Holy Spirit.

The LORD's Prayer (Model Prayer)

<u>Matthew 6: 9-13</u>

After this manner therefore pray ye:

"Our Father which art in heaven, Hallowed be thy name. Thy kingdom come. Thy will be done in earth, as it is in heaven. Give us this day our daily bread. And forgive us our debts, as we forgive our debtors. And lead us not into temptation, but deliver us from evil: For thine is the kingdom, and the power, and the glory, forever. Amen."

The Holy of Holies of the New Covenant:

Jesus longest recorded prayer. His only prolonged prayer. Jesus is the Godly Intercessor. Jesus believes prayer to be a working force. <u>**This is the Prayer of all Prayers.**</u>

Jesus prays in the shadow of the cross. His work is accomplished. Jesus prays for His own life and work. He prays for us given to Him by God. He prays for the multitudes who down through the ages will believe. (That is us.)

<u>John 17: 1-26</u>

1. These words spake Jesus, and lifted up his eyes to heaven, and said, "Father, the hour is come; glorify thy Son, that thy Son also may glorify thee:

[2.] **As thou hast given him power over all flesh, that he should give eternal life to as many as thou hast given him.**

[3.] **And this is life eternal, that they might know thee the only true God, and Jesus Christ, whom thou hast sent.**

[4.] **I have glorified thee on the earth: I have finished the work which thou gavest me to do.**

[5.] And now, O Father, glorify thou me with thine own self with the glory which I had with thee before the world was.

[6.] I have manifested thy name unto the men which thou gavest me out of the world: thine they were, and thou gavest them me; and they have kept thy word.

[7.] Now they have known that all things whatsoever thou hast given me are of thee.

[8.] For I have given unto them the words which thou gavest me; and they have received them, and have known surely that I came out from thee, and they have believed that thou didst send me.

[9.] I pray for them: I pray not for the world, but for them which thou hast given me; for they are thine.

[10.] And all mine are thine, and thine are mine; and I am glorified in them.

[11.] And now I am no more in the world, but these are in the world, and I come to thee. Holy Father, keep through thine own name those whom thou hast given me, that they may be one, as we are.

[12.] While I was with them in the world, I kept them in thy name: those that thou gavest me I have kept, and none of them is lost, but the son of perdition; that the scripture might be fulfilled.

[13.] And now come I to thee; and these things I speak in the world, that they might have my joy fulfilled in themselves.

[14.] I have given them thy word; and the world hath hated them, because they are not of the world, even as I am not of the world.

[15.] I pray not that thou shouldest take them out of the world, but that thou shouldest keep them from the evil.

[16.] They are not of the world, even as I am not of the world.

[17.] Sanctify them through thy truth: thy word is truth.

[18.] As thou hast sent me into the world, even so have I also sent them into the world.

[19.] And for their sakes I sanctify myself, that they also might be sanctified through the truth.

[20.] Neither pray I for these alone, but for them also which shall believe on me through their word;

[21.] That they all may be one; as thou, Father, art in me, and I in thee, that they also may be one in us: that the world may believe that thou hast sent me.

[22.] And the glory which thou gavest me I have given them; that they may be one, even as we are one:

[23.] I in them, and thou in me, that they may be made perfect in one; and that the world may know that thou hast sent me, and hast loved them, as thou hast loved me.

[24.] Father, I will that they also, whom thou hast given me, be with me where I am; that they may behold my glory, which thou hast given me: for thou lovedst me before the foundation of the world.

[25.] O righteous Father, the world hath not known thee: but I have known thee, and these have known that thou hast sent me.

[26.] And I have declared unto them thy name, and will declare it: that the love wherewith thou hast loved me may be in them, and I in them.

Verse 1:	"the hour is come"
Verse 2:	"given him power over all flesh, and eternal life"
Verse 3:	"that they might know thee the only true God, and Jesus Christ"
Verse 4:	"I have glorified thee"
	"I have finished the work"
Verse 5:	"glorify me with that glory that I had with thee before the world was."
Verse 6:	"I have manifested thy name to men:
	"thou gavest them me"
	"they have kept thy word." (Obedient)
Verse 7:	"they know all things are of thee thou hast given me."
Verse 8:	"I have given them Your words"
Verse 9:	"I pray for them: they are mine."
Verse 10:	"all mine are thine, and thine are mine"
Verse 11:	"I come to thee Holy Father"
Verse 12:	"I have kept them none are lost, the scripture is fulfilled.
Verse 13:	"my joy is fulfilled in themselves"
Verse 14:	"I have given them thy word"

Verse 15:	"I pray that thou keep them from the evil"
Verse 16:	"They are not of this world, as I am not"
Verse 17:	"Sanctify them through thy truth"
Verse 18:	"As thou hast sent me I send them"
Verse 19:	"I sanctify myself, that they might be"
Verse 20:	"I pray for these and all those who will believe"
Verse 21:	" That they all may be one"
Verse 22:	" I give them the glory you gave Me."
Verse 23:	"I in them, and thou in me, that they may be made perfect in one; and that the world may know that thou hast sent me, and hast loved them, as thou hast loved me."
Verse 24:	"behold my glory, from before the foundation of the world"
Verse 25:	"I have known them, these have known thee, the world has not"
Verse 26:	"wherewith thou hast loved me may be in them, and I in them."

To Direct Our Prayer:
Ephesians 1:3: "Blessed be the God and Father of our Lord Jesus Christ, who hath blessed us with all spiritual blessings in heavenly places in Christ:"

John 16:23, 24
[23.] **And in that day ye shall ask me nothing. Verily, verily, I say unto you, Whatsoever ye shall ask the Father in my name, he will give it you.**
[24.] **Hitherto have ye asked nothing in my name: ask, and ye shall receive, that your joy may be full.**

Our Prayers Must be Supported by Faith.
Matthew 21:22
[22.] **And all things, whatsoever ye shall ask in prayer, believing, ye shall receive.**

Jesus Prays for us.

John 14:16
[16.] And I will pray the Father, and he shall give you another Comforter, that he may abide with you for ever;

The Prayer of Hypocrites:
Matthew 6:5
[5.] And when thou prayest, thou shalt not be as the hypocrites are: for they love to pray standing in the synagogues and in the corners of the streets, that they may be seen of men. Verily I say unto you, They have their reward.

God Knows When Our Lives Do Not Match Our Prayers:
Luke 18:10-14
[10.] Two men went up into the temple to pray; the one a Pharisee, and the other a publican.
[11.] The Pharisee stood and prayed thus with himself, God, I thank thee, that I am not as other men are, extortioners, unjust, adulterers, or even as this publican.
[12.] I fast twice in the week, I give tithes of all that I possess.
[13.] And the publican, standing afar off, would not lift up so much as his eyes unto heaven, but smote upon his breast, saying, God be merciful to me a sinner.
[14.] I tell you, this man went down to his house justified rather than the other: for every one that exalteth himself shall be abased; and he that humbleth himself shall be exalted.

Matthew 15:8
[8.] This people draweth nigh unto me with their mouth, and honoureth me with their lips; but their heart is far from me.

Mark 7:7
[7.] Howbeit in vain do they worship me, teaching for doctrines the commandments of men.

The Prayer Promise of Jesus (We must be gathered in the name of Jesus.)
Matthew 18:19-20
[19.] Again I say unto you, That if two of you shall agree on earth as touching any thing that they shall ask, it shall be done for them of my Father which is in heaven.
[20.] For where two or three are gathered together in my name, there am I in the midst of them.

Luke 11:9-10
[9.] And I say unto you, Ask, and it shall be given you; seek, and ye shall find; knock, and it shall be opened unto you.
10. For every one that asketh receiveth; and he that seeketh findeth; and to him that knocketh it shall be opened.

John 15:16
[16.] Ye have not chosen me, but I have chosen you, and ordained you, that ye should go and bring forth fruit, and that your fruit should remain: that whatsoever ye shall ask of the Father in my name, he may give it you.

Prayer of Jesus
Matthew 11:25-27
[25.] At that time Jesus answered and said, I thank thee, O Father, Lord of heaven and earth, because thou hast hid these things from the wise and prudent, and hast revealed them unto babes.
[26.] Even so, Father: for so it seemed good in thy sight.
[27.] All things are delivered unto me of my Father: and no man knoweth the Son, but the Father; neither knoweth any man the Father, save the Son, and he to whomsoever the Son will reveal him.

Jesus Gave Thanks Before Meals
Matthew 15:36 (Mark 6:41, 8:6)
[36.[And he took the seven loaves and the fishes, and gave thanks,

and brake them, and gave to his disciples, and the disciples to the multitude.

Jesus Prayer of His Mission Three Times
Matthew 26: 39,42,44 (No answer to this prayer.)
[39.] And he went a little further, and fell on his face, and prayed, saying, **O my Father, if it be possible, let this cup pass from me: nevertheless not as I will, but as thou wilt.**
[42.] He went away again the second time, and prayed, saying, **O my Father, if this cup may not pass away from me, except I drink it, thy will be done.**
[44.] And he left them, and went away again, and prayed the third time, saying the same words.

John 12:27-30 (This prayer answered.)
[27.] **Now is my soul troubled; and what shall I say? Father, save me from this hour: but for this cause came I unto this hour.**
[28.] **Father, glorify thy name.** Then came there a voice from heaven, saying, I have both glorified it, and will glorify it again.
[29.] The people therefore, that stood by, and heard it, said that it thundered: others said, An angel spake to him.
[30.] Jesus answered and said, **This voice came not because of me, but for your sakes.**

Jesus' Three Prayers On the Cross.
Matthew 27:46
[46.] And about the ninth hour Jesus cried with a loud voice, saying, **Eli, Eli, lama sabachthani?** that is to say, My God, my God, why hast thou forsaken me?

Luke 23:34
[34.] Then said Jesus, **Father, forgive them; for they know not what they do.** And they parted his raiment, and cast lots.

Luke 23:46

[46.] And when Jesus had cried with a loud voice, he said, **Father, into thy hands I commend my spirit:** and having said thus, he gave up the ghost.

Jesus Had a Habit of Prayer
Mark 1:35
[35.] And in the morning, rising up a great while before day, he went out, and departed into a solitary place, and there prayed.

Jesus Prayed Alone
Mark 6:46
[46.] And when he had sent them away, he departed into a mountain to pray.

<u>Luke 5:15-16</u>
[15.] But so much the more went there a fame abroad of him: and great multitudes came together to hear, and to be healed by him of their infirmities.
[16.] And he withdrew himself into the wilderness, and prayed.

<u>Luke 9:18</u>
[18.] "**And it came to pass, as He was alone praying, His disciples were with him: and He asked them, saying, Whom say the people that I am?**

Look What Happened to Zecharias (during one of his routine times of prayer.)
Luke 1:11-22
[11.] And there appeared unto him an angel of the Lord standing on the right side of the altar of incense.
[12.] And when Zacharias saw him, he was troubled, and fear fell upon him.
[13.] But the angel said unto him, Fear not, Zacharias: <u>**for thy prayer is heard**</u>; and thy wife Elisabeth shall bear thee a son, and thou shalt call his name John.

[14.] And thou shalt have joy and gladness; and many shall rejoice at his birth.
[15.] For he shall be great in the sight of the Lord, and shall drink neither wine nor strong drink; and he shall be filled with the Holy Ghost, even from his mother's womb.
[16.] And many of the children of Israel shall he turn to the Lord their God.
[17.] And he shall go before him in the spirit and power of Elias, to turn the hearts of the fathers to the children, and the disobedient to the wisdom of the just; to make ready a people prepared for the Lord.
[18.] And Zacharias said unto the angel, Whereby shall I know this? for I am an old man, and my wife well stricken in years.
[19.] And the angel answering said unto him, I am Gabriel, that stand in the presence of God; and am sent to speak unto thee, and to shew thee these glad tidings.
[20.] And, behold, thou shalt be dumb, and not able to speak, until the day that these things shall be performed, because thou believest not my words, which shall be fulfilled in their season.
[21.] And the people waited for Zacharias, and marvelled that he tarried so long in the temple.
[22.] And when he came out, he could not speak unto them: and they perceived that he had seen a vision in the temple: for he beckoned unto them, and remained speechless.

Luke 1:57-80
[57] Now Elisabeth's full time came that she should be delivered; and she brought forth a son.
[58] And her neighbours and her cousins heard how the Lord had shewed great mercy upon her; and they rejoiced with her.
[59] And it came to pass, that on the eighth day they came to circumcise the child; and they called him Zacharias, after the name of his father.
[60] And his mother answered and said, Not so; but he shall be called John.
[61] And they said unto her, There is none of thy kindred that is called by this name.
[62] And they made signs to his father, how he would have him called.

[63] And he asked for a writing table, and wrote, saying, His name is John. And they marvelled all.

[64] And his mouth was opened immediately, and his tongue loosed, and he spake, and praised God.

[65] And fear came on all that dwelt round about them: and all these sayings were noised abroad throughout all the hill country of Judaea.

[66] And all they that heard them laid them up in their hearts, saying, What manner of child shall this be! And the hand of the Lord was with him.

[67] And his father Zacharias was filled with the Holy Ghost, and prophesied, saying,

[68] Blessed be the Lord God of Israel; for he hath visited and redeemed his people.

[69] And hath raised up an horn of salvation for us in the house of his servant David;

[70] As he spake by the mouth of his holy prophets, which have been since the world began:

[71] That we should be saved from our enemies, and from the hand of all that hate us;

[72] To perform the mercy promised to our fathers, and to remember his holy covenant;

[73] The oath which he sware to our father Abraham,

[74] That he would grant unto us, that we being delivered out of the hand of our enemies might serve him without fear,

[75] In holiness and righteousness before him, all the days of our life.

[76] And thou, child, shalt be called the prophet of the Highest: for thou shalt go before the face of the Lord to prepare his ways;

[77] To give knowledge of salvation unto his people by the remission of their sins,

[78] Through the tender mercy of our God; whereby the dayspring from on high hath visited us,

[79] To give light to them that sit in darkness and in the shadow of death, to guide our feet into the way of peace.

[80] And the child grew, and waxed strong in spirit, and was in the deserts till the day of his shewing unto Israel.

Mary's famous prayer when she went to Elizabeth and told her about the angel Gabriel's visit to her announcing that she would be the mother of Jesus. (This is also known as the Song of Mary).

Luke 1:46-55
[46] And Mary said, My soul doth magnify the Lord,
[47] And my spirit hath rejoiced in God my Saviour.
[48] For he hath regarded the low estate of his handmaiden: for, behold, from henceforth all generations shall call me blessed.
[49] For he that is mighty hath done to me great things; and holy is his name.
[50] And his mercy is on them that fear him from generation to generation.
[51] He hath shewed strength with his arm; he hath scattered the proud in the imagination of their hearts.
[52] He hath put down the mighty from their seats, and exalted them of low degree.
[53] He hath filled the hungry with good things; and the rich he hath sent empty away.
[54] He hath holpen his servant Israel, in remembrance of his mercy;
[55] As he spake to our fathers, to Abraham, and to his seed for ever.

A Prayer of Worship
Luke 2:9-14
[9] And, lo, the angel of the Lord came upon them, and the glory of the Lord shone round about them: and they were sore afraid.
[10] And the angel said unto them, Fear not: for, behold, I bring you good tidings of great joy, which shall be to all people.
[11] For unto you is born this day in the city of David a Saviour, which is Christ the Lord.
[12] And this shall be a sign unto you; Ye shall find the babe wrapped in swaddling clothes, lying in a manger.
[13] And suddenly there was with the angel a multitude of the heavenly host praising God, and saying,
[14] Glory to God in the highest, and on earth peace, good will toward men.

The Prayer of Simeon
Luke 2:25-33

[25] And, behold, there was a man in Jerusalem, whose name was Simeon; and the same man was just and devout, waiting for the consolation of Israel: and the Holy Ghost was upon him.

[26] And it was revealed unto him by the Holy Ghost, that he should not see death, before he had seen the Lord's Christ.

[27] And he came by the Spirit into the temple: and when the parents brought in the child Jesus, to do for him after the custom of the law,

[28] Then took he him up in his arms, and blessed God, and said,

[29] Lord, now lettest thou thy servant depart in peace, according to thy word:

[30] For mine eyes have seen thy salvation,

[31] Which thou hast prepared before the face of all people;

[32] A light to lighten the Gentiles, and the glory of thy people Israel.

Jesus' Prayer at His Baptism
Luke 3:21-22

[21.] Now when all the people were baptized, it came to pass, that Jesus also being baptized, and praying, the heaven was opened,

[22.] And the Holy Ghost descended in a bodily shape like a dove upon him, and a voice came from heaven, which said, Thou art my beloved Son; in thee I am well pleased.

Jesus Prayed All Night. (Can we do less?)
Luke 6:12

[12.] And it came to pass in those days, that he went out into a mountain to pray, and continued all night in prayer to God.

Luke 9:28-37 (The Transfiguration)

[28] And it came to pass about an eight days after these sayings, he took Peter and John and James, and went up into a mountain to pray.

[29] And as he prayed, the fashion of his countenance was altered, and his raiment was white and glistering.

[30] And, behold, there talked with him two men, which were Moses and Elias:

[31] Who appeared in glory, and spake of his decease which he should accomplish at Jerusalem.

[32] But Peter and they that were with him were heavy with sleep: and when they were awake, they saw his glory, and the two men that stood with him.

[33] And it came to pass, as they departed from him, Peter said unto Jesus, Master, it is good for us to be here: and let us make three tabernacles; one for thee, and one for Moses, and one for Elias: not knowing what he said.

[34] While he thus spake, there came a cloud, and overshadowed them: and they feared as they entered into the cloud.

[35] And there came a voice out of the cloud, saying, This is my beloved Son: hear him.

[36] And when the voice was past, Jesus was found alone. And they kept it close, and told no man in those days any of those things which they had seen.

[37] And it came to pass, that on the next day, when they were come down from the hill, much people met him.

Prayer From Hell
Luke 16:19-31

[19] There was a certain rich man, which was clothed in purple and fine linen, and fared sumptuously every day:

[20] And there was a certain beggar named Lazarus, which was laid at his gate, full of sores,

[21] And desiring to be fed with the crumbs which fell from the rich man's table: moreover the dogs came and licked his sores.

[22] And it came to pass, that the beggar died, and was carried by the angels into Abraham's bosom: the rich man also died, and was buried;

[23] And in hell he lift up his eyes, being in torments, and seeth Abraham afar off, and Lazarus in his bosom.

[24] And he cried and said, Father Abraham, have mercy on me, and

send Lazarus, that he may dip the tip of his finger in water, and cool my tongue; for I am tormented in this flame.

[25] But Abraham said, Son, remember that thou in thy lifetime receivedst thy good things, and likewise Lazarus evil things: but now he is comforted, and thou art tormented.

[26] And beside all this, between us and you there is a great gulf fixed: so that they which would pass from hence to you cannot; neither can they pass to us, that would come from thence.

[27] Then he said, I pray thee therefore, father, that thou wouldest send him to my father's house:

[28] For I have five brethren; that he may testify unto them, lest they also come
into this place of torment.

[29] Abraham saith unto him, They have Moses and the prophets; let them hear them.

[30] And he said, Nay, father Abraham: but if one went unto them from the dead, they will repent.

[31] And he said unto him, If they hear not Moses and the prophets, neither will they be persuaded, though one rose from the dead.

Jesus Said Men Ought Always Pray
Luke 18:1
[1.] And he spake a parable unto them to this end, that men ought always to pray, and not to faint;

Jesus' Prayer for Peter
Luke 22:31-32
[31.] And the Lord said, **Simon, Simon, behold, Satan hath desired to have you, that he may sift you as wheat:**
[32.] But I have prayed for thee, that thy faith fail not: and when thou art converted, strengthen thy brethren.

Jesus Felt Our Agony As a Man
Luke 22:41-44

[41.] And he was withdrawn from them about a stone's cast, and kneeled down, and prayed,

[42.] Saying, **Father, if thou be willing, remove this cup from me: nevertheless not my will, but thine, be done.**

[43.] And there appeared an angel unto him from heaven, strengthening him.

[44.] And being in an agony he prayed more earnestly: and his sweat was as it were great drops of blood falling down to the ground.

Jesus' Prayer to Give Us the Holy Spirit and Comforter
John 14:16-17

[16.] **And I will pray the Father, and he shall give you another Comforter, that he may abide with you for ever;**

[17.] **Even the Spirit of truth; whom the world cannot receive, because it seeth him not, neither knoweth him: but ye know him; for he dwelleth with you, and shall be in you.**

Jesus Prayed for His Miracles So That We Would Believe
John 11:41-42

[41.] Then they took away the stone from the place where the dead was laid. And Jesus lifted up his eyes, and said, **Father, I thank thee that thou hast heard me.**

[42.] **And I knew that thou hearest me always: but because of the people which stand by I said it, that they may believe that thou hast sent me.**

John 12:27-30

[27.] **Now is my soul troubled; and what shall I say? Father, save me from this hour: but for this cause came I unto this hour.**

[28.] **Father, glorify thy name.** Then came there a voice from heaven, saying, I have both glorified it, and will glorify it again.

[29.] The people therefore, that stood by, and heard it, said that it thundered: others said, An angel spake to him.

[30.] Jesus answered and said, **This voice came not because of me, but for your sakes.**

Rear Admiral Joseph Miller

Prayers in Christ's Name
John 14:13-14
[13.] **And whatsoever ye shall ask in my name, that will I do, that the Father may be glorified in the Son.**
[14.] **If ye shall ask any thing in my name, I will do it.**

John 15:16
[16.] **Ye have not chosen me, but I have chosen you, and ordained you, that ye should go and bring forth fruit, and that your fruit should remain: that whatsoever ye shall ask of the Father in my name, he may give it you.**

John 16:23
[23.] **And in that day ye shall ask me nothing. Verily, verily, I say unto you, Whatsoever ye shall ask the Father in my name, he will give it you.**

In the Upper Room the First Church of Jesus Christ was born **<u>in the first prayer meeting of the church</u>**. They were waiting and preparing themselves, 120 were present. If we wait prayerfully we will hear. I don't believe we can hear in the presence of loud noise.

Acts 1:13-15
[13.] And when they were come in, they went up into an upper room, where abode both Peter, and James, and John, and Andrew, Philip, and Thomas, Bartholomew, and Matthew, James the son of Alphaeus, and Simon Zelotes, and Judas the brother of James.
[14.] These all continued with one accord in prayer and supplication, with the women, and Mary the mother of Jesus, and with his brethren.
[15.] And in those days Peter stood up in the midst of the disciples, and said, (the number of names together were about a hundred and twenty,)

Early Worship
Acts 2:42

[42.] And they continued stedfastly in the apostles' doctrine and fellowship, and in breaking of bread, and in prayers.

There Was an Hour of Prayer in the Temple.
Acts 3:1
[1.] Now Peter and John went up together into the temple at the hour of prayer, being the ninth hour.

Praying Makes us Bold
Acts 4:31
[31.] And when they had prayed, the place was shaken where they were assembled together; and they were all filled with the Holy Ghost, and they spake the word of God with boldness.

Deacons were selected so that the Apostles could give themselves to prayer and the ministry. (Notice that prayer is first.)
Acts 6:4
[4.] But we will give ourselves continually to prayer, and to the ministry of the word.

The First Deacon and First Martyr Prayed the Same Prayer That Christ Prayed On the Cross. (Luke 23:34)
Acts 7: 59-60
[59.] And they stoned Stephen, calling upon God, and saying, Lord Jesus, receive my spirit.
[60.] And he kneeled down, and cried with a loud voice, Lord, lay not this sin to their charge. And when he had said this, he fell asleep.

<u>Saul</u> blinded by the sight of Jesus prayed and was restored and became great in God's work.

Acts 9: 3-6
[3.] And as he journeyed, he came near Damascus: and suddenly there shined round about him a light from heaven:

[4.] And he fell to the earth, and heard a voice saying unto him, Saul, Saul, why persecutest thou me?

[5.] And he said, Who art thou, Lord? And the Lord said, I am Jesus whom thou persecutest: it is hard for thee to kick against the pricks.

[6.] And he trembling and astonished said, Lord, **what wilt thou have me to do**? (**This is similar to what the jailor said in Acts 16:30. These men were both ready to be converted.**) And the LORD said unto him, Arise, and go into the city, and it shall be told thee what thou must do.

Acts 8-11

[8.] And Saul arose from the earth; and when his eyes were opened, he saw no man: but they led him by the hand, and brought him into Damascus.

[9.] And he was three days without sight, and neither did eat nor drink.

[10.]And there was a certain disciple at Damascus, named Ananias; and to him said the Lord in a vision, Ananias. And he said, Behold, I am here, Lord.

[11.] And the Lord said unto him, Arise, and go into the street which is called Straight, and inquire in the house of Judas for one called Saul, of Tarsus: for, behold, he prayeth,

Acts 15-20

[15.] But the Lord said unto him, Go thy way: for he is a chosen vessel unto me, to bear my name before the Gentiles, and kings, and the children of Israel:

[16.] For I will shew him how great things he must suffer for my name's sake.

[17.] And Ananias went his way, and entered into the house; and putting his hands on him said, Brother Saul, the Lord, even Jesus, that appeared unto thee in the way as thou camest, hath sent me, that thou mightest receive thy sight, and be filled with the Holy Ghost.

[18.] And immediately there fell from his eyes as it had been scales: and he received sight forthwith, and arose, and was baptized.

[19.] And when he had received meat, he was strengthened. Then was Saul certain days with the disciples which were at Damascus.

[20.] And straightway he preached Christ in the synagogues, that he is the Son of God.

Peter Prayed and Raised Tabitha (Dorcas) From the Dead.
Acts 9:40
[40.] But Peter put them all forth, and kneeled down, and prayed; and turning him to the body said, Tabitha, arise. And she opened her eyes: and when she saw Peter, she sat up.

Cornelius Was a Gentile and a Man of Prayer. (God heard him and directed him unto Peter. This opened up the ministry to the Gentiles.)
Acts 10:1-5
[1.] There was a certain man in Caesarea called Cornelius, a centurion of the band called the Italian band,
[2.] A devout man, and one that feared God with all his house, which gave much alms to the people, and prayed to God alway.
[3.] He saw in a vision evidently about the ninth hour of the day an angel of God coming in to him, and saying unto him, Cornelius.
[4.] And when he looked on him, he was afraid, and said, What is it, Lord? And he said unto him, Thy prayers and thine alms are come up for a memorial before God.
[5.] And now send men to Joppa, and call for one Simon, whose surname is Peter:

Acts 10: 33-36
[33.] Immediately therefore I sent to thee; and thou hast well done that thou art come. Now therefore are we all here present before God, to hear all things that are commanded thee of God.
[34.] Then Peter opened his mouth, and said, Of a truth I perceive that God is no respecter of persons:
[35.] But in every nation he that feareth him, and worketh righteousness, is accepted with him.
[36.] The word which God sent unto the children of Israel, preaching peace by Jesus Christ: (he is Lord of all:)

Prayer Released Peter From Prison.
Acts 12: 10,12,17
[10.] When they were past the first and the second ward, they came unto the iron gate that leadeth unto the city; which opened to them of his own accord: and they went out, and passed on through one street; and forthwith the angel departed from him.
[12.] And when he had considered the thing, he came to the house of Mary the mother of John, whose surname was Mark; where many were gathered together praying.
[17.] But he, beckoning unto them with the hand to hold their peace, declared unto them how the Lord had brought him out of the prison. And he said, Go shew these things unto James, and to the brethren. And he departed, and went into another place.

Paul and Silas Prayed and Were Released From Prison.
Acts 16:25-32
[25.] And at midnight Paul and Silas prayed, and sang praises unto God: and the prisoners heard them.
[26.] And suddenly there was a great earthquake, so that the foundations of the prison were shaken: and immediately all the doors were opened, and every one's bands were loosed.
[27.] And the keeper of the prison awaking out of his sleep, and seeing the prison doors open, he drew out his sword, and would have killed himself, supposing that the prisoners had been fled.
[28.] But Paul cried with a loud voice, saying, Do thyself no harm: for we are all here.
[29.] Then he called for a light, and sprang in, and came trembling, and fell down before Paul and Silas,
[30.] And brought them out, and said, Sirs, what must I do to be saved?
[31.] And they said, Believe on the Lord Jesus Christ, and thou shalt be saved, and thy house.
[32.] And they spake unto him the word of the Lord, and to all that were in his house.

Scriptures for Life

Paul Prayed When He Was Leaving Ephesus (for the last time.)
Acts 20:36
[36.] And when he had thus spoken, he kneeled down, and prayed with them all.

Paul Prayed That Israel Might be Saved.
Romans 10:1
[1.] Brethren, my heart's desire and prayer to God for Israel is, that they might be saved.

Paul in All of Life's Hope and Problems Prayed.
Romans 12:12
[12.] Rejoicing in hope; patient in tribulation; continuing instant in prayer;

Paul's Prayer of Comfort.
II Corinthians 1:3-4 (This is a great prayer Scripture. I have sent it to hundreds of people in time of bereavement.)
[3.] Blessed be God, even the Father of our Lord Jesus Christ, the Father of mercies, and the God of all comfort;
[4.] Who comforteth us in all our tribulation, that we may be able to comfort them which are in any trouble, by the comfort wherewith we ourselves are comforted of God.

Paul's Prayer For the Saints.
Many pastors, missionaries, teachers, etc. ask us to pray for them. This is natural and a good thing to do, but Paul is taking prayer a step further and is praying for the people. A young man recently asked our church to pray for him. I asked him to tell me about his prayer time and how often he prayed. He obviously was not prepared to answer the question. If someone asks you, can you tell him or her your prayer schedule and what and whom you usually pray for. When someone asks for prayer they should always add, "I will be praying also for you."

Ephesians 1:15-21

[15.] Wherefore I also, after I heard of your faith in the Lord Jesus, and love unto all the saints,

[16.] Cease not to give thanks for you, **making mention of you in my prayers**;

[17.] That the God of our Lord Jesus Christ, the Father of glory, **may give unto you** the spirit of wisdom and revelation in the knowledge of him:

[18.] The eyes of your understanding being enlightened; **that ye may know** what is the hope of his calling, and what the riches of the glory of his inheritance in the saints,

[19.] And what is the exceeding greatness of his power to us-ward who believe, according to the working of his mighty power,

[20.] Which he wrought in Christ, when he raised him from the dead, and set him at his own right hand in the heavenly places,

[21.] Far above all principality, and power, and might, and dominion, and every name that is named, not only in this world, but also in that which is to come:

Ephesians 3: 14-21

[14.] For this cause I bow my knees unto the Father of our Lord Jesus Christ,

[15.] Of whom the whole family in heaven and earth is named,

[16.] That **he would grant you**, according to the riches of his glory, to be strengthened with might by his Spirit in the inner man;

[17.] That **Christ may dwell in your hearts** by faith; that ye, being rooted and grounded in love,

[18.] **May be able to comprehend** with all saints what is the breadth, and length, and depth, and height;

[19.] And to know the love of Christ, which passeth knowledge, **that ye might be filled** with all the fulness of God.

[20.] Now unto him that is able to do exceeding abundantly above all that we ask or think, according to the power that worketh in us,

[21.] Unto him be glory in the church by Christ Jesus throughout all ages, world without end. Amen.

We Have Access to God.

Ephesians 2:18
[18.] For through him we both have access by one Spirit unto the Father.

Ephesians 3:12
[12.] In whom we have boldness and access with confidence by the faith of him.

Prayer to Strengthen the Inner Man.
Ephesians 3:13-21
[13.] Wherefore I desire that ye faint not at my tribulations for you, which is your glory.
[14.] For this cause I bow my knees unto the Father of our Lord Jesus Christ,
[15.] **Of whom the whole family in heaven and earth is named**,
[16.] That **he would grant you**, according to the riches of his glory, to be strengthened with might by his Spirit in the inner man;
[17.] **That Christ may dwell in your hearts** by faith; that ye, being rooted and grounded in love,
[18.] **May be able to comprehend** with all saints what is the breadth, and length, and depth, and height;
[19.] And to know the love of Christ, which passeth knowledge, **that ye might be filled** with all the fulness of God.
[20.] Now unto him that is able to do exceeding abundantly above all that we ask or think, according to the power that worketh in us,
[21.] Unto him be glory in the church by Christ Jesus throughout all ages, world without end. Amen.
Give Thanks Always to God.

Ephesians 5: 19-20
[19.] Speaking to yourselves in psalms and hymns and spiritual songs, singing and making melody in your heart to the Lord;
[20.] Giving thanks always for all things unto God and the Father in the name of our Lord Jesus Christ;

Rejoice in the Lord Always.
Philippians 4:4
[4.] Rejoice in the Lord alway: and again I say, Rejoice.

<u>Request for Joy.</u>
Philippians 1:2-7
[2.] Grace be unto you, and peace, from God our Father, and from the Lord Jesus Christ.
[3.] **<u>I thank my God upon every remembrance of you,</u>**
[4.] Always in every prayer of mine for you all making request with joy,
[5.] For your fellowship in the gospel from the first day until now;
[6.[Being confident of this very thing, that he which hath begun a good work in you will perform it until the day of Jesus Christ:
[7.[Even as it is meet for me to think this of you all, because I have you in my heart; inasmuch as both in my bonds, and in the defence and confirmation of the gospel, ye all are partakers of my grace.

Peace of Mind.
Philippians 4: 6-7, 19
[6.] Be careful for nothing; but in every thing by prayer and supplication with thanksgiving **<u>let your requests be made known unto God.</u>**
[7.] And the peace of God, which passeth all understanding, shall keep your hearts and minds through Christ Jesus.
[19.] But my God shall supply all your need according to his riches in glory by Christ Jesus.

Prayer for Blessing. (How many can you count?)
Colossians 1:9-14
[9.] For this cause we also, since the day we heard it, **<u>do not cease to pray for you</u>**, and to desire that ye might be filled with the knowledge of his will in all wisdom and spiritual understanding;
[10.] That **<u>ye might walk worthy</u>** of the Lord unto all pleasing, being fruitful in every good work, and increasing in the knowledge of God;

[11.] **Strengthened with all might**, according to his glorious power, unto all patience and longsuffering with joyfulness;
[12. Giving thanks unto the Father, which hath made us meet to be partakers of the inheritance of the saints in light:
[13.] Who hath delivered us from the power of darkness, and hath translated us into the kingdom of his dear Son:
[14.] In whom we have redemption through his blood, even the forgiveness of sins:

Prayers of Fellowship for Each Other So That We Can Speak the Truth.
Colossians 4: 2-6
[2.] Continue in prayer, and watch in the same with thanksgiving;
[3.] Withal praying also for us, that God would open unto us a door of utterance, to speak the mystery of Christ, for which I am also in bonds:
[4.] That I may make it manifest, as I ought to speak.
[5.] Walk in wisdom toward them that are without, redeeming the time.
[6.] Let your speech be alway with grace, seasoned with salt, that ye may know how ye ought to answer every man.

We Must Remember Each Other.
I Thessalonians 1:2-3
[2.] We give thanks to God always for you all, **making mention of you in our prayers**;
[3.] Remembering without ceasing your work of faith, and labour of love, and patience of hope in our Lord Jesus Christ, in the sight of God and our Father;

Prayer for Sanctification That We Can be Preserved Blameless.
I Thessalonians 5: 17-18, 21-23
[17.] **Pray without ceasing.**
[18.] In everything give thanks: for this is the will of God in Christ Jesus concerning you.

[21.] **Prove all things**; hold fast that which is good.
[22.] Abstain from all appearance of evil.
[23.] And the very God of peace sanctify you wholly; and **I pray God your whole spirit and soul and body be preserved blameless** unto the coming of our Lord Jesus Christ.

Prayer for Those in Authority.
I Timothy 2: 1-3
[1.] I exhort therefore, that, first of all, supplications, prayers, intercessions, and giving of thanks, be made for all men;
[2.] For kings, and for all that are in authority; that we may lead a quiet and peaceable life in all godliness and honesty.
[3.] For this is good and acceptable in the sight of God our Saviour;

Paul Noted We Must Go Forward or We Will Go Backward.
Hebrews 5: 11-14
[11.] Of whom we have many things to say, and hard to be uttered, seeing ye are dull of hearing.
[12.] For when for **the time ye ought to be teachers, ye have need that one teach you again** which be the first principles of the oracles of God; and are become such as have need of milk, and not of strong meat.
[13.] For every one that useth milk is unskilful in the word of righteousness: for he is a babe.
[14.] But strong meat belongeth to them that are of full age, even those who by reason of use have their senses exercised to discern both good and evil.

Prayer to Do God's Will.
Hebrews 13: 20-21
[20.] Now the God of peace, that brought again from the dead our Lord Jesus, that great shepherd of the sheep, through the blood of the everlasting covenant,
[21.] Make you perfect in every good work **to do his will**, working in you that which is wellpleasing in his sight, through Jesus Christ; to whom be glory for ever and ever. Amen.

If One Lacks Wisdom, Ask God.
James 1:5
[5.] If any of you lack wisdom, let him ask of God, **that giveth to all men liberally**, and upbraideth not; and it shall be given him.

Prayer For Those Who Are Married.
I Peter 3:7
[7.] Likewise, ye husbands, dwell with them according to knowledge, giving honour unto the wife, as unto the weaker vessel, and as being heirs together of the grace of life; that your prayers be not hindered.

We must be filled with the Holy Spirit to be the best in prayer. We must:
- Build up faith
- Pray in the Holy Spirit
- Keep ourselves in love
- Look for mercy unto eternal life
- Have compassion
- Save others
- Hate evil

Jude 20-23
[20.] But ye, beloved, building up yourselves on your most **holy faith, praying** in the Holy Ghost,
[21.] **Keep yourselves in the love of God**, looking for the **mercy** of our Lord Jesus Christ **unto eternal life**.
[22.] And of some **have compassion**, making a difference:
[23.] And **others save** with fear, pulling them out of the fire; **hating** even the garment **spotted by the flesh.**

Prayers Are Described As Incense and Raised Arms as Sacrifice.
Psalm 141:2
[2.] Let my prayer be set forth before thee as incense; and the lifting up of my hands as the evening sacrifice.

(Revelation 5:8) "...twenty elders fell down before the Lamb, having every one of them harps, and golden vials full of odors (incense), which are the prayers of saints."

Revelation 8:3-4
[3.] And another angel came and stood at the altar, having a golden censer; and there was given unto him much incense, that he should offer it with the prayers of all saints upon the golden altar which was before the throne.
[4.] And the smoke of the incense, which came with the prayers of the saints, ascended up before God out of the angel's hand.

Their Praise Goes Up As a Prayer.
Revelation 5: 9-14
[9] And they sung a new song, saying, Thou art worthy to take the book, and to open the seals thereof: for thou wast slain, and hast redeemed us to God by thy blood out of every kindred, and tongue, and people, and nation;
[10] And hast made us unto our God kings and priests: and we shall reign on the earth.
[11] And I beheld, and I heard the voice of many angels round about the throne and the beasts and the elders: and the number of them was ten thousand times ten thousand, and thousands of thousands;
[12] Saying with a loud voice, Worthy is the Lamb that was slain to receive power, and riches, and wisdom, and strength, and honour, and glory, and blessing.
[13] And every creature which is in heaven, and on the earth, and under the earth, and such as are in the sea, and all that are in them, heard I saying, Blessing, and honour, and glory, and power, be unto him that sitteth upon the throne, and unto the Lamb for ever and ever.
[14] And the four beasts said, Amen. And the four and twenty elders fell down and worshipped him that liveth for ever and ever.

One of the most famous prayers in the Bible is the prayer of the saints that were martyred.

Revelation 6:10
[10.] And they cried with a loud voice, saying, How long, O Lord, holy

and true, dost thou not judge and avenge our blood on them that dwell on the earth?

The prayer of the multitude that came out of the Great Tribulation. The Rapture does not occur until after the Great Tribulation and at the opening of the seventh seal. (Revelation 8:1) and is Post Tribulation and Pre-Wrath.

Revelation 7:9-12
[9] After this I beheld, and, lo, a great multitude, which no man could number, of all nations, and kindreds, and people, and tongues, stood before the throne, and before the Lamb, clothed with white robes, and palms in their hands;
[10] And cried with a loud voice, saying, Salvation to our God which sitteth upon the throne, and unto the Lamb.
[11] And all the angels stood round about the throne, and about the elders and the four beasts, and fell before the throne on their faces, and worshipped God,
[12] Saying, Amen: Blessing, and glory, and wisdom, and thanksgiving, and honour, and power, and might, be unto our God for ever and ever. Amen.

The Prayer of the Twenty-Four Elders.
Revelation 11:15-19
[15] And the seventh angel sounded; and there were great voices in heaven, saying, The kingdoms of this world are become the kingdoms of our Lord, and of his Christ; and he shall reign for ever and ever.
[16] And the four and twenty elders, which sat before God on their seats, fell upon their faces, and worshipped God,
[17] Saying, We give thee thanks, O Lord God Almighty, which art, and wast, and art to come; because thou hast taken to thee thy great power, and hast reigned.
[18] And the nations were angry, and thy wrath is come, and the time of the dead, that they should be judged, and that thou shouldest give reward unto thy servants the prophets, and to the saints, and them

that fear thy name, small and great; and shouldest destroy them which destroy the earth.
[19] And the temple of God was opened in heaven, and there was seen in his temple the ark of his testament: and there were lightnings, and voices, and thunderings, and an earthquake, and great hail.

(Note the trumpet in Revelation 11:15 is the same trumpet as in I Corinthians 15:52 and the Ark of Testament [Covenant] in Revelation 11:19 is the Ark of the Covenant which is in heaven and will not be found on earth.)

The Prayer of the Masses
Revelation 15:3-4
[3.] And they sing the song of Moses the servant of God, and the song of the Lamb, saying, Great and marvellous are thy works, Lord God Almighty; just and true are thy ways, thou King of saints.
[4.] Who shall not fear thee, O Lord, and glorify thy name? for thou only art holy: for all nations shall come and worship before thee; for thy judgments are made manifest.

The Prayer of the Saints.
Revelation 19:1-10
[1] And after these things I heard a great voice of much people in heaven, saying, Alleluia; Salvation, and glory, and honour, and power, unto the Lord our God:
[2] For true and righteous are his judgments: for he hath judged the great whore, which did corrupt the earth with her fornication, and hath avenged the blood of his servants at her hand.
[3] And again they said, Alleluia. And her smoke rose up for ever and ever.
[4] And the four and twenty elders and the four beasts fell down and worshipped God that sat on the throne, saying, Amen; Alleluia.
[5] And a voice came out of the throne, saying, Praise our God, all ye his servants, and ye that fear him, both small and great.
[6] And I heard as it were the voice of a great multitude, and as the voice

of many waters, and as the voice of mighty thunderings, saying, Alleluia: for the Lord God omnipotent reigneth.
[7] Let us be glad and rejoice, and give honour to him: for the marriage of the Lamb is come, and his wife hath made herself ready.
[8] And to her was granted that she should be arrayed in fine linen, clean and white: for the fine linen is the righteousness of saints.
[9] And he saith unto me, Write, Blessed are they which are called unto the marriage supper of the Lamb. And he saith unto me, These are the true sayings of God.
[10] And I fell at his feet to worship him. And he said unto me, See thou do it not: I am thy fellowservant, and of thy brethren that have the testimony of Jesus: worship God: for the testimony of Jesus is the spirit of prophecy.
(Note the testimonies of Jesus in Revelation 1:2, 9; 12:17; 19:10; 20:4 and the four Hallelujah's in Revelation 19:1,3,4,6. Hallelujah means, "Praise the Lord.")

The Last Prayer in the Bible is by John.
Revelation 22:20
[20.] "…Even so, come, Lord Jesus."

A Review of Prayer of God's Chosen Biblical Leaders
We know that through prayer we grasp eternity.

Abraham
(Genesis 15:1-5)
"After these things the word of the LORD came unto Abram in a vision, saying, Fear not, Abram: I am thy shield, and thy exceeding great reward. And Abram said, LORD God, what wilt thou give me, seeing I go childless, and the steward of my house is this Eliezer of Damascus? And Abram said, Behold, to me thou hast given no seed: and, lo, one born in my house is mine heir. And, behold, the word of the LORD came unto him, saying, This shall not be thine heir; but he that shall come forth out of thine own bowels shall be thine heir. And he brought him forth abroad, and said, Look now toward heaven, and

tell the stars, if thou be able to number them: and he said unto him, So shall thy seed be."

As Abraham answered Your call. "Here am I", "And it came to pass after these things, that God did tempt Abraham, and said unto him, Abraham: and he said, Behold, here I am." (Genesis 22:1) We answer, "Here we are."

Jacob
"I am not worthy of the least of all the mercies, and of all the truth, which thou hast shewed unto thy servant; for with my staff I passed over this Jordan; and now I am become two bands. Deliver me, I pray thee, from the hand of my brother, from the hand of Esau: for I fear him, lest he will come and smite me, and the mother with the children. And thou saidst, I will surely do thee good, and make thy seed as the sand of the sea, which cannot be numbered for multitude." (Genesis 32:10-12)

Moses
As Moses asked, "who am I?" "And Moses said unto God, Who am I, that I should go unto Pharaoh, and that I should bring forth the children of Israel out of Egypt?" (Exodus 3:11) We ask, "Who are we to do Your work?" We remember Your answer, "Certainly I will be with you."

"LORD, thou hast been our dwelling place in all generations. Before the mountains were brought forth, or ever thou hadst formed the earth and the world, even from everlasting to everlasting, thou art God." (Psalm 90:1-2)

Joshua
You said to Joshua, "Where you stand is Holy Ground." We know that we stand on Holy Ground. "And the captain of the LORD's host said unto Joshua, Loose thy shoe from off thy foot; for the place whereon thou standest is holy. And Joshua did so." (Joshua 5:15)
God said to Moses, Draw not nigh hither: put off thy shoes from off thy feet, for the place whereon thou standest is holy ground. (Exodus 3:5)

Deborah

"And Deborah, a prophetess, the wife of Lapidoth, she judged Israel at that time." (Judges 4:4) "Hear, O ye kings; give ear, O ye princes; I, even I, will sing unto the LORD; I will sing praise to the LORD God of Israel." (Judges 5:3)

(The patriotic woman, judge and prophetess, leads Israel to victory in war. Other prophetess, were: Miriam, Exodus 15:20; Huldah, 2 Kings 22:14; Noadiah, Nehemiah 6:14; Anna, Luke 2:36; daughters of Phillip, Acts 2:9)

Samson

"And Samson called unto the LORD, and said, O LORD God, remember me, I pray thee, and strengthen me, I pray thee, only this once, O God, that I may be at once avenged of the Philistines for my two eyes…And Samson said, Let me die with the Philistines. And he bowed himself with all his might; and the house fell upon the LORDs, and upon all the people that were therein. So the dead which he slew at his death were more than they which he slew in his life." (Judges 16:28,30)

Hannah

We know as Hannah, the ideal mother of Samuel, that, "there is not one Holy like You." "And Hannah prayed, and said, My heart rejoiceth in the LORD, mine horn is exalted in the LORD: my mouth is enlarged over mine enemies; because I rejoice in thy salvation. There is none holy as the LORD: for there is none beside thee: neither is there any rock like our God." (2 Samuel 2: 1-2)

(Mother of Samuel, prayerful, I Samuel 1:10,11; self-denial, 1 Samuel 27, 28; thankful, 1 Samuel 2:1-10; industrious and maternal love, 1 Samuel 2:19)

Elijah

We believe as Elijah believed, "There is power in prayer." "And he stretched himself upon the child three times, and cried unto the LORD, and said, O LORD my God, I pray thee, let this child's soul come into him again. And the LORD heard the voice of Elijah; and the soul of the child came into him again, and he revived. (I Kings 17: 21, 22)

"Hear me, O LORD, hear me, that this people may know that thou art the LORD God, and that thou hast turned their heart back again.Then the fire of the LORD fell, and consumed the burnt sacrifice, and the wood, and the stones, and the dust, and licked up the water that was in the trench. And when all the people saw it, they fell on their faces: and they said, The LORD, he is the God; the LORD, he is the God…And it came to pass at the seventh time, that he said, Behold, there ariseth a little cloud out of the sea, like a man's hand. And he said, Go up, say unto Ahab, Prepare thy chariot, and get thee down that the rain stop thee not. And it came to pass in the mean while, that the heaven was black with clouds and wind, and there was a great rain. And Ahab rode, and went to Jezreel." (I Kings 18:37-39, 44,45)

Solomon
We say as Solomon, "We are like little children who do not know how to come in or go out." "And now, O LORD my God, thou hast made thy servant king instead of David my father: and I am but a little child: I know not how to go out or come in." (I Kings 3:7) Solomon asked only for wisdom. "Give therefore thy servant an understanding heart to judge thy people, that I may discern between good and bad: for who is able to judge this thy so great a people?" (I Kings 3:9)

God answered, "Behold, I have done according to thy words: lo, I have given thee a wise and an understanding heart; so that there was none like thee before thee, neither after thee shall any arise like unto thee. And I have also given thee that which thou hast not asked, both riches, and honour: so that there shall not be any among the kings like unto thee all thy days. And if thou wilt walk in my ways, to keep my statutes and my commandments, as thy father David did walk, then I will lengthen thy days". (I Kings 3:12-14)

Solomon asked, "Who am I?" "But who is able to build him an house, seeing the heaven and heaven of heavens cannot contain him? who am I then, that I should build him an house, save only to burn sacrifice before him?" (2 Chronicles 2:6) "And he set threescore and ten thousand of them to be bearers of burdens, and fourscore thousand to be hewers in the mountain, and three thousand and six hundred overseers to set the people a work." (2 Chronicles 2:18)

"Thus all the work that Solomon made for the house of the LORD was finished: and Solomon brought in all the things that David his father had dedicated; and the silver, and the gold, and all the instruments, put he among the treasures of the house of God." (2 Chronicles 5:1)

Jabez
We ask as Jabez, "Let your hand be with us." "And Jabez called on the God of Israel, saying, Oh that thou wouldest bless me indeed, and enlarge my coast, and that thine hand might be with me, and that thou wouldest keep me from evil, that it may not grieve me! And God granted him that which he requested." (1 Chronicles 4:10)

Jehoshaphet
We pray as Jehoshaphet. "Today our eyes are upon you." "O our God, wilt thou not judge them? for we have no might against this great company that cometh against us; neither know we what to do: but our eyes are upon thee." (2 Chronicles 20:12) "And he said, Hearken ye, all Judah, and ye inhabitants of Jerusalem, and thou king Jehoshaphat, Thus saith the LORD unto you, Be not afraid nor dismayed by reason of this great multitude; for the battle is not yours, but God's." (2 Chronicles 20:15)

David
David asked, "**Who am I**?" "And David said unto Saul, **Who am I**? and what is my life, or my father's family in Israel, that I should be son in law to the king?" (1 Samuel 18:18) "Then went king David in, and sat before the LORD, and he said, **Who am I**, O LORD God? and what is my house, that thou hast brought me hitherto?" (2 Samuel 7:18) "And David

the king came and sat before the LORD, and said, **Who am I**, O LORD God, and what is mine house, that thou hast brought me hitherto?" (I Chronicles 17:16) "But **who am I**, and what is my people, that we should be able to offer so willingly after this sort? for all things come of thee, and of thine own have we given thee." (1 Chronicles 29:14)

We know as David, "Both riches and honour come of thee, and thou reignest over all; and in thine hand is power and might; and in thine hand it is to make great, and to give strength unto all…**But who am I**, and what is my people, that we should be able to offer so willingly after this sort? for all things come of thee, and of thine own have we given thee." (1 Chronicles 29:12,14)

"Let the words of my mouth, and the meditation of my heart, be acceptable in thy sight, O LORD, my strength, and my redeemer". (Psalm 19:14)

"Unto thee, O LORD, do I lift up my soul…O my God, I trust in thee: let me not be ashamed, let not mine enemies triumph over me…For thy name's sake, O LORD, pardon mine iniquity; for it is great." (Psalm 25:1,2,11) (Read all of Psalm 25)

"Be thou exalted, O God, above the heavens: let thy glory be above all the earth." (Psalm 57:11)

"Thy word is a lamp unto my feet, and a light unto my path." (Psalm 119:105)

"Cause me to hear thy lovingkindness in the morning; for in thee do I trust: cause me to know the way wherein I should walk; for I lift up my soul unto thee." (Psalm 143:8)

Asa
"And Asa cried unto the LORD his God, and said, LORD, it is nothing with thee to help, whether with many, or with them that have no power:

help us, O LORD our God; for we rest on thee, and in thy name we go against this multitude. O LORD, thou art our God; let not man prevail against thee." (2 Chronicles 14:11)

Man of Ethan
"I will sing of the mercies of the LORD for ever: with my mouth will I make known thy faithfulness to all generations." (Psalm 89:1)

Nehemiah
"O LORD, I beseech thee, let now thine ear be attentive to the prayer of thy servant, and to the prayer of thy servants, who desire to fear thy name: and prosper, I pray thee, thy servant this day, and grant him mercy in the sight of this man. For I was the king's cupbearer…Then the king said unto me, For what dost thou make request? So I prayed to the God of heaven…And a letter unto Asaph the keeper of the king's forest, that he may give me timber to make beams for the gates of the palace which appertained to the house, and for the wall of the city, and for the house that I shall enter into. And the king granted me, according to the good hand of my God upon me…Then I told them of the hand of my God which was good upon me; as also the king's words that he had spoken unto me. And they said, **<u>Let us rise up and build. So they strengthened their hands for this good work.</u>**" (Nehemiah 1:11; 2:4,8,18) We ask as Nehemiah, "**<u>that you remember us as good.</u>**" "And for the wood offering, at times appointed, and for the firstfruits. Remember me, O my God, for good." (Nehemiah 13:31)

Jeremiah
As Jeremiah we know, "Your eyes are open to all the ways of men." "For mine eyes are upon all their ways: they are not hid from my face, neither is their iniquity hid from mine eyes. For I will set mine eyes upon them for good, and I will bring them again to this land: and I will build them, and not pull them down; and I will plant them, and not pluck them up. Ah LORD God! behold, thou hast made the heaven and the earth by thy great power and stretched out arm, and there is nothing too hard for thee:Thou shewest lovingkindness unto thousands, and recompensest

the iniquity of the fathers into the bosom of their children after them: the Great, the Mighty God, the LORD of hosts, is his name, Great in counsel, and mighty in work: for thine eyes are open upon all the ways of the sons of men: to give every one according to his ways, and according to the fruit of his doings: And said unto Jeremiah the prophet, Let, we beseech thee, our supplication be accepted before thee, and pray for us unto the LORD thy God, even for all this remnant; (for we are left but a few of many, as thine eyes do behold us:)." (Jeremiah 16:17; 24:6, 32:17-19; 42:2)

Isaiah
To the Lord, "Here I am; send me." (Isaiah 6:8)
We know that Your prophet Isaiah was spiritual and knew how to pray. We ask that you make us spiritual and teach us to pray. "But now, O LORD, thou art our father; we are the clay, and thou our potter; and we all are the work of thy hand. Be not wroth very sore, O LORD, neither remember iniquity for ever: behold, see, we beseech thee, we are all thy people." (Isaiah 64:8,9. There are many references in Isaiah concerning prayer.)

Daniel

Chapter nine is one of the most famous prayers of the Bible.
Daniel 9:2-20
[2] In the first year of his reign I Daniel understood by books the number of the years, whereof the word of the LORD came to Jeremiah the prophet, that he would accomplish seventy years in the desolations of Jerusalem.
[3] And I set my face unto the Lord God, to seek by prayer and supplication, with fasting, and sackcloth, and ashes:
[4] And I prayed unto the LORD my God, and made my confession, and said, O Lord, the great and dreadful God, keeping the covenant and mercy to them that love him, and to them that keep his commandments;
[5] We have sinned, and have committed iniquity, and have done

Scriptures for Life

wickedly, and have rebelled, even by departing from thy precepts and from thy judgments:

[6] Neither have we hearkened unto thy servants the prophets, which spake in thy name to our kings, our princes, and our fathers, and to all the people of the land.

[7] O Lord, righteousness belongeth unto thee, but unto us confusion of faces, as at this day; to the men of Judah, and to the inhabitants of Jerusalem, and unto all Israel, that are near, and that are far off, through all the countries whither thou hast driven them, because of their trespass that they have trespassed against thee.

[8] O Lord, to us belongeth confusion of face, to our kings, to our princes, and to our fathers, because we have sinned against thee.

[9] To the Lord our God belong mercies and forgivenesses, though we have rebelled against him;

[10] Neither have we obeyed the voice of the LORD our God, to walk in his laws, which he set before us by his servants the prophets.

[11] Yea, all Israel have transgressed thy law, even by departing, that they might not obey thy voice; therefore the curse is poured upon us, and the oath that is written in the law of Moses the servant of God, because we have sinned against him.

[12] And he hath confirmed his words, which he spake against us, and against our judges that judged us, by bringing upon us a great evil: for under the whole heaven hath not been done as hath been done upon Jerusalem.

[13] As it is written in the law of Moses, all this evil is come upon us: yet made we not our prayer before the LORD our God, that we might turn from our iniquities, and understand thy truth.

[14] Therefore hath the LORD watched upon the evil, and brought it upon us: for the LORD our God is righteous in all his works which he doeth: for we obeyed not his voice.

[15] And now, O Lord our God, that hast brought thy people forth out of the land of Egypt with a mighty hand, and hast gotten thee renown, as at this day; we have sinned, we have done wickedly.

[16] O Lord, according to all thy righteousness, I beseech thee, let thine anger and thy fury be turned away from thy city Jerusalem, thy holy mountain: because for our sins, and for the iniquities of our fathers,

Jerusalem and thy people are become a reproach to all that are about us.

[17] Now therefore, O our God, hear the prayer of thy servant, and his supplications, and cause thy face to shine upon thy sanctuary that is desolate, for the Lord's sake.

[18] O my God, incline thine ear, and hear; open thine eyes, and behold our desolations, and the city which is called by thy name: for we do not present our supplications before thee for our righteousnesses, but for thy great mercies.

[19] O Lord, hear; O Lord, forgive; O Lord, hearken and do; defer not, for thine own sake, O my God: for thy city and thy people are called by thy name.

[20] And whiles I was speaking, and praying, and confessing my sin and the sin of my people Israel, and presenting my supplication before the LORD my God for the holy mountain of my God;

9:2-21 This has the **_Ingredients for True Prayer_**. I count 13 components in this prayer.

v. 2	in **_response to the word_** of the Lord
v. 3	**_pleaded in prayer_** with fasting, self-denial and petitions.
v. 4,5,6	**_with confession_**, recognizes that God keeps his covenant with those who keep His commandments.
v. 7,8	**_God is righteous_**. We are confused because **_we have sinned._**
v. 10,11	**_We have failed._**
v. 12	**_God has judged_** with great evil.
v. 13	**_We did not pray_** and turn from our sins.
v. 14	**_God is righteous_**, but **_we did not obey._**
v. 15	**_admits sin_**
v. 16, 17	**_beseeches God to hear_** our prayers
v. 16, 18	**_ask for mercy_** because of His righteousness
v. 19	**_ask forgiveness_**, we are called by Thy Name
v. 20, 21	**_while speaking_** Daniel was heard

Joel

"O LORD, to thee will I cry: for the fire hath devoured the pastures of the wilderness, and the flame hath burned all the trees of the field. Blow ye the trumpet in Zion, and sound an alarm in my holy mountain: let all the inhabitants of the land tremble: for the day of the LORD cometh, for it is nigh at hand…They shall run like mighty men; they shall climb the wall like men of war; and they shall march every one on his ways, and they shall not break their ranks:" (Joel 1:19, 2:1,7) "But I will remove far off from you the northern army, and will drive him into a land barren and desolate, with his face toward the east sea, and his hinder part toward the utmost sea, and his stink shall come up, and his ill savour shall come up, because he hath done great things. …And I will restore to you the years that the locust hath eaten, the cankerworm, and the caterpiller, and the palmerworm, my great army which I sent among you. And ye shall eat in plenty, and be satisfied, and praise the name of the LORD your God, that hath dealt wondrously with you: and my people shall never be ashamed." (Joel 2:20,25,26)

Amos

Amos said, "Seeking You is seeking good." "Seek good, and not evil, that ye may live: and so the LORD, the God of hosts, shall be with you, as ye have spoken." (Amos 5:14) We seek you, Your mercy, Your wisdom, Your blessings. We bring ourselves and our gifts to You.

Micah

"Therefore I will look unto the LORD; I will wait for the God of my salvation: my God will hear me…Who is a God like unto thee, that pardoneth iniquity, and passeth by the transgression of the remnant of his heritage? he retaineth not his anger for ever, because he delighteth in mercy…He will turn again, he will have compassion upon us; he will subdue our iniquities; and thou wilt cast all their sins into the depths of the sea." (Micah 7:7,18,19)

Habakkuk

"O LORD, I have heard thy speech, and was afraid: O LORD, revive thy work in the midst of the years, in the midst of the years make known; in wrath remember mercy…Thy bow was made quite naked, according to the oaths of the tribes, even thy word. Selah. Thou didst cleave the earth with rivers…Yet I will rejoice in the LORD, I will joy in the God of my salvation…The LORD God is my strength, and he will make my feet like hinds' feet, and he will make me to walk upon mine high places. To the chief singer on my stringed instruments." (Habakkuk 3:2,9,18,19)

Paul
We know as Paul "That the love of Jesus surpasses all knowledge." "That he would grant you, according to the riches of his glory, to be strengthened with might by his Spirit in the inner man; That Christ may dwell in your hearts by faith; that ye, being rooted and grounded in love, May be able to comprehend with all saints what is the breadth, and length, and depth, and height; And to know the love of Christ, which passeth knowledge, that ye might be filled with all the fulness of God. Now unto him that is able to do exceeding abundantly above all that we ask or think, according to the power that worketh in us, Unto him be glory in the church by Christ Jesus throughout all ages, world without end. Amen." (Ephesians 3: 16-21)

"Now the God of peace, that brought again from the dead our Lord Jesus, that great shepherd of the sheep, through the blood of the everlasting covenant, Make you perfect in every good work to do his will, working in you that which is wellpleasing in his sight, through Jesus Christ; to whom be glory for ever and ever. Amen." (Hebrews: 13:20-21)

Mary
"And Mary said, My soul doth magnify the Lord, And my spirit hath rejoiced in God my Saviour." (Luke 1: 46,47)

Jesus
Jesus said, "He loved us even as You loved Him." **"For the Father himself loveth you, because ye have loved me, and have believed that I came out from God. He that hath my commandments, and keepeth them,**

he it is that loveth me: and he that loveth me shall be loved of my Father, and I will love him, and will manifest myself to him. As the Father hath loved me, so have I loved you: continue ye in my love." (John 16:27; 14:21, 15:9)

Jesus prays for all believers: " Neither pray I for these alone, but for them also which shall believe on me through their word; That they all may be one; as thou, Father, art in me, and I in thee, that they also may be one in us: that the world may believe that thou hast sent me. And the glory which thou gavest me I have given them; that they may be one, even as we are one: I in them, and thou in me, that they may be made perfect in one; and that the world may know that thou hast sent me, and hast loved them, as thou hast loved me. Father, I will that they also, whom thou hast given me, be with me where I am; that they may behold my glory, which thou hast given me: for thou lovedst me before the foundation of the world." (John 17:20-24)

Apostles
The Lord knows everyone's hearts. And they prayed, and said, "Thou, Lord, which knowest the hearts of all men, shew whether of these two thou hast chosen." (Acts 1:24)

Other Scriptural Notes on Prayer
Ecclesiastes 5:2 "Be not rash with thy mouth, and let not thine heart be hasty to utter any thing before God: for God is in heaven, and thou upon earth: therefore let thy words be few."

Matthew 6:7 "But when ye pray, use not vain repetitions, as the heathen do: for they think that they shall be heard for their much speaking."

Genesis 4:26 (Prayer is first mentioned.) "And to Seth, to him also there was born a son; and he called his name Enos: then began men to call upon the name of the LORD."

All Men Need Prayer:
Psalm 65:2 "O thou that hearest prayer, unto thee shall all flesh (men) come."

Isaiah 56:7 "Even them will I bring to my holy mountain, and make them joyful in my house of prayer: their burnt offerings and their sacrifices shall be accepted upon mine altar; for mine house shall be **called an house of prayer for all people**." (See Matthew 21:13, Mark 11:17 and Luke 19:46)

Luke 11:1,2 "And it came to pass, that, as he was praying in a certain place, when he ceased, one of his disciples said unto him, Lord, teach us to pray, as John also taught his disciples. And he said unto them, When ye pray, say, Our Father which art in heaven, Hallowed be thy name. Thy kingdom come. Thy will be done, as in heaven, so in earth."
Jesus again gave The Lord's Prayer.

Romans 8:26-27 (Our help in prayer) "Likewise the Spirit also helpeth our infirmities: for we know not what we should pray for as we ought: but the Spirit itself maketh intercession for us with groanings which cannot be uttered. And he that searcheth the hearts knoweth what is the mind of the Spirit, because he maketh intercession for the saints according to the will of God."

A Prayer for the Unsaved.
Our Father, our hearts are today heavy for the unsaved.
- **Some are falling through space with their arms and legs grabbing for something to hold and stop the fall.**
- **Some are going over the highest waterfalls into the worst rapids lined with sharp rocks with more waterfalls to go.**
- **Some are running on this earth being chased by life's lighting bolts.**
- **Some are in the eye of a hurricane waiting to be thrown out into a burning eternity.**
- **Some are eaten up with cancer in a hospital bed and**

> entering a period of multi-system failure and physical death. They open their eyes and death is no longer in the distant future far out in the universe, but is now clearly seen in the top of their room and is imminent.

We know that there are 6,638 people speeding through life and will die today. To those who are unsaved Jesus is saying to them as He did 2000 years ago, **"Thou fool, this night thy soul shall be required of thee: then whose shall those things be, which thou hast provided?" (Luke 12:20)**

"Our Father we are overcome with the magnitude and apparent hopelessness of unsaved people in the world and in our presence. The problem exceeds our capability as human beings. We pray that You will open the hearts and soul of the unsaved in our midst. We pray You will show them the way and joy and hope of eternal salvation. Forgive us, your people , where we have failed Thee. Help us to be better and more in Your will."

A Soldiers Prayer Before Going into Battle
Psalm 121
[1] I will lift up mine eyes unto the hills, from whence cometh my help.
[2] My help cometh from the LORD, which made heaven and earth.
[3] He will not suffer thy foot to be moved: he that keepeth thee will not slumber.
[4] Behold, he that keepeth Israel shall neither slumber nor sleep.
[5] The LORD is thy keeper: the LORD is thy shade upon thy right hand.
[6] The sun shall not smite thee by day, nor the moon by night.
[7] The LORD shall preserve thee from all evil: he shall preserve thy soul.
[8] The LORD shall preserve thy going out and thy coming in from this time forth, and even for evermore.

To some it is known as the travelers Psalm. (David may have penned it when he was going abroad) To some it is know as the soldiers Psalm. (David may have penned it before a hazardous battle.) Either way it encourages us to put our confidence in God, and by faith put ourselves under His protection, and commit ourselves to His care.

David assures himself of help from God (Verse 1) and assures us of it. (v. 3-8)

Verse 1. "I Will lift up mine eyes unto the hills, from whence cometh my help."
(Where does my help come from?)

Verse 2. "My help cometh from the LORD, which made heaven and earth."

Verse 3. "He will not suffer thy foot to be moved:.."(He will not let your foot slip.) (**1Samuel 2:9**...He will keep the feet of the saints.) "He that keepeth thee will not slumber."

Verse 4. Behold, he that keepeth Israel shall neither slumber nor sleep".
(God is never weary and never sleeps.)

Verse 5. "The LORD is thy keeper:" (Shepherd, protector, watches over us.)
"the LORD is thy shade (not only protects, but refreshes us) upon thy right hand". (**Psalm 16:8** ..."because he is at my right hand, I shall not be moved.")

Verse 6. "The sun shall not smite (harm) thee by day, nor the moon by night." (God is our shadow.) (Their father Jacob had complained: **Genesis 31:40** "...in the day the drought consumed me, and the frost by night;..")

Verse 7. "The LORD shall preserve thee from all evil: (harm) He shall preserve thy soul." He will watch over your life. (All souls are His. The soul is the man. God will preserve our soul from perishing eternally.)

Verse 8. "The LORD shall preserve thy going out and thy coming in (Watch over all our journeys and voyages, coming and going) from this time forth, (now) and even for evermore."

(He will keep us in life and death and forever more. It is a protection for life, a guide even unto death, and a promise to preserve us in His Heavenly Kingdom. His Spirit, our Preserver, and Comforter, shall abide with us forever.) (Miller, 25 January 2003).

Our Prayer before Meals
A. The <u>Vocal or Mental Short Prayer</u> (We pray this prayer three times a day.)
"Our Father we thank Thee for this day. We thank Thee for our **<u>Many! Many! Many!</u>** (or **<u>Holy</u>**, **<u>Holy</u>**, **<u>Holy</u>**) blessings, **<u>undeserved</u>** and **<u>too numerous to count</u>**. We ask that you forgive us our sins and continue to be with us. Amen."

B. The <u>Mental Complete Prayer</u>
(Even though God knows what is in our minds; we have written the following so that we will be reminded what is in our minds. Jesus said, (Matthew 6: 7-13 **"But when ye pray, use not vain repetitions, as the heathen do: for they think that they shall be heard for their much speaking. Be not ye therefore like unto them: for your Father knoweth what things ye have need of, before ye ask him. After this manner therefore pray ye: Our Father which art in heaven, Hallowed be thy name. Thy kingdom come. Thy will be done in earth, as it is in heaven. Give us this day our daily bread. And forgive us our debts, as we forgive our debtors. And lead us not into temptation, but deliver us from evil: For thine is the kingdom, and the power, and the glory, for ever. Amen."**)

1. The Short Prayer is repeated (and the whole prayer is added.)
2. The word, "Many", is used three times in our routine prayer. We pray this prayer at least three times a day before each meal. (These notes express our thoughts when we use the word "Many" three times. It is an emphasis.)

All knowledge can be broken down into groups of "three each" as I have proven in my (***"44 Cerebral Software"***)

Many Blessings (3 Groups)

1. The first **"Many"** blessings:
   - **Our salvation: "For God so loved the world, that he gave his only begotten Son, that whosoever believeth in him should not perish, but have everlasting life." – John 3:16**
   - **God's continued love:**

     "As the Father hath loved me, so have I loved you: Now remain in My love". - John 15:9

     "Who shall separate us from the love of Christ? shall tribulation, or distress, or persecution, or famine, or nakedness, or peril, or sword?" Romans 8:35

     "For the Father himself loveth you, because ye have loved me, and have believed that I came out from God."- John 16:27

     "But God demonstrates His own love for us, in this: While we were still sinners, Christ died for us." - Romans 5:8

     How great is the love of the Father that He has lavished on us, that we should be called the children of God! And that is what we are! The reason the world does not know us is that it did not know Him.
     I John 3:1

     "Keep yourselves in God's love as you wait for the mercy of our Lord Jesus Christ to bring you eternal life". - Jude 21

     "And now these three remain: faith, hope, and love. But the greatest of these is love." - I Corinthians 13:13

     "But the fruit of the Spirit is love, joy, peace, longsuffering, gentleness, goodness, faith, Meekness, temperance: against such there is no law." - Galatians 5:22-23

     "And to know the love of Christ, which passeth knowledge, that ye might be filled with all the fulness of God." - Ephesians 3:19

     "And over all these virtues put on love, which binds them all together in perfect unity." - Colossians 3:14

Scriptures for Life

"And so we know and rely on the love God has for us. God is love, Whoever lives in love lives in God, and God in him."- I John 4:16

2. The second **"Many"** blessings:
   - Christian family (being born in a Christian family as we were is one's first blessing.)
     (Our fathers, mothers, children, grandchildren)
     Greatest of all marriages, loving, Christian, dedicated to each other for life.
   - Good bodies and minds
   - Healthy lives
   - Our church (Southern Baptist)
   - Wonderful, Christian, loving, caring people
   - Bible believing
   - Willing to write down what they believe and stand by it. (No other church has done this)
   - Teach it to our children in colleges and universities
   - Profess it through all missionary programs.
   - During our time of recent family illness and death (our son Dwight) by the hundreds our Christian friends from Memphis and the Tampa Bay area responded. (Their love was one of our greatest blessings.)

3. The third **"Many"** blessings:
   - Successful medical career – a large medical practice
   - Associated academic career with medical school teaching opportunities
   - Development of a Neurosciences Center (It has the longest continuously running neuro journal club in America.)
   - A parallel Navy career for 30 years (First reservist as OP093R deputy surgeon general in the Pentagon for 3 years.)
   - 5,238 hour pilot
   - Wonderful retirement (adequately funded)
   - Beautiful place, great climate on unlimited waterways, Gulf and ocean.
   - Loving friendly helpful Christian neighbors

- **Safe neighborhood (children ride their tricycles down the street and leave them in their yards)**
- **Good medical and dental care**
- **Continued interchange with long-term professional friends within the United States and around the world**

"O God you know all our other blessings and love us even when we fail you. Thank you! We pray You will continue to be with us!" ("Admiral" Joe and Cathy)

Prayer for Our Souls
(Restore, redeem, rest, fulfilling)
"This is what the LORD says:
Stand at the crossroads and look;
Ask for the ancient paths,
Ask where the good way is,
And walk in it,
And you will find rest for your souls." (Jeremiah 6:16)

Psalm 62: 5-8
Verse 5. "Find rest, O my soul, in God alone my hope comes from Him."
Verse 6. "He alone is my rock and my salvation, He is my Fortress, I will not be shaken."
Verse 7. "My salvation and my honor depend on God; He is my mighty rock, my refuge."
Verse 8. "Trust in Him at all times O people; pour out your hearts to Him, for God is our refuge."

My Prayer: 7 April 2003 (Paraphrased from the above)
"O God our souls find rest in You alone,
Our hope comes from You.
You alone are our salvation, honor, fortress, and mighty Rock.
O God we pour out our hearts to You, and trust in You at all times."

Other great Scriptures for finding rest in our souls:

Psalm 23:3	"He restores my soul."
Psalm 49: 15	"But God will redeem my soul (from the grave; He will surely take me to Himself.")
Psalm 62: 5	"Find rest O my soul, in God alone my hope comes from Him."
Psalm 94:19	"When anxiety was great within me, Your consolation brought joy to my soul."
Proverbs 13: 19	"A longing fulfilled is sweet to the soul."
Matthew 10: 28	"Do not be afraid of those who kill the body, but cannot kill the soul."
Matthew 11:29	"Take my yoke upon you and learn from me, for I am gentle and humble in heart, and you will find rest for your souls."

A Special Scripture of Comfort from God
(And our ability to comfort others with the same comfort.)

2 Corinthians 1:3-4 (God of all comfort is found only in 2 Corinthians 1:3)

Verse 3. "Praise be to the God and Father of our LORD Jesus, the Father of Compassion and the God of all comfort,
Verse 4. "Who comforts us in all our troubles, so that we can comfort those in any trouble with the comfort we ourselves have received from God."

"Comfort" is found many times in the New Testament:
- **I Corinthians 14:3**
- **2 Corinthians 1:3,4,6**
- **2 Corinthians 2:7**
- **2 Corinthians 7:6,7,13**
- **2 Corinthians 13:11**

The Scriptures give us comfort. "For whatsoever things were written aforetime were written for our learning, that we through patience and **comfort** of the Scriptures might have hope." (Romans 15:4)

The Last Verse In God's Word:
Revelation 22:20
[20] He which testifieth these things saith, Surely I come quickly. Amen. Even so, come, Lord Jesus.

Part II

Some Criteria For The Development
Of
Character

Acknowledgement

To the
Miller and Parker Families
That has made our lives
As perfect as perfect can be
And
To our Friends from all over
the world who are always there when we need them.

To our Family and Friends
Who await us in Heaven!

Dedication

To all my Prayer Partners
And
To the three hundred nineteen Men Who Wear their
Testimony that they are Men of Prayer
and
Patriotic Americans

To My Military Friends of the Navy,
Army, Marines, Air force, and Coast Guard
Who Continue to Give Me Support.

To My Unsaved Friends with Continued
Prayers that God will Open Your Hearts

Classification of Some Criteria for the Development of Character.:

Introduction to Character

- (1.) Conception to Birth (Life in the womb.). 182
- (2.) Care of the Infant (Baby). 183
- (3.) Care of the Child 188
- (4.) A Child's Experience, (The reason for this story):. 191
- (5.) Childhood to Youth 193
- (6.) The Home - The Home is Divinely Instituted. 196
  - a. Love of Children. 199
  - b. Duty to Children 200
  - c. The Place of Training is at Home. 201
  - d. The Mother's Wisdom 203
  - e. Health At Home: 205
- (7.) The Youth. 206
  - a. Choosing a Job-Profession 207
  - b. Education 208
  - c. How do I Look? 210
  - d. Work or Idleness. 211
- (8.) Master One's Self. 212
  - a. The Habit of Thinking. 214
  - b. How to Be Strong? 215
  - c. Love of Books 216
  - d. Strength of Mind 217
  - e. Man's Power 221
  - f. Stability of Mind. 222
  - g. True to Your Word. 222
  - h. The Character of Being Faithful 223
  - i. Good Sense Leads to Excellence 223
- (9.) Make your own way 226
  - a. Help Yourself to Life 227

	b.	Resist Evil	229
	c.	Purpose in Life - Men With a Purpose	230
	d.	A Few Good Men	236
(10.)	Choices		237
	a.	Frugality	242
	b.	Friends	243
	c.	Critics - Negatives	244
(11.)	Behavior		245
	a.	Permanence	246
	b.	Perseverance – Endurance	248
	c.	Indulgence	249
	d.	Stay Calm	250
(12.)	Status		251
	a.	Money	254
	b.	Success	254
	c.	Man's Duty	256
	d.	What Can I do?	260
	e.	Your Harvest	263
	f.	Waste of Time	271
	g.	Job Integrity	271
(13.)	Worldly Morality		272
	a.	Self-Centered or Self-Denial	272
	b.	Live Life With Accuracy	274
	c.	Be Smart	274
	d.	Do Not Live By the Power of Money!	276
	e.	Financial Freedom	277
(14.)	Wisdom		277
(15.)	Science		278
(16.)	Know What Is Important		281
(17.)	Faint Ideas Explode		282
(18.)	The Nones		286
(19.)	Sevens of Character		290
	a.	Gifts of the Holy Spirit	290
	b.	Spiritual Works	291

      c. Corporal Works of Mercy 291
      d. Deadly Sins 291
      e. Pentential Psalms 291
      f. Virtues 292

(20) Character and Importance of Virtue 292

(21.) Nine Charismatic Gifts 293

67 Criteria Noted 294

Final Note: 294

What Is Character

And
What Determines If It Is Present?
Foreword

I was born knowing nothing; these are the things I have learned. The credit I give to God who made available to me learning in extensive reading and study.

I have never met a man, except my father, which I agreed with on every little thing. Most of the men I have met; I felt were smarter than me. As an author, I must confess to you that I am married to a woman (Cathy) smarter than me, but perhaps not always wiser!

I have described the 13 subjects that one must know something about to declare themselves with a Broad Mentality. I am now describing the 67 things a person can review to build their character.

To Develop a Broad Mentality one must have some knowledge of:

1. The Bible, (One is illiterate without a knowledge of the greatest book of all time.)
2. God
3. Man
4. Salvation of man from death.
5. The Church

6. The Lord's Day (Who does not know the meaning of Sunday?)
7. God's Kingdom
8. The Last Things (The End of the World.)
9. Social Order
10. War
11. Religious Liberty
12. The Family
13. Education
    a. **Learn from study and experiences**
    b. **Their professional qualifications (Doctors, lawyers, ministers, teachers, etc.)**

If one does not have some knowledge of these 13 Things they cannot claim to have a **Broad Mentality**. All knowledge is relative as will be mentioned further in this book. A Broad Mentality will widen your vision of all the things to follow. As one specializes in life they are likely know, learn more and more about less and less, and develop a "Narrow Mentality."

Since early January 2011 the idea for this book invaded my mind.

Many years ago I gave several lectures on "Women" at our local all male fraternity. By the fifth lecture I had pretty much proven to my audience that women were actually very simple creatures once one developed a clear knowledge of them. Over the years I have developed a very good small book on **Women**, but my wife, Cathy, absolutely will not let me publish it since I received death threats after the first series of lectures. (The word got out!)

I tried to create a definition of a "Lady". The study was amazing because everyone knows what a lady is, but no one has been able to write it down. Therefore, I retreated to describe a man of character. After several weeks I was flooded with a mental Noah's flood with the waves that make up character.

Introduction to Character
There are at least 67 things that potentially make up our character. One can mix these with 13 things needed to have my definition of a Broad Mentality. The explosion of ideas is louder than atomic bombs. When ideas migrate to thoughts and thoughts explode into action they are more powerful than any Army, Navy, Marines, Coast Guard, or Air Force.

Education is not learning. It is an exercise to develop the power of the mind God gave each of us. It is done in the institute of learning and in the experiences and conflicts in life.

It makes little difference who we are, it matters more what we are!
The brain has circuits for character as it does for music.
Here are 67 diamonds of life that build character that I have discovered and are hereby discussed.

The information below was in a newspaper article found in the pocket of a man drowned on the ship "Henry Clay" that sunk off of Riverdale, New York on 28 July 1852. The author was not listed. It is a good beginning on the study of character.

- <u>Keep good company, or none.</u>
- <u>Never be idle</u>. If your hands can't be <u>usefully employed</u>, attend to the <u>cultivation of your mind</u>.
- <u>Always speak the truth</u>.
- <u>Make few promises</u>.
- <u>Live up to your engagements</u>.
- <u>Keep your own secrets, if you have any</u>.
- When you speak to a person <u>look him or her in the face</u>. <u>Good company and good conversation are the very sinews of virtue. Good character is a above all thing else. Your character cannot be essentially injured except by your own acts. If anyone speaks evil of you, let your life be so that none will believe him</u>.
- <u>Drink no kind of intoxicating liquors</u>.
- <u>Ever live</u> (misfortune excepted) <u>within your income</u>. When you retire to bed think over what you have been

<u>doing during the day</u>. Make no haste to be rich if you would prosper. Small and steady gains give competency, with a tranquil mind.
- Never play at any game of chance.
- Avoid temptation through fear you may not withstand it.
- Earn money before you spend it.
- Never run into debt unless you see a way to get out again. Never borrow if you can possibly avoid it.
- Do not marry until you are able to support a wife.
- Never speak evil of anyone.
- Be just before you are generous.
- Keep yourself innocent if you would be happy.
- Save when you are young, spend when you are old.

Read over the above maxims once a week.

(1.) Conception to Birth (Life in the womb.)

The parents must have the knowledge to protect the baby in the womb. The baby has a highly developed brain two months before they are born.

There is a new light in the last few years upon the nature of man. One is not born with a human nature, they develop it. One must learn to be human. Man has been classified physically of his species as Homo Sapiens. He has not had his psychological classification revealed. Man is born with the potentialities for being human, but he must learn how. A baby can't walk or talk, but they are human. There have been a few children that have not had human contact and have been physically blind, deaf, been unable to walk or run, and could make only the most elementary sounds. If children are trained they have remarkable capacity to learn complex symbols and their relationships. <u>**Human nature is actually an acquired behavior of the person**</u>.

The Chinese begin counting age at conception. Because to them life begins nine months before actual birth. Scientifically this is "A very much more sound manner of reckoning age than our own system." When we see a child at birth we label him a "tabulo rasa" (A blank slate.) This is a horrible error and is one of the many learned errors. I recently

Scriptures for Life

had a person in my lineage that did to want to know the sex of their child until birth. There is so much to learn before birth, but I understand that it is not a rare decision to wait. It is now known that there is a very intimate relationship between the nervous system of the mother and the fetus. This is through a neuro-hormonal system.

An emotionally disturbed pregnant woman may communicate her disturbance to the fetus. This is revealed by a marked increase in the activity of the fetus. When the mother is fatigued there may be hyperactivity in the fetus. The babies are, after birth, sometimes, hyperactive, irritable, squirming, and have feeding problems. A neurotic infant may have been born.

It is now well known that the fetus responds to touch stimuli, vibrations, loud and particularly sudden sounds, differences in pitch, tone, taste, and various gasses, and a trip thorough the birth canal with the screaming mother. The touch stimuli, if uncomfortable, such as an umbilical cord around the neck of the fetus in the womb or if the infant is in an uncomfortable stroller, bed, etc., may cause changes in their behavior.

Remember that 270 days (9 Months) of life in utero may play a part in the epidemiology of mental illness. It is now known that in a mother who smokes, particularly with a father who also keeps the baby's room full of smoke are likely to have a baby with a smaller brain. An alcoholic mother will also produce an alcoholic baby. Babies born of drug addicts are already drug addicts and have been known to have withdrawal reactions. There has been much talk and no action for legislation to protect the baby during uterine development. The baby is developing from the time of conception. **<u>This is usually even before the mother knows she is pregnant</u>**. The gestation period is 8-9 months before the baby is born. There can be mental illnesses based on the mother and father's activities during this period.

(2.) Care of the Infant (Baby)

Show me a murderer, a hardened criminal, a juvenile delinquent, a psychopath, and in almost every case I will show you the tragedy that results from not being adequately loved during childhood. An unloved child by the mother feels that the whole world is unloving. More than one in eight prisoners in the United States has a serious mental illness. It is said that our jails have become "psychiatric hospitals".

I learned fifty years ago in my study of the reticular formation of the brain that it was stimulated by sudden loud sounds and this affects the infant. I had visitors who came to see all my babies upset with me because I told them before they went into the room that I did not want loud noises such as screaming, "horse-laughing", etc. One has only to see a baby almost jump out of their crib with a sudden loud sound because a visitor screams, "Oh, What a beautiful baby!" During a thunderstorm a baby should be held close with soft humming to counteract thunder and lightening. Two months before a baby is born they have a highly developed brain.

The brain doubles in size the first year. A baby's personality is reported to be developed by the age of six weeks.

Where does aggressiveness or destructive aggression, hate, jealously, hostility, greediness, egotistic, and selfishness, come from? They are all acquired sick reactions. They are thought to be a response to frustration brought on by the baby not having their needs satisfied. (Poor feeding, ignorance about diaper rash, lack of vitamins, etc.) Added to the usual needs is a lack of loving care in the nursery or childcare center. There may be a lack of social status in school. (The lack of good clothes or shoes, etc. that match their peers.) This on top of a chronic lack of love at home can cause an explosive reaction in a child. The family provides the social inheritance. Society in both children and adults can be heinous. Human beings are **naturally** inclined to develop their potential for being warm, loving, and healthy people. They are created like this to do good.

Science says our human nature is born good and without "One iota" of aggressiveness, hostility, badness, "Original Sin", or innate depravity. Human nature has highly organized drive to confer the benefits of love upon all. Here is where the function of religion comes in. We have faith in science and faith in the beliefs that the good man has in his religion.

Human babies are born with the desire for love, beyond and above all other needs. They need to be loved and also need to love others. David Brooks in the **New York Times** article *"Using Biology to Understand Beliefs, Passions Can Be done". Tampa Tribune*, 15 May 2008, p.9, confirmed that Love is vital to brain development.

The evidence is that love is the best stimulus to the baby's development and the best stimulus to the development of its own potential for loving others. <u>**There is no evidence in which this can be doubted**</u>. The baby is born to love and be loved. Love is the best communication to others that one can have for them. People involved in the welfare of others must show this stimulation. Love and education cannot be separated. The baby when conceived in the womb has the capacity for the stimulation of love because that is what he is born <u>**as**</u> and <u>**for**</u>. With the proper stimulus their love develops into an ordered, harmonic view of human creative beings of which they are one. The western world is a matrix of confusion and disorder because they never had the stimulation of love in their lives. The mother stands at the core of humanity. It is the mother, the loving mother, who teaches her children the most important trait, which is the ability to love. They then give the survival benefits of love to all they come into contact with. Females have the best potential for this love as a communication tool. They must learn it in their first six months of life. We need to restore the mother to her inheritance as the educator of humanity. "Man is born with a highly organized system of drives all of which are directed toward development in terms of goodness and love." (**Montagu**)

Love, in the vernacular (the native language), may be defined as the communication to others of the attitude that they are all for them.

We must consider the origin of man.
"And God blessed them, and God said unto them, Be fruitful, and multiply, and replenish the earth, and subdue it: and have dominion over the fish of the sea, and over the fowl of the air, and over every living thing that moveth upon the earth. And God said, Behold, I have given you every herb bearing seed, which is upon the face of all the earth, and every tree, in the which is the fruit of a tree yielding seed; to you it shall be for meat." **(Genesis 1:28,29)**

The Lord must build the "house".
"Except the LORD build the house, they labour in vain that build it: except the LORD keep the city, the watchman waketh but in vain." **(Psalms 127:1)**

God's reward to us.
"Lo, children are an heritage of the LORD: and the fruit of the womb is his reward."**(Psalms 127:3)**

Jesus gives various profound truths that concern both us and children.
"And said, Verily I say unto you, Except ye be converted, and become as little children, ye shall not enter into the kingdom of heaven. Take heed that ye despise not one of these little ones; for I say unto you, That in heaven their angels do always behold the face of my Father which is in heaven."(Matthew 18:3,10) Their angels behold the Face of My Father.

"Whosoever shall receive one of such children in my name, receiveth me: and whosoever shall receive me, receiveth not me, but him that sent me."(Mark 9:37)

Parents must make known God to their children.
"That the generation to come might know them, even the children which should be born; who should arise and declare them to their children that

Scriptures for Life

they might set their hope in God, and not forget the works of God, but keep his commandments:"**(Psalms 78:6-7)**

"And thou shalt teach them diligently unto thy children, and shalt talk of them when thou sittest in thine house, and when thou walkest by the way, and when thou liest down, and when thou risest up."**(Deuteronomy 6:7)**

"Tell ye your children of it, and let your children tell their children, and their children another generation."**(Joel 1:3)**

"Hear, ye children, the instruction of a father, and attend to know understanding."**(Proverbs 4:11)**

"Now therefore hearken unto me, O ye children: for blessed are they that keep my ways. Hear instruction, and be wise, and refuse it not."**(Proverbs 8:32,33)**

"Children, obey your parents in the Lord: for this is right. Honour thy father and mother; (which is the first commandment with promise;) That it may be well with thee, and thou mayest live long on the earth."**(Ephesians 6:1,2,3)**

"Train up a child in the way he should go: and when he is old, he will not depart from it."**(Proverbs 22:6)**

We must learn early that we as Christians are the children of God. (Deuteronomy 14:1, Galatians 3:26; 4:5,6,7; Romans 8:14, 16, 17; I John 3:1,2,10; Ephesians 5:1; Luke 20:36; Mark 10:14; John 1:12) There are many Scriptures that refer to us as children of God. This has to be a part of our character.

From birth to death we reach. We reach for good or we reach for bad. The hand that rocks the cradle controls the world. (William Ross Wallace

1819-1881) The infant is close to God and the hope of mother and father. The helplessness draws our love and demands our best tender care. These moments of joy are to be built unto the joys of Heaven. The father is to make the child a man, but the mother plants the root of the manly tree. A life of eternal activity has begun. The voiceless child may someday master great problems. The child is ignorant of truth. The education of God's Word must begin before reading, writing, and arithmetic. This begins by the gentle feeding by the mother. Soft religious music follows. Visitors are to be quiet and not scream, "Oh, what a beautiful baby!" I have seen babies almost jump out of the crib when someone came in the room and in ignorance screamed out. Movements must be slow, smooth, and without jerks. The head is to be supported as the small body is moved slowly. Don't ever shake a baby. Many states have adopted programs and hospital policies that require that all new mothers have an opportunity to view, with the father and other persons of the mother's choosing, a video on the dangers of shaking a baby and "Shaken Baby Syndrome", before the mother's discharge from the facility. Shaking a baby may cause the "Shaken Baby Syndrome", which is fatal, and leaves characteristic hemorrhage in the brain stem.

The pathology will convict the murderer. It is not rare. I have seen several cases. The guilty person is not aware of what shaking a baby can do. The world wants and is looking for goodness. Here it is, keep it that way, and direct the earliest brain to begin storing goodness. Newborn babies are not spoiled. When they cry there is a problem. Solve it even if it demands a trip to the pediatric emergency room. The death of a firstborn being laid in a grave leaves anguish in the home and a burst of sorrow that, without prayer, and spiritual help may result in a life-long bitterness of heart. The loss of a child changes one forever. The memory is sealed in the circuits of the brain. The mortality of a child renders an immortal child who is blessed into an eternal innocence.

(3.) Care of the Child
(Father, mother, other children, grandparents, maid, child care hired from the public or private, etc.)

Evil Is Not Inherent in Human Nature, It Is Learned.
Aggressiveness, hostility, hatred, is nothing but forms of love frustrated, and so is evil. A baby does not cry when their needs are supplied. If they do one must look for a painful problem of some kind. Children are not afraid and anxious because the times are violent and threatening. The times are violent and threatening because the times are afraid and anxious. Give a child love and security and he will not be anxious if the times are violent and threatening. When a child hears a preacher or teacher relate the notion of "Original sin" there is created in the child a regimen for systematically frustrated needs for the child. The **frustration dwarfs the expected satisfaction. The newborn is not egocentric**. He has no ego. He acquires ego from other egos. This may be from the mother or father. An infant's egocentricity is usually not an ego, but a result of their dependency on needs not provided. Age fifty is the gateway to a liberation passage in a woman's life. Her children are leaving the nest. Mother leaves home for her hobbies, but she still has children with problems. The greatest source of stress between human begins is sibling rivalry. They learned competition without love at home.

Keep in mind that our infants are not wild animals. Their brain and all the symbols and other experiences are making them what they will be. When we accept a new concept of the correct nature of human nature our cultures will see fewer fears and anxieties. The infant seeks only to be loved when they have their basic needs supplied. Their environment is slow, peaceful, quiet, and loving. **Remember they want to love you too.**

I learned quickly that children are also very forgiving when given the chance. As far as I know none of my children ever had the tension of insecurity. One must think of and watch for this. It may come from some external action in their social environment. In any fierce competitive society everyone may at times feel some insecurity and even fear. A child who is loved and loves will be strengthened and strong enough to handle anything life may offer. For the unbeliever it is impossible to put love and competition together. It presents no problem when love of selflessness is learned. Love is a relationship between two persons, which contributes to the development of each other. A successful and growing social life depends on human beings behavior to their fellow men. Ones self in society is not the only right person in it. Our society is a conflict producing one. Our children are taught to love their neighbors as themselves. At the same time we tell them to compete with the same love.

Solomon (The wisest man who ever lived) in God's Word says: "Train up a child in the way he should go: and when he is old, he will not depart from it."(Proverbs 22:6)

They love their homes. The child who is still in a helpless state must eat, sleep, and dwell in a happy, quiet, peaceful place. The baby is an individual whose personality is developed no later than six months of age. It takes planning with love, attention, holding, rocking, humming, and eye-to-eye contact. The house must be pleasant in all its ways. There must be room for the children's treasures. Children are taught to develop and have their own collections of toys, books, music, games, etc. It is the mother who at first must teach them the love of nature by watching and naming the birds, squirrels, etc. They must teach the love of the beautiful and the sky, stars, moon, trees, flowers and all the colors. They are developing swiftly maturing as we are also maturing and growing older. Our life has changed. The husband and wife now have a strong competition. This new baby is first in priority and with love between husband and wife that is great joy. The baby becomes inquisitive and must be given opportunities to develop a broad home education. The baby's expectations must be recognized. A little thought can fill the little brain with new things. Childhood trials are real and we become the mentor, friend, supplier of food, and clothes, the sympathetic, and listening counselor. We lead them by successful planning without them knowing it. They always want to hear something new. It must be a source of good and never a source of evil. The television is off until the child is asleep or in school. Heed this warning. Guard the child. Do not allow evil to enter his life. It will force itself soon enough. If the nursery is well modeled and Sunday School developed at their level they will not be spoiled at this age. We, slowly by stories and our lifestyle, bring our children to their Savior. They are led so that they know they depend on us and now they must also depend on Jesus, who we teach that He loves them as much as love can love and He is love. There can never be any doubt about our love and the love of Jesus. They must continue to fill our thoughts. We never rest from this, we think of them by day and dream of them by night. We are constantly there for their activities, hopes and fears. The earliest and only indisputable knowledge is the knowledge of God. It has been said that it is better to be unborn than unloved with an unloving and irresponsible mother and father. We must give them a body, mind, and help them develop their soul. God, who is infallible, will make our efforts a success. Our teaching should begin at birth.

(4.) A Child's Experience, (The reason for this story):

How does a pick-up fit in for teaching children? I lived in Bethesda, Maryland, but taught a large men's Sunday School class at the First Baptist Church in Downtown Washington, D.C. about four blocks from the White House. There came a snow. so big that even Washington D.C. was "snowed-in". Nothing was moving. I looked out the window at the snow-covered pick-up. It seemed to say, "Get the snow off me and let's go!" My oldest son, Joe III said, "Dad, I'm going with you!" Joe III was 5 years old. I said, "Come on cowboy. Let's show the world how two boys from the south live!"

On Connecticut Avenue about halfway to the First Baptist Church and the White House a car had slipped on ice and was off the road, against the curb. Stuck there with a woman looking out. Joe and I jumped out, hooked our chain on her car and pulled her back onto the road. **<u>She declared Joe and I her two angels</u>**.

When we arrived at the church for Sunday School there was about 750 people present. The church was in an area of many apartment buildings and they had walked to church, but I was the only teacher there. They were gathered into a large auditorium. Joe sat on the front seat and I taught the lesson.

When we got home Joe said, "Dad, I'm glad I went with you." Joe died at age 17 (1973) of Ewing's Syndrome. He was president of the Student Body at a large high school. 1200 students came to his funeral. He is buried in the Miller plot in Memphis at the famous Pre-Civil War Elmwood Cemetery where my mother and father are buried. Since 1973 and up to 2011, some unknown person has put flowers on his grave at Christmas Time!

Regulate your child's sleep time. It has been noted that young people in America do not get enough sleep. They need 7-8 hours each night. Irritability in children is usually the result of overwork. Teach your child to practice saving something. This is very important in a "me, me" society where learning self-denial in our economy is a must.

As you make out your church envelope have your child make out theirs. They should give 10% of their allowance. It will surprise and bless you when they give extra to a special mission or hunger program in the church. When they give their coat away at school, it may cost you, but throw yourself on the floor and pray a thanksgiving prayer.

Singing mothers usually have singing children. Children's choirs at church have eternal effects.

Plan a systematic course of Christian education in the doctrine of the Bible. It is a daily, not Sunday only, effort. If a child has not learned syncopation (A shifting of regular musical accent) between the ages of 8-12 the musical brain not used can never be developed.

An unanswered question that prevails over us in this age of television and public speakers in schools is with the differing levels of sensitivity in a group of children. What do they need to hear of the world's problems? I have lectured to many children from the 4th grade and young people through age 30. I am amazed at how much a 4th grader knows, which is much more than I knew at that age. I was just learning to put a worm or grasshopper on a fishhook. In a discussion with 4th graders, one of them informed me she wanted to be a neonatologist. I had finished medical school (1955) before I heard that term.

When is a child old enough to hear about abortions, homosexuality, euthanasia, and persecution in religions or terrorism? A child in North Korea told her teacher she did well on her test by "God's grace". When she got home her parents had disappeared. (Bob Mall, **Christianity Today**, March 2010, p.13.) When can a child hear the Voice of the Martyrs? Does this encourage children's faith or burden them with inappropriate information? Allen of John Brown University said, "Six or seven year olds can process these stories." When can the deeper truths be told?

Katy Kiger, a former missionary to South Africa said, "It is awesome to hear how kids talk about their own struggles." Are we in the dark ages? A mother told her aggressive son that he needed to talk to his father about sex. The boy did this and asked the father what he wanted to know!

Different levels of communication may be impossible. A teacher knew one of her students had alcoholic parents. To teach him a lesson on alcohol she put a worm in a glass of water and it began to swim around. She then put a worm in a glass of clear alcohol and the worm died. She asked what lesson had he learned. He said, "If you drink alcohol you will not have worms."

(5.) Childhood to Youth
The Technique of Learning Became Lost Sometime in History.
In my library I have fourteen Bible translations, twenty Bible commentaries, ten Bible dictionaries, fifteen books on theology, forty books on the Reformation, almost uncountable books on religious history, etc. I read three Baptist state papers, one national Baptist paper, and multiple magazine articles. It is clear that the "Golden Age" of theology has vanished. The only religious leader today is the Pope. The theologians from many schools produce hundreds of amateur-like papers. Most of them are not in any sense of the word academic and

are frequently prejudiced by personal aberrations. The "Golden Age" of theology is over.

Charlemagne (742-814) was "shocked by the decay of Christian learning." He also said, "Written books are better than planting vines, for those who plant a vine serves his belly, but he who writes a book saves his soul." **Charlemagne** reformed language and education. His school at Yorkshire became the most famous in Europe.

Without education there can be no division of work, and without division of work social improvement.

"The kingdom of God cometh not with observation: Neither shall they say, Lo here! or, lo there! for, behold, the kingdom of God is within you." (Luke 17:20-21)

It is said, "Children are what their mothers are." Little children have sharp eyes and ears. We are all "teachers" for children. Our very manners become the "application of their truth." The earliest impressions are the deepest and instilled into the hearts of children and last forever. The memories of children never disappear from their minds. It is our job to make their memories so that their hearts will be stronger and their lives better. The mind is the heart's mouth. Reveal truth into the child and it becomes his bread of life. The hunger will grow and grow for truth. **"Blessed are they who hunger and thirst for righteousness for they will be filled."** (Matthew 5:6) Through life they will be "filled again and again." Teach, feed, and teach, feed the truth it lights the little lamps and it will become their bread of life. The first things invade the child's receptive brain. The first words, the first music, the first looks, the first colors, the first flowers, the first birds, the first toys, the first books, the first bed, the first chair, the first love, and on and on. We paint the first pictures in the child's mind. Let the child remain a child-like be as long as nature allows. No one understands why some people are motivated to success and others are not, but motivation may come from some seemingly little good or little bad thing. We cannot give the child too much love. He will learn the bad things in life soon enough. If one cannot say something good in the presence of a child then do not say anything at all. Teach our children rightly the first years of their home education and they will manage our country well when they grow up. Learn to talk with them and not to them. Any progress they make becomes not a part only, but a part of the whole. They must be helped to advance physically, mentally, morally, but without interference and certainly not with violent oppressive speech instructions. Pitching to your child as he learns to use a bat will endure him to you forever. The number one thing to teach your children (boys and girls) is golf. They can play it around the world and until they get to be 100. At age 100 when they are beating their friends at golf, they will say, "My dad taught me to play!"

Do not ever be guilty so that you will never hear, "my dad or mother taught me to smoke, drink, be lazy in a soft chair watching television, over-eat and be fat, gossip or sleep late on Sunday mornings. Have your children in church three times a week from the time they are 6 weeks old until they leave for college. You cannot teach them that church is important by telling them. You must show them by always going yourself.

My grandfather bought a new ¾ ton pick-up truck one week before WWII started in December 1941. He was a machinist, welder, oil driller, and farmer. Mr. H.L. Hunt himself called my grandfather to return to the oil field for the war effort. At age 13 I was allowed to drive it and do the farm work while he was away in the oil fields. I milked six cows morning and night and took care of all he animals; pigs, chickens, etc. His last ambition was to alone, no labor help, to build a house. He finished a two-bedroom house. He did it all. Poured the concrete, plumbing, electrical wiring, painting, roofing, etc. Grandmother found him dead in the front seat of the pick-up where he always ate his lunch.

The pick-up was mine. I drove it as a second car as a resident and to Bethesda for my 2 years of military service. It was in perfect condition.

My grandfather oiled every joint, including the door hinges, etc. This was before pick-ups were popular. I was the only person I knew that had one. I had many friends that used it when they needed to move, etc. It had a reputation like a person.

(6.) The Home - The Home is Divinely Instituted

Let parental authority be with a loving tone. Discipline by fatherly love is from a powerful hand of love. The blessings and pleasure of God will be forevermore.

The home is divinely instituted:
"So God created man in his own image, in the image of God created he him; male and female created he them. And God blessed them, and God said unto them, Be fruitful, and multiply, and replenish the earth, and subdue it: and have dominion over the fish of the sea, and over the fowl of the air, and over every living thing that moveth upon the earth."**(Genesis 1:27,28)**

"And the rib, which the LORD God had taken from man, made he a woman, and brought her unto the man. And Adam said, This is now bone of my bones, and flesh of my flesh: she shall be called Woman, because she was taken out of Man. Therefore shall a man leave his father and his mother, and shall cleave unto his wife: and they shall be one flesh."**(Genesis 2:22, 23,24)**

"So shall thy barns be filled with plenty, and thy presses shall burst out with new wine. My son, despise not the chastening of the LORD; neither be weary of his correction: For whom the LORD loveth he correcteth; even as a father the son in whom he delighteth."**(Proverbs 3:10,11,12)**

"It is better to dwell in the wilderness, than with a contentious and an angry woman."**(Proverbs 21:19)**

"Children, obey your parents in all things: for this is well pleasing unto the Lord. Fathers, provoke not your children to anger, lest they be discouraged. Servants, obey in all things your masters according to the flesh; not with eyeservice, as menpleasers; but in singleness of heart, fearing God. And whatsoever ye do, do it heartily, as to the Lord, and not unto men; Knowing that of the Lord ye shall receive the reward of the inheritance: for ye serve the Lord Christ."**(Colossians 3:20,21,23,24)**

The most affectionate and excessive attentive parent is not the one that attains the most lasting love. This is most commonly seen when father and mother, mother and grandmother, etc. compete for a child's love. A most crude example is from a patient of mine years ago. This man was so fat that he could not reach around and wipe his bottom. His mother and his wife cooked him four meals a day each. They competed to see which one would get to wipe his bottom.

He was referred to me because he was loosing the use of his legs because of spinal stenosis. No one else would operate on him. I had to put him on two operating tables pushed together.

I did a spinal decompression, put him on a rigid weight reduction, and did not discharge him until he lost 200 pounds. He was walking well. His wife and mother both insisted that they were responsible for him coming to me. They never thanked him for the fact that he could now wipe his own bottom.

Denying a child the proper education of the **discipline of self-denial** is worse than criminal and never to be atoned. It is an injury to a child who is helpless in the parents care. Just as if a child does not learn certain types of music between the ages of 8-12 their brain circuits will be closed at age 12 and they cannot be learned later. This is true in many other things that must be learned early. From age 5 upwards a child must be in the preaching service. That is where he learns about church. If he can only attend one service on Sunday, it must be the preaching service and not Sunday school. That is where he learns the spirit of reverence. The family should sit together when the sound of the music and gospel sounds overcome all other thoughts. There is a blessed "magic" for children who are in God's house **more frequently than shopping or "eating out"**. Make first things first in their lives. The most stupid statement a father can make is, "Let them do as I have done, and make their own way in the world." Give them the proper training to be better. This is the only way generations can progress. Wrinkles and pallor may come on a faithful and dutiful mother, but **they come earlier in one that smokes and wastes herself in other ways**. The wrinkles of one shows dignity, the other uselessness and shame. It is said that in America that three-fourths of mothers are ignorant of their motherly duties. They do not know what their children should wear, hear, or read, or what to watch on television. This cripples their bodies, taints their purity, spoils their manners, and **destroys their souls**.

A Mother should be a praying mother. I repeated in my autobiography one of Cathy's (my wife) writings when she listed 29 praying mothers of famous men. This included: Constantine, Augustine, Charlemagne, Gutenberg (inventor of the printing press), Martin Luther, and Bunyan, Watts, Wesley, Newton, Judson, "Fanny" Crosby, Spurgeon, Moody, and Billy Graham. "The mothers' love for her child is the truest type of Christ's love for us." **The child believes it when they see it is their mother.**

A Navy friend of mine, when he left for duty, agreed with his wife that they would pray for each other at the same time every day. Another friend of mine who became Mother of Tennessee and the United States told me that when each of her children were born she prayed everyday not only for her child, but for the child who someday would be her child's spouse. Each one of her children, who are now parents and even grandparents have all been successful with a wonderful marriage. There had not been a single divorce. The superior and prayerful minds of parents with God direct their children's immortal souls to the will of God as He has entrusted to them. God sees the child at the rising and setting sun, the coming and going of the moon and stars, and with all the glory of the heaven. Talk to your children of God's role in the rain, falling snow, the dew and frost, and the formation of ice. Teach them the songs of birds, the hidden flowers in the grass, trees, and the origin of the new form of babies. Children are adults in miniature. God rules and reigns over all.

Teach them that God created animals that are to be respected and not abused, but animals are not created in God's image. They do not do noble works, broaden the merits of civilization, have memories that change the world, are not eternal, and do not have souls.

"Fathers, provoke not your children to wrath, but bring them up in the nurture and admonition of the Lord." (Ephesians 6:4)

"God hath not appointed us to wrath, but to obtain salvation." (1 Thessalonians. 5:9)

"A soft answer turneth away wrath: but grievous words stir up anger." (Proverbs 15:1)

God watches us parents. We should not fail in his commands.

(6.) a. Love of Children
Where the love of children is found we find the other virtues. We never enter an age when we are under no obligations to our children. It is said that, "Our love for them keeps many men from sins, crime, and particular divorce. As they grow older their need and love from us grows stronger. Our love does not go unrewarded." No boy or girl can become truly great who neglect the comfort of father or mother. The love that one is born to is the sweetest you will have on this earth. The love of a wonderful wife that over-shadows it at a time in life is a different kind of love. Our stories go back to our home. Looking back at age thirteen when I decided to be a "brain surgeon" it was impossible for me in our situation. My father and mother made it possible by a great sacrifice to themselves. **I think of them everyday and with every blessing**. A wife who does not love her husband's mother has a real serious deficit in her life and creates a deficit in his for her. "The eye that mocketh at his father,

and despiseth to obey his mother, the ravens of the valley shall peck it out, and the young eagles shall eat it". (Proverbs 30:17)

The greatest satisfaction of a parent is to see their children grow up to be Christians: They have become sons and daughters of the Lord Almighty.

(6.) b. Duty to Children

Parenthood is fatherhood **and** motherhood. The father is the head, but he is no more essential to the perfection of the family than the mother. They are both commanded in God's word to instruct and discipline their children. It is shameful when a father's business keeps him from instructing his children. (I wish I had done this better.) True knowing, true being, and true doing involve both parents and all their children. Teach them that the only way to appear good is to be good. Never punish them when you are angry. Never smile or laugh at things that are not good. **Never give them anything because they cry for it**.

Jesus is the example from the Word of God. Be patient, meek, love, teach, pray morning and evening, and once during the day or sooner. As they grow up the defense against sin and error and weakness is prayer. Teach them to be holy and it will come back to you. "We cannot commit a wrong without some retribution from it." An idle word or bad word never dies (Matthew 12:36-37). The memory of life does not perish with life itself. I attended the funeral of a friend where the minister said glowing things about him. When I walked out of the church I heard, "That was not the man I knew." **The air is a library where whispered words are written forever**. If bad foundations are laid there will be a bad citizen, bad husband, bad son, bad father, and a bad neighbor. There is no easy lesson for parents.

At a time our bodies will wear out and we become ugly physically. **We must make our "young" life live long after our ugly life begins**. Here there is a lesson to be learned. At age seventeen my English teacher was so ugly to my young mind that I could not look straight at her. By the end of that year she became one of the most beautiful people I have ever known. **Only the revealing of God's love to a young person can do that**.

A parent is not born, they are made. A man is not born, he is made. A lady is not born, she is made. I have never met anyone who could describe a "lady" including Webster, but we adults know one when we see one.

"Home Sweet Home"

(6.) c. The Place of Training is at Home
Home is the place for training the young, where **culture**, discipline, love, beginning of education and the learning process is begun. To the young and helpless it is a sacred place and the starting of a new life. A bad home environment for the child is like "sand in the eyes and rocks in the shoes." Under crystal chandeliers, imprinted rugs, and curved carved oak stairways doted, and collected by ignorant mothers come wild or unfaithful children. The home has no sunshine. There are no smiles and the mothers' eyes do not reveal sunbeams of love. The mother is unhappy and irritable because she is not "somebody." She is a homebody mother. The children spend as much time someplace else as possible. There is a group of crystal glasses and a large hand-cut wine decanter on a glistening expensive table. They learn to drink wine at the back door of the country club or the large clubhouse. There are no books for the young souls. **The unwritten philosophy of that house is that there is no eternity, no judgment, and no Hell**.

Let no one in our home become morally worse. Do not allow temptation or intemperance (alcohol, etc) under our roofs. Let no quarrels continue. There must be love and peace at all costs. A child cannot be made to be good. He must be helped to be good. Help him in rooms of confidence, kindness, love and trust with plans to make dreams for travel, play, reading, and church. By the time the child finishes high school he should have been on several mission trips. If their dirty clothes are all on the bed and floor at home then they will be in the dorm at college or when they are guests in another home.

One must learn to be independent, but also dependent on each other in the family. When the family are allies there is beauty, loveliness, humility and they are the cornerstones of happiness. Love and order in the home will be powerful direction to it in Heaven. The dispositions must be filled with blue skies, rainbows, and music and natures happy sounds. There is full play and blessings for all.

The family that works together and prays together stays together. Let the family add beauty to their home by planting little trees, flowers, and a family painted fence. On a special occasion I planted a small white cedar tree in a bare curved driveway in front of a three-story house. It grew like the children. After they were all gone to college and had their own house the big house was sold. The new owner cut down the cedar because it hid the 3-story house from view from the street. Do good family things now. They will soon be gone. I asked one of my partners how he could play golf every day off with the same four friends. He said our families are all gone. They day will come where one comes home and you and your wife will be all alone. Young people must have fun. Help elevate their buoyant spirits. No unhappiness in life is equal to unhappiness at home. Homes are like instruments of music. The strings give melody and with leadership and training there will be harmony. One single string…Perceive the moment and don't let it happen.

(Tears, Hallelujah, Hallelujah, more Tears, but don't worry the hungry babies will return with hungry babies and diapers.)

Training at Home
In the struggle for life, remember other people's rights; this is a demand for Christians. A youth today with good manners stands out in the

crowd, it has been said they are, "like perfume is to a flower." **Politeness is to goodness what words are to thoughts**.

Sympathy is the very essence of a Christian. "Move through life like a band of music filling the air with sweetness as do orchards of ripe fruit." Men can be trees of righteousness dropping their fruit wherever they go. "**It is the royal gift of the soul**." Say "good morning" to everybody you meet starting with your parents. It will do you good and do good to all you meet. If you add, "**Have a good day" you become a prophet**.

No words can describe a lady, but Hannah Moore does pretty well. "They promote the most useful and elegant conversation, almost without speaking a word. The modes of speech are little more than the modes of silence. The silence of listless ignorance and the silence of sparkling intelligence are separately marked in the most unequivocal language. A lady's illuminated countenance of attention is the most flattering encouragement in the world of men. A pretty simpleton who sits near a man puts an end to his remarks and hears his regret of departure of such reasonable company." (Hannah Moore 1785-1833), is historically famous for several reasons. She established Sunday Schools where the poor were taught reading, personal hygiene, and religion. Her letters published in 1834 are vivacious and highly informative. She wrote two ethical tragedies, *"Percy and Fatal Falsehood"* and *"Thoughts on the Importance of the Manners of the Great to General Society,"* and the novel **"Colebs in Search of a Wife."** She was a highly educated social reformer. At age twenty-two she became engaged to a wealthy man, 20 years older. He never married her but left her an annuity that made her financially independent.

(6.) d. The Mother's Wisdom

She must be the most informed and wisest person in the community. To raise children it takes care and intelligence. **You will not know if you are successful until your children get age 60 and their children age 30**. I am almost there and must admit there are a few failures. I was busy doing the necessary things of a busy surgeon. I knew the effect of this and made it a point to return home daily for dinner with the family at six. I returned to the hospital to finish my work. I know now that neither their mother nor I had regular times of prayer and Bible reading with the children. This was an inexcusable deficiency in my life. I wrote an introduction to a book I finished sixty-two years later and termed the coin at age seventeen, "The Great Beyond" describing my life from age seventeen to eighty. Looking back it was "My, My, My" visions. It is impossible for a proper life to be all "My, My, My." I substituted "things" for "myself" and gave them "things, things, things," travel, cars, and private clubs for golf. That is not the proper life. **The effects as defects will be revealed**.

If religion is practiced with tears and prayers for children there will be an echo of gladness in **several generations**. The mother is not only rocking a child, but may be rocking the fate of nations and the glories of Heaven. In one study 100 out of 120 successful Christian men attributed their conversion to their mother. The mother is the center of attraction. That attraction can be good or evil. There were 19 kings of Israel, but no good kings. There were 20 kings of Judah, but only 8 were good kings. The good kings all had "God-fearing" mothers. Eve became a good mother. Her children were the first to "call upon the name of the LORD". (Genesis 4:25, 26) The nursery of the church is the nursery of the family. We all know of dedicated people that have spent most of their lives in the church nursery. They, no doubt, will have the biggest mansions of Heaven, and it **will be filled with "their" children**.

A daughter came to her mother and said she was praying all night for her sins. Her mother said, "Stop praying, I have given you a $500 dress for the prom next week." A few months later as the child was dying she asked for the dress and said, "**Mother, that dress is the price of my soul!**" Moody said, "Many a young man in this city wants a mother more than a preacher." No language can show the power, beauty, heroism and majesty of a mother's love. It is eternal like a star in Heaven. The battles of a mother are what we hear, drink and wear. Her opinions last forever. The true mother lives for the interest of her husband and her children. The "biggest job on earth"! The eyes of a child form the first sweet page of their education. The language is a light from Heaven. The education begins. The character and beliefs of a mother are repeated in her children. Her work is essential to her children's success.

(6.) e. Health At Home:

Good health is more valuable than money. Health animates all the enjoyment of life and the soul. With poor nourishment, obesity, alcohol, drugs and parental neglect strength loses to weakness, youth loses its vigor, beauty loses its charms, music is harsh, conversation is lost for good, homes become prisons, riches are useless, honor is unknown, and fake crowns are a sorrow. The diseased may be painful as violence to the body. Health must be watched continually.

I had a patient who was an identical twin. During the time of growth in one year one twin was a head taller than the other. Upon examination the smaller twin was also blind. She got her movements by copying her twin. I removed a pituitary tumor. She regained vision in one eye and almost caught up with her twin in growth.

We cannot sell or give away sleep. The mother must make sure it happens. I can't sing, but that seems to help me sing them to sleep. Learn several nighttime stories and by repeating them the developed familiarity will make them relax and go to sleep.

I frequently quote scripture at night with the light out in bed. On occasion when I awake in the morning I realize I went to sleep before finishing the quote. I recently heard an old pillar of the church say the same thing. Don't think about anything troublesome at night.

Learn the eating and sanitary laws of health. When a child is hurt and cries do not try to hush it by threat and ridicule. Be a human mother. Divert the attention to a toy and solve the problem of the pain, but if you can't, take him to the emergency room.

During the growth period, children need love, vitamins, orange juice, milk, proteins, sunshine, and more love, exercise, and learning God's love from a literal Bible.

(7.) The Youth

Who are they? What are they? Do they have anything to offer us? Should they learn, teach, produce for God and man? A boy begins, but ends as a man. A boy who won the Latin prize and practices shooting bagged the most game. The clerk who studied in his spare time is promoted. **<u>Happy-go-luck presidents of their class are frequently dead weight at age 45</u>**.

Choose an occupation that you like and one that will provide you with a living for you and your family. When a young lady today marries it is usually to a man that will require her to work all her life. Their family life is very restricted and both of them, particularly the wife has more temptations in the world.

When President Garfield was suffering he said that since his boyhood having a "reverence for God" had strengthened his influence and kept it under control. This boy with a well spent boyhood and youth became president of the country.

The youth time is preparation days for youth. If it is good and true now it will be good and true later. One must learn early that evil thoughts and vulgarity degrades the humanity of the person and destroys his soul. Follow only good examples. An older person's experience is of no value unless the youth uses the time and effort to learn about it. Your building is not on the future, but on the past and present. If a youth sees no good in his past he has nothing good to build on to become an "experimental test pilot of life". He may be killed or go to Hell. A youth does not inherit scholarships. If he is to be capable he must cultivate his heart and mind. Youths may learn regard for duty, obedience to authority, and the law, and not learn respect for parents, sound morality and God at home. A boy needs something of a man in him and a man needs something of a boy in him. (One must consider the cost of raising a child to age seventeen. The Agriculture Department for Nutrition Policy and Promotion reveals that the cost to age seventeen is $235,000.)

(7.) a. <u>Choosing a Job-Profession</u>

The wisdom of God shows in the happy divinity in the works of man. Some work from their hands, some with their backs, **but all with their minds**. Human progression requires that all of us need to change the human race over the world. Cities, roads, bridges, dams, steel for railroads, wood for lumber, furniture, science for power, theology, and called ministers healing are required to make us what we are. This is a working world that requires labor, physical and mental. **An idle life is always a selfish one**. Days without labor bring nights of restless worthlessness, **which is the scourge that destroys a man's mind and soul**. Young men see how much you can do, not how little you can get by with. Life's course is to be won and will not be accepted as a gift. Remember, all work set by God and done divinely is of equal honor.

Prepare your body and soul for a battle of life that will bring you dawn and build you up. It will bring on gray hairs and success. Even with restlessness, and near exhaustion the brain will continue to function. In my specialty of neurosurgery I assigned myself a schedule of reading about Pathology on Monday nights, Physiology Tuesday nights, Anatomy on Wednesday nights, Surgery on Thursday nights and special needs for Friday nights, such as medical journals, etc. I reserved Sunday morning for surgical rounds, Sunday School and church. Sunday afternoon was for rest. I learned something that was astounding which has never before been reported. Some nights I would be too tired to read, but I forced myself to read at least a paragraph in the assigned subject. With the tired brain I would never forget that paragraph. Someone has described life as a muddy road covered with deep mud holes. I never paid any attention to what was under my feet or on my back. When I wrote my autobiography, the word work is never described because I did not know what it was. I loved everything I did everyday because I knew I was called to be in my early teens what was impossible for me to be. I also did not know about the word impossible, so with my parents, and God's help paving the way, I did not know the impossible. I have since learned and for those who do not know the Bible nothing is impossible with God. (Matt 17:20, 19:25, Luke 1:37) We are under the Divine Teacher and the Holy Comforter.

"And I saw a new heaven and a new earth: for the first heaven and the first earth were passed away; and there was no more sea."(Revelation 21:1) The final dwelling place for the righteous is noted in Isaiah 66:22, and II Peter 3:13)

(7.) **b. Education**
Education is the responsibility of every person.
All education depends on effort of the individual. A book under your pillow will not educate or a Bible on the shelf will not reveal to you the doctrines of God. You must teach yourself, be your own scholar, and be in control of your mind. Education is the development of the **method of learning** in one's mind. The mind must be prepared to learn. One can never learn it all. Education is like sanctification it never ends. Learning brings on and builds up the soul. **A life of learning builds upon itself**. Truth builds on truth, love builds on love, giving builds on giving, good builds on good, strength builds on strength, and loyalty builds on loyalty.

Learning grows when one waters the tree with more learning. Man is the only animal that can establish his own culture. The school of life and the making of the mind require strength, and endurance to expand ones life. Learning is a duty of life. God did not intend for us to remain a baby forever. To be a scholar requires hard work that is **planned with an intellectual objective**.

Planning Begins In College.
To the college group entering a four year academic curriculum in August-September 2012:
Start planning for your life now. Choose a major that will enable you to

make a living. Begin thinking about all the people you meet that might help you accomplish your goals. (Writing letters of recommendation, career counseling, etc.)

Your first Year:

The first year try to complete all your required courses early so that you will have a good choice of electives your last two years. Learn public speaking and also a foreign language, particularly Arabic. Apply for a job or internship related to your career interest. A pre-medicine course must start the first year. Study hard for good grades.

Your Second Year:

The second year take a business course, accounting, or a specific professional or personal finance course. Volunteer for things that you are good at. Get to know people. Some type of externship or internship will be helpful in the summer.

Your Third Year

The third year make sure you have all the requirements for your major. Some study abroad related to your major is very valuable. Again, get a summer job related to your interest.

Your fourth year

The fourth year should be aimed at getting a job or postgraduate study required for your career. Be sure to get a Teachers Certificate if applicable to you. Look at all the people you know and plan your life of success!

Look for better things. Be a self-made man. Be a self-made scholar. Do this and virtually on almost any subject one chooses to learn they will find themselves in the clouds. So what? Why be a scholar? Why be in the clouds of knowledge? Why have a polished education? Why have mental discipline? When one has knowledge that only they know by study that it is knowledge something has been planted in the soul. What is it? Knowledge just as love forces one to action. The action is to love to teach. This is what makes the world grow. Who can "**little me**" teach? Who does God command you to teach as a start? One of the most famous commands of the Old Testament, "Teach them thy sons, and thy son's sons." (Deuteronomy 4:9; 4:40; 11:19; Psalms 78:5; 103:17; 128:6) Our children are like the "stars of heaven" (Nehemiah 9:23), and "heritage of the LORD, His reward" (Psalms 127:3) "glory of their fathers"(Proverbs

17:6). "That they may teach the young women to be sober, to love their husbands, to love their children." (Titus 2:4) **This is the only scripture instructing women to love their husbands.**

(7.) c. How do I Look?

Do not take the appearances or the picture of the thing itself that is the exterior, because the interior of a person is what counts. "God knows the secrets of the heart." (Psalms 44:21) Don't bathe in the exterior world and don't dirty the exterior grace. Don't agitate the soul while the mind is in an uproar. Don't lose control of the voice while the passions are running away. This would be like throwing bad smells in a polluted river.

The temper of the mind shows in the faces "Wisdom makes the face shine" and produces a serenity of the soul. Some of you feel good and bad in the soul and don't know it. You confuse the soul with conscious. Conscientiousness is a learned sense of right and wrong. The soul has always been there and was implanted by God. Outward appearances and resemblances are transitory not to be confused with external facts. Their notoriety is of no eternal consequence. The holiness of our force forward is the only thing that counts. If our human person fails, forget it. Every Christian knows he is "nothing" without God. With God we can do all things. (Matthew 19:26, Mark 9:23, 10:27, 14:36; Luke 18:27) (Note that God says this over and over for us who are dull of wit.)

What is a good appearance? No one can answer that, but it is to say the least, " to be neat and tidy in your personal appearance. A little girl who was a good student went to school and always sat alone at lunchtime. The teacher advised her to go to the lunchroom and be with the other students. The next day the teacher went to the little girls' desk to get her lunch and escort her to the lunchroom. She said, "Please don't touch it teacher, it is only blocks." She had no lunch to bring. A very good Christian friend of mine who was always neat and tidy, but never wore a necktie said to me, "Jesus never wore a necktie." All people are human and all humans have problems so never worry about your appearance if it is your best. Who are the humble poor man and the proud rich man? The humble poor man at his wood table with bread and milk is as proud as those of royal birth. Don't ever pay attention to one single emotion of flattered vanities.

(7.) d. Work or Idleness

The body and the mind are our beasts of burden, and victory depends on how we drive them along the highway of life. The human mind and body are instruments for the **steady pull** of a successful career. We need to learn early what we need. We should do work for which we are fitted until the end of our days. **Benjamin Disraeli** said, "By a wise adaptation to our needs and body literary men in their authorship find ability in labor until the lighter."

Many a new business has been reached by our active and beautiful old age with the tenors of youth being left behind. The long-term saddle fits with the end of days in some people of faith.

Hannah Moore said, " **Idleness among men and children is the root of all evil**."

Find something good to do. Those who work also find good healthy play. The surprising changes in life are seen day and night, at labor and rest, hurrying and coasting to retirement will keep the mind active: work is given to us by God. Work in love and it becomes a divine action. We can be a servant of the Almighty as a plowman, laborer, weaver, mechanic, and in my experience the hardest labor includes clearing a right of way away for a road, and picking cotton. One must not be ashamed to do any hard work. It has been clearly shown that on occasion idleness leads to wandering vagabonds, which leads to crime, murder, theft, burglary, and rape.

"If any man would not work, neither should he eat." (II Thessalonians

3:10) "All men should be required to work at something." There are no lazy and idle true Christians. **The undeserved disability checks and parking stickers corrodes the human being in his character, purity, sense of worthiness, and his very soul**. Live so that you are not ashamed to die. I have seen this. It is by far the worst experience of life. There is a mental agony and extreme pain of the mind. Just to see it makes one sick. "One will be ashamed to die until they have done some good for humanity". (**Horace Mann**) "For being born, or, being born, to die?" (*"Life"* by **Frances Bacon**, 1561-1626) "Be ready. Know thyself you are born to die and with reasoning there is error". *("Essay on Man"* by **Alexander Pope**) "Die with your boots on like a pioneer." *("The Ballad of William Sycamore"*, **Stephen Vincent Benét**, 1898-1943) "Die not drunk while asleep". (**Walter Stephens**) "Die as our fathers die." (**Algernon Charles Swinburne**, 1837-1909)

Work is the true thinkers "rock." An unknown writer said, "Remember, my son, you have to work whether you handle a pick or pen, a wheelbarrow full of rocks or a set of books, or digging or editing." "We are God's fellow workers." (1 Corinthians 3:9) Jesus said, **"I know your works."** (Revelation 2:2) **"Behold, I come quickly; and my reward is with me to give every man according or his work shall be."** (Revelation 22:12) This is repeated in Psalm 62:12, Proverbs 24:29, and I Peter 1:17.

"The mind was God's best work" (Robert Burns). Use it. Solomon, the wisest man said, "God will bring every work into judgment." (Ecclesiastes 12:14) He (God) is the rock, His work is perfect: for all His ways are judgment, a God of truth." (Deuteronomy 32:4)

"Men must work, and women must weep." (**Charles Kingsley**), but, "Woman's work is never done." (Anonymous) "To pray is to work, to work is to pray." (**Motto of Benediction Order**) And finally, Jesus warns, **"The night cometh when no man can work."** (John 9:4)

(8.) Master One's Self
The training for this must begin young in life. Never reward anyone

Scriptures for Life

for crying or temper tan-trums (when a child cries there is usually a real problem). It has been said that, "crying in an adult woman is a physiological process, but not in a child." I have a book on **"Famous Last Words"**. It is almost meaningless on the subject of death. Very few live the heroic self-control when dying. The famous **Thomas Paine** in his book **"The Age of Reason"** denied the Christian faith and upon dying alternated between blasphemous oaths and pitiful cries to the Lord for mercy. One of his associates who saw the infidel shivering in his bed said to him, "Die a man, die a man Paine!" God said to Job, "Gird up not thy loins like a man, for I will demand of thee, and answer thou me." (38:5) Julian, a pagan, said, "O, Nazarene, thou hast conquered!"

Voltaire said to his doctor, " I shall go to Hell and you shall go with me." When being burned at the stake, **Latimer** said to **Ridley** to encourage him, "Ridley, be thou of good cheer." **Judson** said, "Death will never take me by surprise!" **John Wesley** said, " The best of all is, God is with us." **Elizabeth the Queen of England** with 10,000 dresses in her wardrobe said, "Millions of pounds for another inch of time." She could not buy it. I had a patient ask me for six months which I could not give. He died slowly over two weeks.

Enoch was "translated" by God, but did not say anything (Gen 5:24, Hebrews 11:5-6). Is there a message for us here? Maybe there is. When I was a small boy, my beloved great Christian great grandmother was dying at home. The room was filled with people. I was standing with my chin on the high bed and she opened her eyes and said to me, "The only thing I hate about dying is leaving you." She died in a few minutes after that. That was her last words and her only words for 24 hours. If she had awakened after that she probably would not have remembered those words, but deep in her brain when she saw me she had a loving message just for me. I have encouraged all my friends and students to leave your message in writing to your family and friends. It could be the best thing you ever did. Burke said, "Manners are more important than laws." Never show a lack of courtesy. Be patient when a friend keeps you waiting. Never say anything that you will later be ashamed of.

God said to Hezekiah for the sins of the kingdom of Judah for my servant David's sake I will preserve a remnant (2 Kings 19:20, 31, 34). Do not let your tongue be your master. In difficult times the powerful Christian mind will be the tongues master. Take all suggestions kindly. If they violate your character say kindly, "That is not the way I think."

(8.) a. The Habit of Thinking

"As a man thinks, So is He." (Proverbs 23:7) We are commanded to "Think no evil." (1 Corinthians 13:5). The habit of thinking and doing good is a mighty tide in life that sails us to a good hope, free grace and a happy landing at life's end, which launches us to an eternal mansion.

A Christian must think so he can do. He will do what he thinks. So "think good." "One knows what he practices." (**Savonarola**)

"Go boldly with a white standard and follow it yourself." (**Joan of Arc**) A standard of white thoughts leads to a white action. **Thinking and doing are like two lovers; Neither one has anything without the other**. (**Miller**)

We sleep in our grave but our works follow us on and on. **There are millions betrayed by the visible church to Biblical illiteracy**. This includes at least three generations that I am aware of. Generation after generation has grown up in sin and suffering and false religions and left to die. Value the things of life as you will on judgment day. Money that you give to the work of soul saving is the greatest of all works which is for eternity. The 90% of your dollar for the local church is sacred and a blessing. The 10% to the Cooperative Program is not. Only 2% or 2 dollars gets to the International Mission Board. The current president (2011) of the Southern Baptist Convention directed 5% to foreign missions and 5% to the Cooperative Program, which is a good start. **We continue to ignore the lack of academically acceptable Biblical education in our Sunday schools**. Our students as they go to college continue to be Biblically literate as are their parents of the 2 previous generations or our Sunday schools. Let us connect them with brain and brawn for Christ's sake.

"A tree will lie as it falls, but also will fall as it leans." In every beginning think of the ending. "The happiness of our lives depends on the quality of our thoughts." (**Marcus Antoninus**)

It is silly to preach to drunken men; it is casting pearls before swine; get them sober and talk to them soberly; if you lecture to them while they are drunk, you act as if you were drunk yourself. Do not try to serve the Lord with a cold heart and drawn soul. Are you riding a snail that thinks he is on the way to Heaven? He who stares with his mouth open will stare until he is dead. Rabbits do not run into the mouths of sleeping dogs. He that has time and looks for a little time will not find it until he repents of time. He who lies down and cries, "God help us" will be crying out judgment where he is his own witness. It is an old, old saying, "God helps those who help themselves." Some men think if they made hats men would be born without heads. If they went to sea they think the water would dry up. No one can help those who for a long time have refused to help themselves.

(8.) b. How to Be Strong?
The world needs strong men to help the weak. (Romans 15:1) Our command, " Be strong in the grace that is in Christ Jesus." (II Timothy 2:1) "Be strong in the Lord." (Ephesians 6:10) "For Christ's sake: for when I am weak, then I am strong." (II Corinthians 12:10)

The true strong man is needed today as never before. In the hour of battle the commander in a stimulator voice is heard to say, " Be brave; be bold; stand your place in honor; conduct yourselves like me and be strong."

In life's battles the Right Truth is against Wrong, Truth against Error,

Sin against Holiness, the Hosts of (Armies) of God are with you. To fail in truth is to destitute the mind!

If you look up you can feel yourself being dragged downward. Be prepared to fall like a martyr of old during their days of blood and persecution as those days exists today in many parts of the world. Teach your children to be as big as truth and to never say, "I can't." With the power to conquer fate, fate is not a word in the vocabulary of one who has truth. The things that will not make a man happy give him power to be strong. To be great in the truth man must die to himself and cease to exist in his own thoughts, then he becomes great. The soul knows justice and truth creates conscience. A youth without character will absorb whatever sin is easiest for him. The "truth mind" becomes a low within itself and follows the leadings of conscience. He becomes true to himself and true to all others. The secret loyalty to his right is the essence of all true freedom.

Right is bound to do right! Strong drink is the curse of the country and to the strength of youth. A true son can be as free as the singing bird above his head. Freedom is not on a signpost or coin; it is that which is within one of truth.

(8.) c. Love of Books

My son, Dwight, had cancer that had metastasized. He lived five years after the cancer was discovered. He taught his children to love books. He read the Bible regularly to them. Even the five year old could quote scripture. When his children of all ages (my grandchildren), visited me I witnessed the most amazing thing. I would buy them anything. They did not want toys, they wanted books. They had rather go to a large bookstore than to Disney World. Cathy and I love books and bookstores, but they would keep us there for hours. Each one would collect stacks of books, I think they studied my eyes and knew when they had reached their limit with me. How can you refuse a child who wants a good book?

Before every trip the whole family would quote Psalm 121. A heavenly blessing came to Cathy and me when we heard a five year old quote the Psalm alone and with confidence. Books strengthen our love for our fellow man. They teach us the minds of men from many lands. Books come from the genius of another human frequently from another land and culture. **They expand our mind and soul**. They give us sensation, knowledge, and imagination that make our mind seek for more. The right books as well as the Bible should be part of every Christian and patriot. If truth is not known it is lost. When truth is lost the Devil gains. Books will penetrate our children. If they do not get good books from us, they will be exposed to bad books from the world. God is the enemy of evil.

(8.) d. Strength of Mind
An old saying, "Knowledge is power" is true. Anything added to the mind good or bad in a sense makes it stronger. Bad things will eventually make the mind weaker and good things will make it stronger. Both good and bad have eternal effects. One pleases God and one does not. Knowledge, wealth, and power as Solomon says are all "vanity". I add that knowledge, wealth, and power frequently become man's master. A pure mind will direct all three to higher levels. I have heard at funerals the most uneducated men referred to as being wise and good by all who spoke. **The advertisement for Christianity is a wise and good Christian**. Who can argue if Christ is the cornerstone for one's life? A good education may be forced by various situations and the desire for more knowledge may continue forever.

If it had been left entirely up to me I would probably still be a neurosurgical resident at age 80. When I finished the Neurosurgical Board requirements I wanted an extra year. I was going to spend a year in Sweden with a world famous neurosurgeon on vascular lesions of the brain. He contracted hepatitis and my time with him was cancelled. I applied for a research position that would give me an extra year of neurosurgical credit and satisfy the Doctor's Draft Law. I was transferred from the Navy to the United States Public Health Service as a senior assistant surgeon. To stay clinical I made neurosurgical rounds across the street at the National Naval Medical Center. The Chairman of Neurosurgery was the senior neurosurgeon in the Armed Forces. He liked me, and as a result, I was transferred from the United States Public Health Service back to the Navy. The youngest neurosurgeon in the United States was to replace the senior neurosurgeon in the United States. I learned how lonely it was to be at the top alone. I was the only trained neurosurgeon. A neurosurgical resident was called out of his residency at the Mayo Clinic to assist me on this big neurosurgical service. I had no one to call for advice when I had a question about a patient.

Dr., Professor Gayle W. Crutchfield, the long-term, great, famous neurosurgical consultant came to Washington once a month to "Get out of Dodge". His excuse was to come and be my consultant for one or two hours. He was not only my consultant in Neurosurgery, but he was my shining light in neurosurgery. Looking back I must consider that my young mind was a young mind because at times I felt I was the smartest man in the world and at times the dumbest man in the world.

Being the teacher of a large all age adult men's Sunday School class at the First Baptist Church of Washington, D. C. for two years kept me on track. In our formal education we learn facts and pass tests to prove it. Where does knowledge begin? What is wisdom? My definitions after years of study include: Facts with understanding of their meaning becomes knowledge and understanding knowledge becomes wisdom. (**Knowledge plus Understanding equals Wisdom**.)

From whom can you learn? Who can be a mentor in life? People who don't know the answer pick "a buddy" they like. I know a non-surgical doctor who picked a "buddy" surgeon to operate on one of his relatives. The "buddy" surgeon opened his relative's abdomen and found a problem he was not competent to handle and sewed him back up. He was referred to a competent surgeon in a well-known medical center. It is good to have "buddies" in life, but "buddyism" is below specialized competency when needed. Pick the best for the best. A mentor as described by Webster

Scriptures for Life

describes is *"a trusted counselor."* There are mentors of professional facts and there are mentors of life. Who are the creditable mentors of life? I will list a few who left their name in history as one conspicuously religious:

- Abel (Genesis 4, Hebrews 11)
- Noah (Genesis 6-9)
- Abraham (Genesis 12, 15, 17, 18)
- Jacob (Genesis 29,32)
- Moses (Exodus 3, Deuteronomy 32:33)
- Jethro (Exodus 18)
- Joshua
- Gideon (Judges 6,7)
- Samuel (I Samuel 3)
- David (See his Psalms)
- Solomon (I kings, 18,19)
- Jehoshaphat (II Chronicles 17,19,20)
- Jabez (I Chronicles 4)
- Asa (II Chronicles 14,15)
- Josiah (II Kings 22,23)
- Daniel (Daniel 6)
- The Three Hebrews (Daniel 3:1-30)
- Zacharias Luke 7)
- Cornelius (Acts 10)
- Eunice and Lois (II Timothy 1:5)
- **Jesus, Eleven Apostles, Paul and Stephen**

Beware of school and church counselors without certification. I have a long list of "bad" counseling. I know of a "psycho" wife of a prominent man in a church who was picked to counsel young people. This is why the statement was made that the most dangerous place for children and youth is church. The lawsuits abound in this area. Ignorance teaching ignorance never works out right.

What is a testimony? It is not God giving you the faith to learn to ride a bicycle. I have heard testimonies just that absurd. Recently at a funeral **<u>I heard a family member who had nothing to say, say it for fifteen minutes</u>**. He was having great fun.

So what is a testimony?
- Sing praises to the LORD (Psalms 9:11)
- Give thanks to the LORD among the heathen. (Psalms 18:49)
- Understand the way and talk of His wonderful works (Psalms 119:27)
- My tongue shall speak thy word. (Psalms 119:172)
- The heart understands knowledge and the stammers speak plainly. (Isaiah 32:4)
- Do not be afraid, ye are My witnesses. (Isaiah 44:8)
- Declare the word of our LORD. (Jeremiah 51:10)
- "Whosoever therefore shall confess me before men, him will I confess also before My Father which is in heaven." (Matthew 10:32)
- "Speak so that they may see the light." (Luke 8:16)
- "And ye are witnesses of these things." (Luke 24:48)
- "Ye shall receive power to be My witness." (Acts 1:8)
- Be a witness to His resurrection. (Acts 1:220
- No man can say that Jesus is the Lord, but by the Holy Spirit. (I Corinthians 12:3)
- Be not ashamed of the testimony of our Lord. (II Timothy 1:8)
- I will declare thy name unto my brethren in the midst of the church. (Hebrews 2:12)
- Be ready always to give an answer. (I Peter 3:15)
- Let the elders be a witness among you–be a witness of the sufferings of Christ and a partaker of the glory that shall be revealed. (I Peter 5:1)

Composure is very often the highest result of strength. A spiritually strong man always has composure even when being burned at the stake.

The human soul through the sanctification of struggle, sometimes suffering, and victories is going toward the final perfection. Virtue fashioned by the will to resist temptation gives a strength that cannot be defeated. **<u>Not to plan is to resolve to do nothing</u>**. Religion is necessary and indispensable as an inheritance for eternity and the connection of man to his Creator. We are not aiming to a mansion, but to a throne.

Scriptures for Life

Without God in the world man is in another space away from the purpose of his creation.

(8.) <u>e. Man's Power</u>
<u>Every man can be productive and destructive</u>. No man lives to himself, and his books. Be careful what you read. We are all part of the whole. If you don't like this world you are probably part of the reason and conversely if you like the world you are probably part of the reason. Your influence can be buried with you or it can be carried on. Don't be not what you should have been. Do your best and there is never any reason for regret. In the grave you are your only friend so give it an aroma of strength. You fought a good fight. My Dad used to say to me, "Boy, be sure they know you have been there." The mother of **John Newton** died when he was seven years old. Because of her religious teachings he recovered from being a dissipated sailor and through him **Claudius Buchanan** was converted to be a missionary to India and wrote *"The Star in the East"* that converted **Adonia Judson** to be a missionary to India. **Adonia Judson** attributed his success in Burma as a missionary to <u>a life of prayer</u>. Newton was responsible for the conversion of **Tomas Scott** and through him **William Cowper** was rescued from depression and turned to religion. He influenced Wilberforce who influenced the abolition of slavery. **William Wilberforce** wrote, *"A Practical View of Christianity"*, which led to the conversion of **Legh Richmond**, the author of *"The Dairyman's Daughter"*, which saved thousands and all this because of John Newton's mother's teachings to him before she died when he was seven years old.

Individuals reform the world and bring it back to God. Secular learning is not related to goodness and happiness and changes humility to pride. True virtue saves man to seek good for its own sake. The touch of nature makes us kin to the whole world. One emerges humble, but noble and man's power has arrived.

(8.) f. Stability of Mind

Without stable minds there would be no love or virtue in the world. **Spasmodic enthusiasm goes nowhere. The best modern examples** are the numerous church committees that meet with ideas and enthusiasm and nothing happens before the next meeting. They are zealous in speech, but no action. Deep convictions, however, set the right direction and hold the soul steady. Where there is hope, hope can never go away. Hope in a youth that looked above to the All Powerful is held by infallible words, **"Lo, I am with you always."** (Matthew 28:20) The biggest mistake of Christians is agreeing with the world. If our lives are above the world we will have a true Christian power. God does not change. He is not unstable. Words are to be stable before God without the influence of self love.

(8.) g. True to Your Word

"God hates those who don't keep their word."(Proverbs 12:220 "A promise made is a debt unpaid." (**Shakespeare**) When you break your word it will always be with you. The one thing that you can give and keep is your word. This is deep from an unknown writer. "Does it pay to be honest? No, my son, if you are honest for pay, it doesn't." If you find someone's purse and return it for reward it becomes a duty and is not a blessing. Jesus said, **"Render what belongs to man and what belongs to God."** (Matthew 22:21) This is a Divine Order. Honesty to man means pay your debts due to him, but makes you dishonest if you do not render to God what is due him. God wants our praises and our service to Him. It is dishonest not to. To be trusted brings on success. I had a patient rendered permanently disabled because two concrete blocks being used to hold up his car fell on him. It was determined that due to dishonesty the makers of the blocks had not applied the specified amount of concrete. There are many examples like this of walls falling down, roofs collapsing, etc, due to dishonesty of builders knowingly using inferior building materials and inferior workmanship.

(8.) h. The Character of Being Faithful
Allegiance, Loyalty, Devotion, and Fidelity
"Thy people shall be my people, and thy God my God: Where thou diest, will I die."(Ruth 1:16,17)

"Most men will proclaim every one his own goodness: but a faithful man who can find?" (Proverbs 20:6) I have pushed prayer and loyalty for four years in the church I attend. More than three hundred men have stepped forward to make that their testimony, but there are many men in the church and even staff members who have not stepped forward. One should not refuse to show loyalty when asked, if they do not one must wonder which side they are on. "We are all in a storm sea of life and we owe each a terrible loyalty." (**G.K. Chesterton**) Loyalty in little things is a great thing. Faithfulness or loyalty to the best of our strength is rewarded by a larger chance for advancement. He that is faithful falls into a larger world. Do your available activity faithfully and see yourself rise to something nobler. It goes higher and higher. One sees that no human hand could have delivered my blessing to me. Virtue is its own reward as noted by the death of Socrates. **John Milton** said, "Who best can suffer, best can do." God does not ask our opinion, but gives us orders sometimes for the impossible. A true follower of Jesus will say yes. "Ours is not to reason why, ours is to do and die." (**Alfred Lord Tennyson**) If we are not big in little things we will be little in big things. Do your work as unto God, and to unto men. If you are an educated man who is digging a ditch, let your education show as beauty in the ditch. However, you should be preaching, teaching, or doing surgery. The real "making out" in this world is fighting its evil and the sins in our own hearts. The guard dogs of Pompeii never left their post. Their skeletons have been found at their posts where they died of suffocation in agony under the lava from the eruption of Mount Vesuvius in AD 79.

(8.) i. Good Sense Leads to Excellence
"Common sense is not common." (**Breese**, 1883) Genius is not common sense. Genius is a natural trait given by God to a few people. "Common

sense" according to Webster is ***"ordinary good sense and judgment."*** In a 40-year-old Collegiate Webster Dictionary it is defined as, ***"a sound prudent judgment or the <u>unreflective opinion of ordinary men</u>."*** I like the 1973 New World Webster's Dictionary definition as, ***"intelligence that comes from experience"*** or "<u>**the sense to dress warmly in cold weather**</u>." "Do not go in deep water until you can swim." We then note that there are people that don't learn from experience. In my study, it appears that common sense should be teachable. Boy or girl, dress warmly in the winter, short sleeves in summer, eat well, rest well, work hard, pray well, study well etc, etc.

Common sense is not science, but it is a conceived idea of the above. It is said to have a moral influence on morals and manners. My father told me that the big thing when he was a teenager was eating live-grasshoppers. That is not common sense, but is a cultural aberration, a deviation from the standard or common sense. Cultural aberration today includes youth addictions to food, alcohol, drugs, and loud banging rhythm-less music, etc. (Many of our youth will have a severe hearing loss by the age of fifty due to loud music. God will hold the religious music directors in churches accountable for that.) The only evidence for evolution that I have seen is young peoples dress in this age.

Common sense, whatever it is and wherever it comes from, improves conduct and regulates every day life's activities. Common sense is said to reveal to every man that the "moral laws are building upon every intelligence in the universe."

Christianity is common sense with grace and love for truth, right and virtue. It produces a golden growth of happiness, peace and other holy blessings. Common sense gives one blessings in abundance. While we are in the world we must live with the living relatives of the world. For years I have had a lot of fun telling my close minister and other religious friends that I am a "spiritual" man. 100% of the time, there is at least a slight shock to the recipients' face and when I immediately say I am also a "man of the world" there is a sudden, relaxed, peace that comes over their face. But, this is true for all Christians who live in this world. There is a "master of evil" that surrounds all of us, but we have the master of power, the Holy Spirit, within us. With common sense we can enjoy and improve the present. The living reality is that we can grab the attainable and do what some say is the impossible. There is no scripture that says we all disregard the natural laws of security and success. "Negativism", an attitude of skepticism and denial of nearly everything suggested by others is frequently seen among Baptists.

About 30 years ago, a motion was brought before the church to adjust church policies to new income tax law regarding supporting of church members going on mission trips. A loud spoken deacon objected because he did want the church to support anything that allowed people to save on income tax. This man also refused to sign any type of pledge to the church. A secretary in the church office related that there was no record of his giving anything. The ushers who passed the collection plate watched him and noted that he only occasionally put in a dollar. One can imagine the uproar. Two things happened. He moved to a "smaller" church and the church passed a rule that no member of the church could be a paid employee. All church secretaries were members of some other church.

Another example of one's sins finding them out was reported 128 years ago (1883) where a man's sin was revealed after his death. A benevolent society had proposed giving life insurance policies to missionaries who made a few hundred dollars per year so that their families would be supported after their deaths. One of the "Fathers of Grace" argued that the future of their families was in God's care. The "brothers" wretched logic prevailed. When he, himself, died he left his family without a dollar. They had to depend on charities for "barest necessities of food and clothing!"

In 1960 I was a teacher in a large men's Sunday School class in the prominent First Baptist Church in Washington, D.C., which has been attended by several of our Presidents. Five men in the church came to me and wanted to develop a group of trustees to invest their money into investments and spend only the profits. That church is now financially independent. At about the same time this was presented to another Baptist church. They turned it down because it would take away the incentive and blessings of giving for its members. The truth prevails that 4 of 5 church members never give anything to the church over a years time. The one in five who do give, would give anything and would be able to give to things not normally required - the budget. The concept prevails that common sense is not common. The world goes on year after year. **Goethe** used to sing, "by never resting, never wasting we could live double the years of the average spanned American."

Common sense promotes a cheerful disposition. Recently in an Amish restaurant I read on the wall, "Plant kindness in life and gather love-life in Heaven."

(9.) Make your own way
(Don't depend on surrounding conditions)

If you can't find your place make one for yourself. There is a divinity that will shape our little world for us. Conditions do not make the man. The man makes the conditions. He who fills his world makes or breaks it. A free man may be a slave and a slave a free man. It is something inside, not outside, that makes one free. The stake was the martyrs throne. **Their deaths caused the conversion of millions**. Never complain or murmur of problems in life. Put them under your mental feet and charge to glory. Do not run away from the sound of life's guns. Moses went from the emperor's son to forty years of tending sheep to being called by God. Jacob was the only person ever to see God face to face and his life preserved. (Genesis 32:30) I treated patients for forty years and loved every minute of it. As Moses I was where God put me. Man is to be the master of his conditions whether it is front line battle, operating on people, or filling sand bags in the 117-degree sun to build a barrier to protect a battle field hospital. "Sands make the mountain and **moments make the life**." Life's events come quickly and are the garden of the soul. The day may do its worst, **but you will never meet that day again**. Use your time in a godly manner. Do not allow wickedness to enter into your mind or actions. Do your part in feeding the hungry, visiting the sick, and spreading the gospel. Whatever your circumstances, attempt to **glorify God whether it is with "two mites" or more**. You can do as much or more.

(9.) a. Help Yourself to Life
"Commit to the LORD whatever you do, and your plans will succeed." (Proverbs 16:3) "The father of success is work, the mother of accomplishment is the desire for success." (Reference unknown) "The man is a success who has lived well, laughed often and loved much; who has gained the respect of intelligent men and the love of children." **(Robert Louis Stevenson)**

"A just man falls seven times, and gets up again: but the wicked shall fall one time into mischief." (Proverbs 24:16) A dead fish can float downstream, but it takes a live fish to swim upstream.

Temptation is life's eternal danger. **It is the decisive times of life**. Satan entered Judas. (Luke 22:3) Jesus said to Peter, "Satan hath desired to have you." (Luke 22:31) Eternal Hell reaches into life on earth time. **Life's desires are the powers of Hell**. They are the undertow that takes us out into Hell's ocean. A hot hand from Hell that feels cold to us reaches out from Hell to grab us into darkness. The battle for our soul is fought in our soul for our soul. Sin is illogical, but it takes advantage of the evil part of man's will. Sin takes place with our desire. Temptation causes us to enter an "I wish" mode of thinking. Our morals fall to a logical intellect. Our character falls apart. We lie to ourselves to accomplish our evil wishes, but this deceitful purpose causes collusion in our minds. To live is to be tempted. This is where the Holy Spirit that Christ left us comes in. In Him comes the strength for victory over Satan's temptation.

"Submit yourselves therefore to God. Resist the devil, and he will flee from you." (James 4:7) This says, "Take a stand!" "Help yourself to Life!" "There hath no temptation taken you but such as is common to man:

but God is faithful, who will not suffer you to be tempted above that ye are able; but will with the temptation also make a way to escape, that ye may be able to bear it."(I Corinthians 10:13)

Be faithful, help yourself, God always provides away to escape sinful temptations. Christ lifts up the young and old and makes them holy men and women, but **all of us must reach up to Him**. He sets us free. He made us His children. Our earthly father is due great honor. I honor no man more than my earthly father, but I look up to my heavenly Father. A Father that has re-created us; who has given us a re-birth. Who has made us to be "born again" and it is free, paid for by His Son's life. He loved us first. Our only effort is **repentance** and **faith** and **acceptance**. We can have victory over every temptation. "Watch ye and pray, lest ye enter into temptation. The spirit truly is ready, but the flesh is weak." Mark 14:38) *"Watch"* is like a military sentry or a guard. They are not to fight, but warn the commander of the harm so he can prepare to meet them the foe. The holy learned the skill of believing is to yield oneself to God. Know you are helpless and permit yourself to be rescued. Allow God to perform a miracle in your life and show you the way to holiness. This is the **struggle of faith** and the **victory of faith**. Faith humbles oneself before God and reaches up to Him like a helpless child that we are. The Devil is stronger than we are. Our mental sentry guard sees the enemy and notifies the commander who defeats the enemy and sets us free. Jesus Christ the Chief Force is always with us, but we have to look up to Him for victory. Do you understand? "At that time Jesus answered and said, **I thank thee, O Father, Lord of heaven and earth, because thou hast hid these things from the wise and prudent, and hast revealed them unto babes.**"(Matthew 11:25) "Call on the LORD while He is near." (Isaiah 55:6) God draws us into His Holy Presence. God calls us. That is our spiritual awakening. **C.S. Lewis** said that God calls on people many times and at certain times God gives up and calls on them no more. I believe this as noted in my experience with certain people, however we cannot give up on anyone because we do not know when God leaves a person on their on. It happened to King Saul in the Bible, so it happened. "Choose you this day whom you will serve. (Joshua 24:15) "Today if ye will hear his voice, harden not your hearts,

Scriptures for Life

as in the provocation." (Hebrews 3:15) Human beings have a mind of their own. We are not to mold our mind on some one else, but we are to develop our mind to be at the highest level possible. When one loses their individuality it is fatal for the development of their own character. Self-reliance is what makes humans different than animals. The more we see ourselves, the more will be our personal efforts. Our prayers are only heard if we work at life as well as prayers. A child learns to walk by walking. We learn an excellent nature by pursuing an excellent nature. We don't learn to be lazy, that is natural. The first requisite to know is **to want to know** and then to have a plan with a purpose. Unseen personal mental glory is to have a will that cannot be subdued or conquered. Help yourself to life, be a success, and be happy.

(9.) b. Resist Evil

One must look at the consequences of sin. An ounce of prevention is worth a pound of cure. (Old proverb) Life can be visualized as weaving a beautiful "rug". When life is finished one can look back at the "rug" that can be filled with magnificent moments of beauty or blotched with irregular marks of wicked wrongdoings. There will always be defects or mistake in the "rug". There is still the possibility of a magnanimous moment (The word *"magnanimous"* is the highest word in the English language to describe greatness) to think, reason, and talk with God. "Come now, and let us reason together, saith the LORD: though your sins be as scarlet, they shall be as white as snow; though they be red like crimson, they shall be as wool."(Isaiah 1:18) The only promise from any religion or in other sources of authority isn't the world that can and will wipe out the past. **God will remember our sins no more**. (Jeremiah 31:34; Psalms 79:8; Isaiah 43:25; 65:17; Hebrews 10:17) To yield to temptation provides only **moments of pleasure** and gratification. The big difference between a true "born again" Christian is that the Christian is **always** sorry when he sins. **When one brags about his sins**, **evil habits, or the abuses of pure life he is not a Christian**. Prevention prevents a need for a cure of sin, but God wants to cure us and if we believe, he will remember our sins no more. People are not God and many people will never forget a sin of others. If one cannot forget their own sins they do not know God. Man's economy of life is not God's economy of life, but God gives it to those who ask. (Matthew 7:7-8; Mark 11:24) Keeping your mouth shut is never overshadowed by ones explanation when they should not have opened it. Greasing a squeaky mouth can only be greased by the grease of God's grace. Prevention is God's Grace in the mind. The currents of the soul if directed into the proper channels of joy and hope always return larger to the soul. Fires are friendly when used for benefit, but when they blaze uncontrolled they devastate all in their path. Man can control nature and the direction of his own soul. Evil strained through moral strainers simply become increased diluted evils. "Overcome evil with good." (Romans 12:21)

(9.) c. Purpose in Life - Men With a Purpose

"Turn not to the right or left: remove thy foot from evil. My son, attend unto my wisdom, and bow thine ear to my understanding, respect distinction, keep knowledge." (Proverbs 4:27, 5:1,2) To be a successful man with a purpose requires hard work. Some say it is "painful", but it was never painful to me. The "non-medical" people in college took their courses in the mornings and were free in the afternoon. The pre-medical group took their lectures in the morning and their lab work in the afternoon. I clearly remember looking out the lab window one afternoon and seeing my friends at play. I learned to like a test table and a microscope better than a football. I was where I was supposed to be and "I loved it". It was not work or painful to me. I felt good about falling into the bed exhausted at night. If one becomes **"burned out"** in their profession they have wandered away from God. He gives us the strength we need.

"There hath no temptation taken you but such as is common to man: but God is faithful, who will not suffer you to be tempted above that you are able; but will with the temptation, also make a way to escape, that you may be able to bear it!" **(1 Corinthians 10:13)**

"Thou therefore endure hardness, as a good soldier of Jesus Christ." **(2 Timothy 2:3)**
Walk worthy of vocation wherewith ye are called." **(Ephesians 4:1, 1 Thessalonians 2:12, 2 Thessalonians 1:11)**
"I can do all things through Christ which strengtheneth me." **(Philippians 4:13)**
"Let us hold first the profession of our faith." **(Hebrews 10:23)**
"Wherefore the rather, brethren, give diligence to make your calling and election sure, for if ye do these things, ye shall never fail." **(2 Peter 1:10)**

Learn from the Bible. It will be in place as long as we live. Have certain competent verses to memory, if you don't, when you need them it will be like a gun with no bullets.

Do good work in your profession if you don't it is mere professional suicide. The word of your poor work will get out. Build a reputation of excellence. **Luther** said, "The greatest temptation of a Christian is comfort in what he is." We must continue to strive to be better. Have interest in what you do. "Interest is the mother of attention" and another said, "Attention is the mother of memory."

A mind that is receptive draws to itself things others do not use.

Have courage to live or die for a moral purpose.
I have heard it said, "Everyone and particularly every child needs a hero." Our country is getting bored, we have need of a real hero. The term *"hero"* has as many colloquial definitins as there are minds of men. Webster's second definiton of the term *"hero"* is as good as any, "A man admired for his achievements or abilty." He does not include women in the definition, but I know at least two heroic women. **Mikhail Lermontov** (1814-1841) wrote, *"A Hero of Our Time,"* in 1840. Each genreration has their heroes, but most of them are obliterated by time. There are many herose of the Bible whose names have lasted thousands of years.

To Name A Few:
Noah, Abraham, Moses, Jacob, Joseph, Joshua, Gideon, Samuel, David, Jonathan, Solomon, Elijah, Elisha, Daniel, Enoch, Isaac, Samson, Asa,(physician), Jehoshaphet, Joash, Hezekiah, Josiah, Ezra, Ethan, Job, Isaiah, Jeremiah, Ezekiel, Hosea, Jonah, Micah, Zechariah, Malachi, John the Baptist, Stephen, and the 11 Apostles: Peter, Andrew, James, John, Philip Bartholomew, Thomas, Mathew, another James, Thaddeus, and Simon. The list goes on and on: Melchizedek, Luke, Nicodemus, Joseph of Arimathea, Timothy, Barnabas, Simeon, and Paul. A few of the heroic women include: Abigail, Bathsheba, Deborah, (the patriotic woman"), Esther, Hannah, Rahab, Ruth, Sarah ("Mother of nations"), Anna (She may have been the first to recognize baby Jesus as the Messiah), Elizabeth (Mother of John the Baptist), Mary (mother of Jesus), Mary of Bethany (She was at Jesus; feet three times. She anointed Jesus feet and wiped them with her hair). John 12:3 for Comfort John 11:32 and for instruction Luke 10:39 Mary Magdalene (stood near Jesus at His crucifixion), and Mary (mother of James and Joses)

I have listed six – six heroes from the Bible whose names have lasted and are still strong at 2000 Years. Add Jesus the Christ as the hero of all heroes in and out of the Bible. How many people not in the Bible can you name as heroes whose name is still prominent in history after 2000 years. An interesting fact of history is there is a continuing without interruption of Christian heroes to the present time:

Ignatius (30-117) Peter appointed him to be **Bishop of Antioch**. He was the first to refer to the church as "universal" (Catholic). Here the followers of Christ were **first called Christians**. Several church writers refer to Ignatious as the young child that Jesus took in his arms in Mark 9:36. **Ignatius** was taught by John the Apostle. He wrote letters to: The Ephesians, Magnesians, Trallians, Romans Philadelphians, Smyrnaeans, Polycarp, Bishop of Smyrna, Tarsians, Antiochians, Philippians, Mary at Neapolis, and two letters to John the Apostle. He is noted as a Deacon at Antioch. **He welcomed death and was thrown to the lions**.

Scriptures for Life

Polycarp (69-155) He was also a pupil of the Apostle John. He received and transmitted the doctrine of faith. He was a link in church history between the Apostle John and Ireaneus whom he taught.

Irenaeus was the church's chief literay historian of the second century. He descirbes hearing Polycarp speak of the "conversations he had held with John and with others who had seen the Lord." **He was burned at the stake**. The fire did not kill him and he was pierced with a sword.

The History of Christian Heroes Goes On and On:
- **Martyr (101-163)**
- **Perpetua (185-211) Martyred for Christ**
- **Cyprian (200-258)**
- **Constantine (280-337) The "Founder of Christian Freedom"**
- **Athanasius (295-373) The Defender of the "Orthodoxy of Immortality"**

These Names Continue From 329-2011:
- **Basil of Caesarea**
- **Gregory of Nyssa**
- **Chrysostom**
- **Augustine**
- **Patrick of Ireland (A Slave who returned to the land as a missionary)**
- **Clovis**
- **Benedict of Nursia**
- **Columba (Ireland)**
- **Isidone of Seville**
- **Bede (Introduced the terms B.C. and A.D.)**
- **Charlemagne**
- **Cyril**
- **Methoduis**
- **King Alfred, the Protestant upon Protestants**
- **King Wenceslas (Martyred as a lover of Christ, 935 A.D.)**

- Vladimir (Made Christianity the official religion of Russia)
- Anslem (The "Second Augustine", his work guided the church for a thousand years)
- Bernard of Clairvoux (Greatest of the 12th century)
- Peter Waldo (Founder of the Waldenses and one of four Pre-reformers with Wycliff, Huss, and Savonarola)
- Aquinas (Author of the classic *"Summer Theologica"*)
- Wycliff ("Morning Star" of the Reformation)
- Savonarola (Martyr)
- Albrecht Dürer
- Luther (Leader of the Reformation)
- Latimer (Leader of the English Reformation)
- Knox
- Anne Askew (Daughter of the Reformation who was martyred at the stake.)
- Joan Mathurin (Died with her husband at the stake to give him strength.)
- John Bunyan (The Christian Dreamer, author of *"Pilgrim's Progress"*)
- Sir Isaac Newton (Great Christian and scientist who cherished the Biblical doctrines)
- Isaac Watts ("Father of English hymnody")
- John Wesley (Founder of the Methodism)
- Whitfield
- John Newton (Wrote "Amazing Grace")
- Adoniram Judson (India and Burma-Founder of modern American Missions)
- John Charles Ryle (<u>The Bible is the first book in the child's mind and the last one of the dying man</u>)
- Fanny Crosby (Blind Christian hymn writer)
- Charles Spurgeon
- Dwight L. Moody
- J.R. Miller (His writings since his death in 1912 continue to reach millions)

- Karl Barth (The leading theologian of the 20th century. He inspired the renaissance.)
- C.S. Lewis
- Dietrich Bonhoffer (Martyred)
- Billy Graham

I have wondered why depressed people did not rise up against their masters. (Some do) The reverence in them has been killed and this kills the hero in man. (**Ayn Rand**, 1905-1982, *"The Fountainhead"*.)

The beauty of the hero was truth. (**Tolstoy**, Sevastopol, 1855)
"A hero must think great thoughts as well as be an idealists." (**Oliver Wendell Holmes**, Jr., *"The Path of the Law"*, 1886)

"Heroes are created by popular demand, sometimes out of the scantiest materials, or none at all." (**Gerald Johnson**, *"American Heroes and Hero-Worship"*, 1942)

"A lady with a lamp shall stand, In the great history of the land, A noble type of good, Heroic womanhood."
(**Longfellow**, "Florence Nightingale," *"Santa Filomena"*, 1858)

Helen Keller (1880-1968) was one of the greatest figures in American history was born blind and deaf. Don't forget her teacher, **Anne Sullivan**. Helen graduated with honors from Radcliff College. She became an author, lecturer, and an advocate of social causes.

Mother Teresa (1910-1997) She worked to help "the hungry, the naked, the homeless, the crippled, the blind, the lepers, all the people who felt unwanted, unloved, uncared for throughout society, people who have become a burden to society and are shunned by everyone." She organized the "Missionaries of Charity" which grew from twelve nuns in 1950 to 4,500 nuns at the time of her death.

There are many viewpoints of what constitute a hero. One view is that **it relates to a person with courage who combats great obstacles, great burdens, or great danger without personal or selfish interest**.

Other names that virtually are in the minds of most educated people include:
- **Socrates (469-399 B.C.)**
- **Plato (429-347 B.C)**
- **Aristotle (384-322 BC.)**
- **Shakespeare (1564-1616 A.D.)**
- **Benjamin Franklin (1706-1790 a. D.)**
- **Thomas Jefferson (1743-1826)**
- **Albert Einstein (1879-1955)**
- **George Washington (1732-1799)**

We all know that there are forms of greatness that make no earthly sign. My father and mother were examples of this.

(9.) d. A Few Good Men

The U.S. Marines say they need a "few good men." The world needs a "few good men." The Mangoday of Genghis Khan as a title means, "Exposed to Death." Mangoday means, "Consecrated to God." The leader of the Mangoday said, "40 selected men can shake the world." The Mangoday never consisted of more than a few thousand warriors. They conquered half the world including the Gobi desert in Central Asia, which is one of the largest deserts in the world being 1000 miles from East to West. He dug out the Afghanistan army from their caves in one month. He chased the Shah to Tehran and to Baghdad killed all persons and destroyed the Islam army. He defeated the Christian Teutonic Knights, the Hospitallers, and the Templars when all fought to the death. Genghis Khan is the only one in history to have defeated the Chinese Army. He moved the capitol to Beijing. It was said that a virgin could ride from the silver sea to the shores of China with a rock of gold and be safe? The penalty of death was included for robbery, spying, rape, indecent arts, lying, stealing, desertion, refusal to carry out an order, leaving a casualty in the field, abandoning battle while the play was still fledging. He destroyed whole towns for general immorality. He proved immediate capital punishment works. **The mentally aberrant criminals were soon eliminated**.

A Baptist paper 127 years ago states, "The demand for ministers for first places was never greater in our denomination than it is today"(1883). "Ministers abound, but not the kind needed." The greatest need of their age is men, men who are not for sale and men who will condemn wrong in friend or foe, in themselves as well as others.

Who can tell the truth and look the Devil in the eye? :
- **Men who are careful of God's honor and careless of men's applause.**
- **Men who know their duty and do it. Who know their places and fill them.**
- **Men who are not too lazy to work, nor too proud to be poor.**
- **Men who are strong with wisdom from above and love from the love of Christ.**

Young man you are placed in life to build up your manhood, not your wealth. Men fall more for moral reason than business ability. Look in the mirror, will you not remember more than the insects of the world or will you live and die and the people of the world be better off. You are the greatest creation of God. You can be the best athlete in the world and be one third of a man and useless to society. If you fill your mind full of knowledge from education and be two thirds of that can be useless and maybe dangerous. Put Christ in your heart, control yourself, and fulfill His purpose and you are an ideal man with character.

(10.) Choices

Man was made free. He has the free will of choice. He makes his life what he makes it. It may not turn out like he wanted to make it, but it is the result of his wide latitude of the many choices of life and death. It takes the greatest of wisdom to time the activities of ones life because the gates of opportunity open and close.

Do You Have a Decision to Make?
If so, be grateful. **To have a decision is the opportunity to make choices**. Today because so many young people cannot make decisions at the proper time they later have no decision or choice, but must take the first job offered out of necessity.

The first decision to make, which many times is an unconscious one because of ones parent training. The result of training at home frequently decides whether a person's character is good or bad. **This is the most important of all human qualities**. The man who can step forward and do the job that needs to be done reveals himself as a man. **When the golden opportunities of youth are lost because of inability to make a decision, they are soon replaced by middle age seasonal depressions**. The next stage is clay to be molded by others and then on to **spiritual dust and cremation** with the ashes thrown wherever your beneficiary wants to sprinkle them. No man can serve God by doing it tomorrow. **Everybody's work is nobody's work**. To everyone God gives a gift. (I Corinthians 7:7; I Peter 4:10) Don't neglect it. (I Timothy 4:14) **Not to decide is to decide**. A dead and alive Christian, is one who is spiritually alive one day and spiritually dead the next. They do nothing for God and His Church. The pulpit quote is **"Alive on Sunday and dead on Monday."** My sixth grade teacher was scolding me for something I had done. I answered, "Everyone else is doing it." She replied, "I guess if everyone went down to the muddy river and jumped in you would go too?" I answered, "Yes, mam, there would be nothing to do here." That answer did not help my position. "Doing as the rest did has ruined many people."

The mind and the effects reach everyone according to their decisions. A very close admiral friend of mine called me today to tell me of the death of his son. After high school his son's only choice was to join the Navy. He was an excessive smoker. After 16 years he failed to be promoted by three successive selection boards, he was thus, by requirement discharged. He developed Chronic Pulmonary Obstructive Disease (COPD). He carried around an oxygen tank several years and was in and out of a respirator. He had a stroke and died at early age. "O decision of your

Scriptures for Life

youth where are you now?" Eli a deeply religious man and high priest whose service to God was unblemished, but was a lax father who had not properly disciplines his sons. They were both killed carrying the ark into battle. The Philistines captured the ark. (I Samuel 4:10) Eli, when he heard this, at age 98 fell back and broke his neck. (I Samuel 4:17,18) The house of Eli is no more due to Eli's sins related to his neglected sons. (I Kings 2:35) (Abiathar was his last relative). **Hesitation is frequently negligence** when interest and effort is not used to make a decision. "I will do it tomorrow", **leads to eternity without a decision being made**. No decision is a decision. Chronic hesitation without decision reveals a weakness of mind and is also a weakness of the body. There are millions who never make up their minds. They, therefore, have not prepared for life, for the maintenance of a family, and their only retirement is begging for disability in order to survive. They really don't care who pays for their gravesite or cremation. The process of no decision as a youth, which was a decision, led them to a useless and dependent existence until death gives them relief. Every life is cut out by ones decisions. "You cannot help men by doing for them what they could and should do for themselves." **(Abraham Lincoln)**

I had finished my neurosurgical training and at age twenty-nine I was serving the required two years of military duty. I did this in research at the National Institute of Health. I was given a lab of a neurophysiologist who was on a year's sabbatical leave. My lab assistant and I would spend all day trying to with hand made glass microelectrodes, penetrate the neuron in the brain of a cat. It would require at least three hours to prepare the cat's head in a frame. Any movement or even vibrations would break the electrode. A large truck passing by or even the closing of the elevator door down the hall would break the electrode if someone running to catch the elevator stopped the door from closing. We would spend eight to ten hours together at the operating monitoring table. There would be hours when noting was happening. My assistant I got to know each other quite well. I asked him what his career pathway was. He said I have not decided yet. He was thirty-two years old.

One of the publications about Harvard University says that if one desires admission to Harvard they should begin preparing in the fifth grade. The son of a personal acquaintance of mine was entering a local college with a high academic rating. He asked me for advice. (I have been through this same scenario several times with the same negative result. I have only had one that was positive and that person became world famous. The others never made their goal). I asked him his career pathway and he had not decided. I suggested he take pre-medicine because along the way he could convert to any other college major without losing a year. He did not take my advice. At the end of two years because he did not work at study and with medium grades he came back to me with determination. With his fingers he struck me in the chest and said, "I'm going to be a doctor because I am as good as you are!" I replied, "That is not the question. The question is, are you willing to work as hard as I." After an extra year to get the pre-medicine requirement he graduated and did well his last two years. He was never accepted to a medical school. The gate had closed. He taught his "minor" in a small school until he retired.

Another person asked me about college. I asked him what he wanted to be. He said he had not decided. I said, "Don't go to college until you decide." College was going to be a financial hardship for him. In the next two years of working and college he finished with no college credit. I asked him if he had decided what he wanted to be. He said, "Either a minister or a lawyer". I said, "You are going from one sphere to the other." He had several children and was working and in school part time. The last time I talked with him he was considering a nursing career. Because of the lack of decision the gate had closed. I can repeat the gate-closing situation several times.

Recently I have been counseling young military enlisted and young officers. The enlisted seemed to know what they wanted to be, but did not know how to accomplish it. Two years ago I spoke to two hundred fifth graders. In the discussion two of the girls said, "I want to be a neonatologist." I was stunned. One of the girls' mothers was a nurse and was the source of the term to the fifth grader. The second one in a separate class was not sure where she heard about neonatology. Several of

Scriptures for Life

the small weak looking boys wanted to be professional football players. Through all of this I have learned at least two things. Number one the young people today are very smart and some educated by television and computer are far beyond their age. **Second the counselors in our schools and churches are not trained for it and make "dumb" suggestions**. I know of a professional man's wife who has had psychiatric care, but functions in a church as a young peoples counselor. I know of a **church staff person who serves as a counselor** who also has had psychiatric care. At this time, this age, unless a person had the proper certificate to a counselor they should not be allowed to counsel our children. I know of a church "mentor" program where the "mentors" were themselves or their buddies without any presentation of professional certificates to be a mentor for our young people. The blind are leading the blind or more appropriately the dumb are leading the young and innocent. Our young go into the world (college) Biblically illiterate, innocent and wandering into a time in life that is most likely to affect their future. Academic jealousy with the concept, "That is my domain, I know it all, keep out!" I know of a young man who was going to another institution to an additional year or post-graduate training. His professor said to him, "Be sure and not learn anything." The presumption was that he had taught him all he needed to know.

We never learn it all. To learn what is available to us we must use "all that is within us" and also that which is without us, including hours of prayer, soul, love, thought, time, and strength. God will give us knowledge with grace. What are our dangers and some of them are; pleasure is a shadow, wealthy is a vanity, power a play, emotional knowledge for show, and fame limited in space and as of short descriptions. In God's will we "fear no danger, look into volcanoes, dive into oceans, perforate the earth, fly in the skies, explore the sea and land, know the minute from the great, no place is too remote, no height too high for us to reach. Note that this shows our ability to do God's will, not charging like a mouse or a ball on our own. Don't let your lips be sealed by those who don't know how to do anything, but, "hear before speaking, think before judging, hold our angry tongue, be kind to the distressed and patient with everybody." We must be selective in our choice to think. Our imagination may be close to reality. Do not mingle with the impure. One can only approach God with "clean hands and a pure heart." (John 4:8)

(10.) a. Frugality
I have been trying to break my wife's, Cathy, frugality for the 34 years we have been married. Webster defines ***"frugal"*** as being economical or thrifty. It has been said that there is a true frugality, and there is a false frugality. Cathy is like a little child and filled with much economic innocence that I have a problem with defining economical. An example that I will never be able to explain is as follows. Cathy had 17 children and grandchildren, as our guest during the Christmas holidays-it was wonderful at Disney World, etc. When they were all gone I took Cathy out to dinner to celebrate at a nice and I thought fairly luxurious restaurant. We were well dressed. After ordering our meal I was looking at her natural and sweet beauty. I was thinking of something great to say for the moment. Before I could say anything, she said I would like to say something. I was expecting something, at this romantic moment, like, "You are so wonderful, so good looking, and so smart." She, in her innocence, said, "I think I have a $3.00 coupon for this place." She looked so sweet and beautiful, so innocent that I was carried away to glory that only comes from clouds. After all these years Cathy will not buy anything unless it is 2 for 1 or on a 50-75% sale. On occasion when I was shopping with her I virtually forced her to buy something that I liked and she liked, but thought was too expensive. One of her mottos is, "The wasteful shall come to want."

Everything I have ever bought her she cherishes and loves and takes extreme care of it all. She wipes off her pearl necklaces before putting them away, even if it is late. She wears a scarf around her neck to keep off body oil from her dress and coat collar, etc. I cannot tell if she likes the expensive things I have bought anymore than the things she has from a sale. All I can say is that she is one of a kind and has kept me confused about worldly things since we were married. She is frugal and I am not when it comes to buying for her, but the fall out is that she has made me so frugal that I cannot buy for myself. She literally buys all my clothes now and she is not frugal when doing it. So what is frugal and what is not frugal? Don't ask me because I do not know. Cathy has the most expensive clothes bought at super sales and with her extreme care they still look new after ten years. She has an excellent oriental seamstress, but I frequently see her at night mending her own things as well as mine.

An Englishman has said we have warped the word *"economy."* Economy no more means spending money. **Economy is wise management of money and time**. Economy involves three levels of intelligence: apply your money and labor rationally, preserve them both carefully, and save and distribute them with common sense. Economy is not carelessness in dress or time. Make things last and be productive. God holds us responsible for our talents and blessings. Our economy should not consider the pocketbook before the needs of the soul. **Don't cheat God to enrich a worm**. David felt like a "worm" when he sinned (Psalm 22:6). Spiritual worms do not die (Isaiah 66:24, Mark 9:44,46). Education of time if neglected is lost forever. Moral education when weakened to add power for physical reasons is blight forever. Parents devoted to giving their children are blind to the result. Where will they learn to earn their own "bread" as their fathers did before them? **The failure of many rich men's sons shows this by their becoming insignificant and worthless.**

A gospel that cost nothing is an absurdity. It cost Jesus his life. A gospel that cost nothing is worth nothing. Money hoarded is poor pay for minds and souls dwarfed.

(10.) b. Friends

Friendship increases joy and diminishes sorrow. Without friends what is a man? Recently I was looking at the membership list of my last Sunday School class of older men. Of the thirty-eight on the role, eighteen attended regularly. As I looked at each one of these eighteen men I recalled a serious medical problem that each one of had had. I prayed for them and I know they prayed for me. Two more of the clan has died. One had been ill for years. I gave his eulogy. Two of their wives died and both are happily remarried. I learned from them that sorrow, serious illness, and prayer produces close friendships. I would trust my life with any one of these eighteen men. What a valuable group of friends I have in these men. As we grow old together our bodies decay and our minds begin to fail, but the beauty remains. Never is virtue without sympathy. Our family and friends are the closest things to Heaven on this earth. Help one another is the motto of a friend. "Bread cast upon the waters returns after many days." (Ecclesiastes 11:1). Friendship is reciprocal benevolence, kindness to kindness, good to good, love to love, help to help, prayer to prayer, and on and on and on. With a friend you can "seem to be what you seem to be, and be only what you are." An outlet for sympathetic listening, helping hand, and kind words are likely to be available from a friend than from anyone else. To listen wisely may be the first duty, which calls us.

(10.) c. Critics - Negatives

A young person going to the city has the windows of his soul opened toward Heaven. Cities have been blessings and lamps for humanity of religion, but there is reported a case of a youth changed into a profane, vulgar man, consumed by his vices, and fired for dishonesty and he was surrounded by a Christian community. I moved from the country to the city, back to the country and back to the city. If you are a strong person conflicts make you stronger. You are better being in the world of the great battlefield for life. If one is weak say good-bye to the salvation of your soul. The odds are against you. City life crushes much of the beauty seen in the country. "Ignorance of school spelling books is bad, but ignorance of hard work is worse." Wisdom does not always speak Latin.

Wisdom in a poor man is like a diamond set in lead where few can see it. Wisdom walks after patched shoes, but men do not see it, but you can find ignorance in site of St. Paul's.

Scriptures for Life

(11.) Behavior

Our behavior is put together by small lines of reasoning of thought every day. It becomes a continuing element. It becomes a habit of mind toward good or bad. It is strong, and if bad difficult to break. If good the power of God prevails to make it better. We do it almost as an unconscious act. I have a wealthy lady friend raised in private schools and high society who used profanity as a natural part of her conversation. We brought her to our church and in Sunday School she shocked the other ladies without even being aware of it. They loved her and her life changed. Her profanity went away and she asked the ladies for prayer when she had major surgery. Habits of speech are the most intractable of all natural actions. They are like thorns in the heart. The seeds bring forth weeds. It has been said that no one example is as bad to us as our own. Self-control is the preference of genius. Our divine freedom is a gift of God. We are all equal at the foot of the Cross and He will judge us according to our devotion and purity to Him who made us. Many bodies go to the grave because of the addiction or habit of drunkenness. Burns said, "If a barrel of rum was in one corner of the room and in another corner the barrel of a gun was to be fired at me I would go for the rum. I would have no choice but to go for the rum." We like freedom, but habits can become our dictator. It is said that every person has at least one "King Habit" that he bows before. It slowly becomes our "King Habit or Habits". A "baby" pleasure may become a "King Habit" or a giant. It is like flakes of beautiful snow that becomes an avalanche that buries us. Augustine said, "**A habit not resisted becomes a necessity**". "The small chains of habit become too strong to be broken." (**Dr. Samuel Johnson**) Great change may come over the character without being conscious of any change. Habitual thought or the hands of angels may frame our lives. Lightening was striking all around a profane man. He survived and was asked what he was thinking. He said I was afraid to say anything for the fear of God. In an hour of personal danger he was overpowered by the blackness of profanity. He was alone without the love of God that **he so greatly feared**.

(11.) a. Permanence
Permanence is the absence of change:
"But thou art the same, and thy years shall have no end." (**Psalms 102:27**)
"For I am the LORD, I change not; therefore ye sons of Jacob are not consumed."(**Malachi 3:6**)
"Jesus Christ the same yesterday, and to day, and for ever." (**Hebrews 13:8**)
"Every good gift and every perfect gift is from above, and cometh down from the Father of lights, with whom is no variableness, neither shadow of turning."(**James 1:17**)
"One generation passeth away, and another generation cometh: but the earth abideth for ever."(**Ecclesiastes 1:4**)
"Fear before him, all the earth: the world also shall be stable, that it be not moved."
(**I Chronicles 16:30**;Pslams 93:1; 96:10)
"Thy faithfulness is unto all generations: thou hast established the earth, and it abideth."(**Psalms 119:90**)
"And saying, Where is the promise of his coming? for since the fathers fell asleep, all things continue as they were from the beginning of the creation."(**II Peter 3:4**)
God's Word will not pass away.
"**Heaven and earth shall pass away, but my words shall not pass away.**"(Mathew 24:35; Mark 13:31; Luke 21:33

Permanence in Behavior
This is the number one feature of character. Ones character paints a picture of uniformity or one of haphazardness. Uniformity of character embraces it not for character, but for truth. Seeking and sharing truth is the goal of every Christian. It is a state of mind conformed to the will of God that directs our actions and practices. The scriptural virtues include: "Who shall ascend into the hill of the LORD? or who shall stand in his holy place? He that hath clean hands, and a pure heart; who hath not lifted up his soul unto vanity, nor sworn deceitfully."(Psalms 24:3,4) **Also:** "He that walketh uprightly, and worketh righteousness, and

speaketh the truth in his heart.backbiteth doeth evil his eyes contempts a vile person, receives no reward against the innocent." (Psalms 15:2-5) The blessing of free will is to choose the good or the evil. "See, I have set before thee this day life and good, and death and evil." (Deuteronomy 30:15) Our "righteousness should run as a mighty stream." (Amos 5:24)

<u>Being persistent is a trait of character</u>, which is noted by those who know us or work with us. If one is not persistent their character cannot claim that as a trait. Persistence is more than being constant or unchanging. It is less than being persistent when it is an act toward certain objectives. Without it that part of a person's character ceases to exist or does not exist. He who works and is persistent in his work conquers. A man was observing an ant carrying a kernel of corn larger than himself up a wall. The ant dropped the corn over sixty times, but finally made it to the top with the corn. This reminds one of the question, "How does an ant move a mountain?" The answer is, "One grain at a time." An ant never gives up until he is dead. It seems in this modern age that everything that is good must fight for existence. A person true to their natural obligations such as faithfulness to religion, etc. must also **have an action of courage to ring true to their heart**. I have seen hundreds of patients completely paralyzed and without sensation from the waist down. Most of them do not get proper care and without it 100% will develop "bed sores". These can be larger than a baseball with all the tissue gone outside the bone. This is a horrible thing to see because even with perfect care it will take months to heal. I saw such a case on hospital rounds. I was stunned because I knew that I had nothing to offer this patient. An older nurse making rounds with me looked at it and said, "Doctor, I will take care of this." She knew this patient required attention constantly twenty-four hours a day. Persisting is the only care. It takes weeks to months of keeping the patient padded in such away that the bedsore is never for one minute allowed to touch the bed. There can be no pressure on the area or it will not heal regardless of treatment. The best hope is that it will granulate in enough so that plastic surgery can be used to speed up the skin closure over the wound.

The will to live and not worrying about it, and staying active are forces that determine longevity. I studied a series of patients who were above eighty years of age, healthy, and looked younger. (One had a 67-year-old daughter that looked older than her mother.) We studied them beginning with their personal history, past history, lab work, etc. There was noting to suggest their longevity. I was looking at the data at midnight and it suddenly "hit me". They were all happy with a sweet **honest** facial expression. They were totally self-reliant and were not dependent on anyone else, including their doctor. If their doctor missed them on hospital rounds one day it was all right. Their comment was, "He will come by when he needs to." They are not fussy or dependent; they are themselves. They do not try to be or copy anyone else. **Breese** reports that **Socrates** learned to play a musical instrument at an old age. **Cato** at age 80, learned Greek, **Plutarch** at age 80 learned Latin, and **Ludovocio Mandaldesco** wrote his memoirs at age 115.

Did I hear you say you were too old to learn? A 78-year-old friend told me he was "too old for Sunday School". Don't confuse a strong "I will" with a strong "I won't." Everyone has troubles, but the darkest day will pass away. "For his anger endureth but a moment; in his favour is life: weeping may endure for a night, but joy cometh in the morning." (Psalms 30:5)

(11.) b. Perseverance – Endurance

Perseverance is to persist in an undertaking in spite of difficulties. Endurance is to understand hardship or stress or to suffer firmly or patiently. To bear or endure pain or the exert pressure of influence. Some of the most dramatic words of Jesus, **"But he that shall endure unto the end, the same shall be saved."** (Matthew 24:13) "When we "take of the divine nature and diligently apply it our faith it grows to virtue, knowledge, temperance, patience, perseverance, godliness, brotherly kindness, and charity." (Love) (II Peter 1:4-7) "Happy are those that endure as in the patient Job and have seen the end with the Lord as pitiful and of tender mercy." (James 5:11) The Christian doctrine is a manner of life of purpose, faith, perseverance, love, and patience. (II

Timothy1: 10) Perseverance is a virtue. They add to each other. The more perseverance the more virtue and vice versa. **One adds to the beauty of the other**. It is like the sunset of patience with its golden radiation of perseverance. Good builds on good and beauty builds on beauty. This is the building that allows good and beauty to overcome evil or wickedness. A man must get into the water to swim or get on a horse to ride. The initial action of man is the start toward becoming a better swimmer or rider. Men learn to be a good citizen by exercising the rights and freedom of being a good citizen. Perseverance builds the **character** of man and starts him toward perfection. The purity of a soul seeks its destiny of goodness. The soul that always murmurs finds its destiny of cruelness. When one loses perseverance they never find it again as self-control has been lost. Endurance opens our life to success, honor, and eternity.

(11.) c. Indulgence

Toleration can be totally passive. "I just put up with it and endure it because I can do nothing about it." Or one can be sympathetic. "I share their feelings even thought I do not agree." The question is do you mentally fight or do you mentally love? The Christian by looking at God's Word finds the answer. **Epictetus** said, "A man hurts himself by hurting me; should I hurt myself by hurting him?" Is it a disgrace not to be outdone and take another person down? Or does one get the better by taking the hurt?' **Real sympathy is sympathy expressed**. It is all right to let it be known that one disagrees, but be sure to relate that one respects the others feelings. **A kindness only becomes real when it is expressed**. **Reverend John Elliot** preached peace and love to the American Indians. He taught three little words, "bear, forebear, and forgive." With love the heart reveals a real sorrow to see sorrow in someone else. When my successful and beautiful lawyer son was dying, but slightly conscious, the whole family came in the room one at a time and went to his bed to speak their last words to him. I stayed seated until last and then it came my turn to do it. One of my other children told me that they had never before seen tears in my eyes. Since I have become more spiritual I have many tears, almost daily in my eyes. If sorrow is present a true Christian will always feel it inside himself. As we grow spiritually and older we become tender to harshness. We have a tender heart for one who seems to hate humanity in general. When others have faults we look at their virtues. Study God's Word and I think you will find that there is no sin that one has not committed. We have all had murder in our hearts, lust in our minds, stretched truth in our conversation, covetousness that blackens our soul, pride that overshadows our love for others and points itself back to us. Bibles that are not read and learned, idols of bank accounts, cars, and houses, which God calls committing adultery in his presence. Let what God has pleased to give thee please thee. Your friend is not perfect, but guess what, neither are you? Human nature has all the weaknesses, but God only gives the strength to conquer, but you must ask Him and obey Him.

(11.) d. Stay Calm

One cannot think, fight, or see things in a true light when they **are angry or in a hilarious state of mind**. Learn to abide by the facts and see the truth of things. The world is full of excitement and horror. We can become "drunk" in mind as well as in body. Alcohol is a unique drug when used excessively. There remains a conscious human control. The classic example is if one when they get drunk wants to be mean their inhibitors are removed and they become meaner. On the other hand if when one gets drunk and they want to be sad they can be sadder. Take your time and be calm. It is said that **a man always in a hurry is a man always behind**. They are trying to pass every car on the road, which is not possible and they many kill themselves trying. I can count at least thirty-four Biblical references regarding patience. I have had a lot of fun with some of my peers with Jesus' Words, **"In your patience possess ye your souls."** (Luke 21:19) I have in a humorous manner said, "This means there will be no neurosurgeons in Heaven." I have only seen two that seemed to have patience, but they did not have the other credentials for Heaven or even to a top place in neurosurgery. Paul gives other credentials that go with patience. "Follow after righteousness, godliness, faith, love, patience, meekness." (I Timothy 6:11) "But let patience have her perfect work, that ye may be perfect and entire, wanting nothing."

(James 1:4) **<u>Anxiety is the poison of life and it is worry that kills men</u>**, not work. Success pumps us up with energy, but never makes us drunk.

My father in law was a neat and calm man. One could tell him that the Russians had invaded California and I am sure he would say, "I've got to go out in the garden and check on my gourds." It was said that some world leaders were discussing whether or not England should go to war. They all agreed except one at the table. They asked him, "What are you waiting for"? His answer was, "I am waiting for someone to pass the potatoes." On should always be happy while eating. A happy waiter frequently "makes one's meal"! A sour-puss face can dampen any meal. One can open the door of tomorrow with **faith or anxiety**. One must always recognize danger such as skydiving, bungee jumping, or kissing a girl. "There be three things which are too wonderful for me, yea, four which I know not: The way of an eagle in the air; the way of a serpent upon a rock; the way of a ship in the midst of the sea; and the way of a man with a maid." Proverbs 30:18,19) It is said that laughter is a friend to every virtue and an enemy to malice and scandal. Laughter makes the heart alive and brings light. Happiness relates to the heart and judgment of man if we remember that God sees it all.

(12.) Status

Useful men with exertion, natural energy, and self-help grow upward to high places in society. Examples:
- **The Apostles as fisherman**
- **Luther (1483-1546) from a miner's cottage**
- **Elijah from Tishbe was a Teshhite from a small village of unknown location**
- **Justin Martyr (103-163) in a small colony in Samaria learned from Plato and became the first Christian philosopher and beheaded and his name changed to Martyr.**
- **Cyprian (200-258) from a Pagan family in age of persecution and when professions of Christianity began**

falling away from truth was born in North Africa and died a martyrs death there.
- Athanasius (295-373) whose name means *"Immortality"* was born in the metropolis of Alexandria in "disturbing" circumstances. He was a defender of orthodoxy and helped form the famous Nicene Creed.
- Anne Askew (1520-1546) her husband "kicked her out of the house" when she became a Christian. She became the "Daughter of the Reformation." She died a martyr at age 25. She bore her sufferings with a firmness and gentleness never surpassed in the "Annals of Christian heroism."
- Joan Mathurin (1539-1560) was born poor south of Turin on the bank of the PO River. She and her husband were Christians. He was to be burned at the stake. She was afraid he would weaken in his faith so she revealed that she was also a Christian so that she could be burned with him. They died as heroes without crying out, tied to each other.
- John Bunyan (1628-1688) spent 14 years in prison where he wrote the immortal *"Pilgrims Progress."* His father was a poor tinker (who repaired household utensils), but sent Bunyan to school until he could read and write.
- Sir Isaac Newton (1642-1727) was born premature and remained weak and feeble in infancy and was not expected to live. He never knew his father. He became the greatest of Christian scientists discovering the law of gravity, calculus, the three laws of motion, and invented the telescope and other things also.
- Isaac Watts (1674-1748) his father was imprisoned for his beliefs. His mother nursed him while visiting his father in jail. He became the "Father of English Hymnody" beginning at age 7 wrote 700 hymns. He was a powerful preacher, children's poet, and author of Christian Literature.
- John Wesley (1703-1791) the founder of Methodism, one of 19 children, was rescued from a burning house fire by neighbors' standing on each other's shoulders to reach him. He said, "Preach faith, till you have it; and then because you have it, you will preach faith." He organized

Scriptures for Life

the famed "lay-preachers" the faith, which works by love, purifies the soul."

- John Newton (1725-1807) father was a master on a Spanish trading ship in the Mediterranean and a stern and severe man. His mother was religious and taught him to read by the time he was age 4 and his mind stored much scripture, Isaac Watts' Catechism and hymns. She committed him to God and died when he was age 7. His father took him out of school and put him on a ship and he became a slave-trader. He almost lost his life in a storm at sea. The fierce winds upon the deck and though of death changed his heart and mind from, "the great blasphemy" to this past and God when he had so often profaned. He pleaded with God to give him the faith of his mother. He began preaching at age 39 and preached 28 years. He wrote, "Amazing Grace", 280 poems, and 68 hymns were collected. It is said he composed a new hymn for each Sunday evening service. Some of his last words were "When I think of heaven I am amazed at three things, there I will see some I did not expect, I will not see some I expected to see, and I myself will be there."

I can name many many others who under the will of God did the impossible when it was not possible. **In every case there were high and right aims**, a strong will, **fixed perseverance** and success came thought not expected. No one knows how long it takes for success to come. **De Maister** said, "in knowing how to wait, and I add work. A governor of Massachusetts ran for office for 16 years and finally won by one vote. We had a resident that applied for our neurosurgical residency for seven years. He was accepted because of his perseverance. **Daniel Boone** (1734-18290) at age thirty-five wanted to move to Florida. His wife refused to go with him; with thirty men he blazed the famous Wilderness Road. His enduring courage and determination gave the world a name in history.

(12.) a. Money
Many people including theologians believe "the winning of wealth to be a perfectly legitimate pursuit." It may have great beneficial uses. The rich man whose only desire is to be richer becomes "inhuman and un-Christian." It's right to seek wealth if the purpose is to serve God with it. "There is no sin in being rich and no virtue in begin poor. Rich men are needed in the churched, colleges, and society. **John Wesley** said, "Get all you can, save all you can, give all you can. By giving all I can I am laying up treasures upon earth." You can't take it with you, but you can send it to Heaven in advance. God sends every bird its food, but he does not throw it in the nest. He gives us "our daily bread" through our own labor. Do not be greedy. Covetousness is always poor. **To get on poverty by faking it is not virtue and destroys the soul**. On an old gravestone is written, "What I spent, I had, what I saved I lost, what I gave I have." A saving woman at the **head of a family** is the very best savings bank. All of us know that saving is a pleasant activity **once the habit is established**. Activity is essential to man. The sluggard in the Bible is denounced. (Proverbs 6:6, 19:24, Matthew 25:26) Do business in the name of the Lord, as we are missionaries among the non-Christians particularly.

There is the "dollar a day" concept, which means different things to different people, but do not confuse "the dollar" with "the day". They are entirely different. **The dollar you leave on earth**, the day you live with in Heaven or Hell.

(12.) b. Success
- "Commit thy works unto the LORD, and thy thoughts will succeed." (Proverbs 16:3)
- "He that winketh with the eye causeth sorrow: but a prating fool shall fall." (Proverbs 11:10)
- "Accept the challenges, so that you may feel the exhilaration of victory." (General George S. Patton)
- "**Recipe for success:** Study while others are sleeping; work

Scriptures for Life

while others are loafing, prepare while others are playing and dream while others are wishing." (W.A. Word)
- The father of success is work; the mother of ambition is the achievement.
- "Success has many friends." (Greek proverb)
- "The height of success is when you become uninterested in money, compliments or publicity." (Eddie Rickenbacker)
- "The man is a success who has lived well, laughed often and loved much; has gained the respect of successful men, and the love of children, who leaves the world better, has rescued a soul, and looked for the best in others and gave the best he had." (Robert Louis Stevenson)
- Success is industry, frugality, and perseverance.
- Make experience your counselor. Have high aims and an earnest will.
- To make success be faithful, never lie, think that nothing is too small to do, and write good letters.
- If you are asked what are your best recommendations, the answer is, "My mother!!"
- To insure success develop ability, show integrity, and originate industry. Everyone has ability as it is the power of doing a thing well." Whatever is worth doing at all is worth doing well." Be fruitful in every good work. (Colossians 1:10) "Let every man prove his own work, and then he shall have rejoicing in himself alone!" (Galatians 6:4)
- It is better to be a first-class carpenter than a fourth-rate lawyer; a good machinist than a poor doctor."
- Attack life with whole heartedness. Integrity and an honorable name must be earned. The most industrious are the most successful. Have knowledge that will show the way to service.
- The memory book –the brain can only be read by the owner. It is always present, gets better and bigger with use and it is reliable. It gives out knowledge that one puts into it. A trained brain is better than a trained hand. Knowledge and experience grows into a large pyramid.

I developed a new word *"gnosis empeiria"* that means, "Knowledge gained by experience. Almost every young man has at least one chance of success. Teach them to open their minds to it. He needs ability, integrity, and industry. Save by one dollar at a time!

(12.) c. Man's Duty

The Duties of a Christian are noted in Romans 12:1-21.
Outline
- **Present your bodies a living sacrifice (12:1)**
- **Renew your mind (12:2)**
- **Think soberly (12:3)**
- **One body, different office (12:4)**
- **One body in Christ, every member one of another (12:5)**
- **Have different gifts (12:6)**
- **Ministry or teachers (12:7)**
- **Exhorteth, giveth, ruleth, show mercy (12:8)**
- **Love without dissimulation (12:9)**
- **Prefer one another (12:10)**
- **Good in business (12:11)**
- **Rejoice in hope, trials, prayer (12:12)**
- **Give to the saints (12:13)**
- **Bless your enemies (12:14)**
- **Rejoice and weep as needed (12:15)**
- **Be the same one to another (12:16)**
- **No evil for evil (12:17)**
- **Live peaceably with all men (12:18)**
- **Avenge not yourselves (12:19)**
- **Feed your enemy hunger (12:20)**
- **Overcome evil with good (12:21)**

Romans 12:1-21
[1] I beseech you therefore, brethren, by the mercies of God, that ye present your bodies a living sacrifice, holy, acceptable unto God, which is your reasonable service.
[2] And be not conformed to this world: but be ye transformed by

Scriptures for Life

the renewing of your mind, that ye may prove what is that good, and acceptable, and perfect, will of God.

[3] For I say, through the grace given unto me, to every man that is among you, not to think of himself more highly than he ought to think; but to think soberly, according as God hath dealt to every man the measure of faith.

[4] For as we have many members in one body, and all members have not the same office:

[5] So we, being many, are one body in Christ, and every one members one of another.

[6] Having then gifts differing according to the grace that is given to us, whether prophecy, let us prophesy according to the proportion of faith;

[7] Or ministry, let us wait on our ministering: or he that teacheth, on teaching;

[8] Or he that exhorteth, on exhortation: he that giveth, let him do it with simplicity; he that ruleth, with diligence; he that sheweth mercy, with cheerfulness.

[9] Let love be without dissimulation. Abhor that which is evil; cleave to that which is good.

[10] Be kindly affectioned one to another with brotherly love; in honour preferring one another;

[11] Not slothful in business; fervent in spirit; serving the Lord;

[12] Rejoicing in hope; patient in tribulation; continuing instant in prayer;

[13] Distributing to the necessity of saints; given to hospitality.

[14] Bless them which persecute you: bless, and curse not.

[15] Rejoice with them that do rejoice, and weep with them that weep.

[16] Be of the same mind one toward another. Mind not high things, but condescend to men of low estate. Be not wise in your own conceits.

[17] Recompense to no man evil for evil. Provide things honest in the sight of all men.

[18] If it be possible, as much as lieth in you, live peaceably with all men.

[19] Dearly beloved, avenge not yourselves, but rather give place unto wrath: for it is written, Vengeance is mine; I will repay, saith the Lord.

[20] Therefore if thine enemy hunger, feed him; if he thirst, give him drink: for in so doing thou shalt heap coals of fire on his head.
[21] Be not overcome of evil, but overcome evil with good.

A man who joins the military for money is never a good military man. A man who becomes a physician for money is never a good physician. I know because I have seen them. There is some basic learning required here and a baseline as to where one begins. God loans you life and you make it a **life.** God will take your life back someday. You can make it a good life or a bad life. Jesus reveals an interesting option. He said of the man that betrayed Him, **"It had been good for that man if he had not been born."** (Matthew 26:23-24) Believe it or not the same thing can be said today of all people who do accept Jesus and betray Him with their lives.

When a Bible scholar goes into a "mode" of deep thought one learns that a call to a mind that opens it to be receptive to God may be a rare event. "Seek ye the LORD while he may be found, call ye upon him while he is near." (Isaiah 55:6) One of the horror stories of the Bible is when Samuel told Saul, "Wherefore then dost thou ask of me, seeing the LORD is departed from thee, and is become thine enemy?"(I Samuel 28:16) Samuel concluded with "Tomorrow you and your sons will die." (I Samuel 28:19) The Bible, God's Word, goes on and on with the warning, "Choose you this day whom ye will serve." (Joshua 24:15) God will not tolerate unbelief - the so-called Christians who are bungling, vacillating, whining, sighing, and complaining. God said to the people of Israel whom He had delivered from Egypt that because of their disbelief, "Your carcasses shall fall in this wilderness; and all that were numbered of you, according to your whole number, from twenty years old and upward, which have murmured against me shall die."(Numbers 14: 29, 35) Only Caleb and Joshua were allowed to enter the land. (Numbers 14:30; 32:13) Because of Moses sin he was not allowed to enter the Promised Land. (Numbers 20:12) God allowed Moses to see the Promised Land, but he could not enter it. God buried Moses at the age of one hundred twenty and said, "There arose not a prophet since in Israel like unto Moses, whom the LORD knew face to face." (Joshua 34:5, 6,7,10)

Scriptures for Life

A Washington Politician, the richest man in the world, and the man on the street have the same obligation of obedient faith in the overall divine plan for the world. The rich man had plenty, but he was going to build more and get richer and "rest, eat, drink, and be merry. Jesus said to him, **"Thou fool, this night thy soul shall be required of thee."** (Luke 12:19,20) (A doctor wrote this.) We cannot neglect our duty without disregarding our consciousness of right and wrong. We cannot run away from our duty. It will follow us. If we contrive this course we will be hopeless in our ministry. Happiness will be beyond our vision. We cannot escape the power that created each of us as a part of the human race. On the other hand the work of the faithful with a steady energy is always rewarded.

Vanity fades away and man of character emerges. There is light in the human action that aids the eternal with the human race. We do not live for ourselves alone. A mother may feel her life deficit by other obligations besides her baby's cradle. The father may feel his wife is not a companion, but a baby produces a **love between** a father and mother not paralleled in any other blessing of life. The message must be repeated over and over. **We do not live for ourselves alone**. Our manifest motive is for a good cause and a good cause is always to do for the benefit of others. The beauty is that the benefit of our actions for others in some ways returns to us. To not do our duty is not an acceptable choice. Duty calls like a sound in the woods; it must be heard to be duty. **Duty is the opportunity to hope for, work for, and die for**. A person has the choice of the last words being, "O No, or here I am Lord." Life is a book. There is a time when it will be closed for the last time. Life is a short day, but it must be a working day and it must lead to something good. We write the pages with love, understanding, courage, truth, tolerance, and self-denial to benefit others. The first "others" includes our parents, then our brothers and sisters, then our husbands or wives, then or children, our grandchildren, and all others in the human race and all of God's creation. We must honor his animals, trees, flowers and water including streams, rives, lakes, and oceans. Look at nature. God made it for us. Do not destroy it or make it dirty. Our work can cover the gauntlet from using a pen, to teaching, preaching, or banging a hammer. Remember whatever we do we are a part of the divine plan for all of us. At the end of life, don't look in the mirror and see nothing or something ugly.

(12.) d. What Can I do?

One learns early that with a computer one must ask the right question to get the right answer. What is the right question? Look at the problems of the world; what can I do? Look at the problems of the mankind; what can I do? You have not asked the right question. 2000 years ago someone smarter than you asked the right question. It's not about the world. The right question is, "What shall I do that I may inherit eternal life?" (Matthew 19:16; Mark 10:17; Luke 10:25) This must be an important question since it is recorded three times in the New Testament and was directed to Jesus each time. To a thinking person this is an important matter. Can anyone say anything about a person who must know that he will someday die and not ask that question? From the theological point of view nothing good can be said when a person does not ask the question. Is there anyone who has never asked it? If so, they can only be described as having extreme apathy, a completely suspended sense of feeling, dull, or dullness of mind, and to use the crude but truthful answer, they must simply be considered stupid. This is an example of the man with six academic degrees who has not properly addressed or considered the options of the question. This proves that academic degrees do not always relieve one of being "stupid". The answer is that I must do nothing, but accept it. Even in the worldly courts an individual does nothing to accept his inheritance except to accept it. The court may actually seek the heir as God does all of us. The inheritance seeks the heir. Our inheritance is seeking us. Our Savior, "Who will have all men to be saved, and to come unto the knowledge of the truth." **(I Timothy 2:4)** One must have certain knowledge to be saved. This is why we support missions. We can hope, as Jesus, that all men will be saved. It is free and is looking for us.

We are all "ambassadors for Christ." When God reconciled us to Himself, He gave us "the ministry of reconciliation." (II Corinthians 5:18-20) We are in touch with a spiritual awakening, but we must be

Scriptures for Life

awake to see it. Jesus' Words, "**Because thou knewest not the time of thy visitation.**" (Luke 19:44) God was there, but one was not listening and thus did not hear. We see it, we accept it, and we have conversion, rebirth, a changed life, become a new person, and are a person who has eternal life. We need surgery, but we must ask the surgeon to operate. We die and God makes us alive. The majesty of God is revealed in our heart and mind. Suddenly the major change in our life causes us to love, to look up, love to be in the light, love to read God's Word, love to pray, and love to worship in God's house on Sunday and every chance we get. We suddenly hate the "darkness" of the world. In all of God's creation we see the beautiful even in the worldly darkness we see the beauty in his created creatures. The unlovable person becomes lovable. To be saved is to know and believe. Our confidence is not in our dying bodies, but it is in the only proven power of resurrection, Jesus Christ. There is "bliss" of complete happiness and joy that cannot be written down or understood unless one has it. You have to know it to get it and you have to get it to know it. The experience is not a momentary event or derived from observation. It is something encountered which is alive! It is a mental movement that is in you and goes with you wherever you go. It is always there and it is always getting better by building on itself.

Sanctification is separation from the world, building to purification, righteousness, and holiness. "Boot camp" is over in a second and you feel the concept of "Send me in coach!" I am read for service, loyalty, and action that leads to wherever it leads. Sanctification is the believer's work working with God. We are sanctified by faith in Him. (Acts 26:18) Remember God created the world by saying "Be ye world and the world appeared." "We must walk in the Spirit to display the fruit of the Spirit." (Galatians 5:25, 22, 23) We are commanded to be holy, (Leviticus 11:44, I Peter 1:15-16) and be servants of righteousness for holiness. (Romans 6:19)

We need to speak to our youth. It is the "seed-time" of life. If we adults do not plant the seed of the knowledge of God's Word it may never be planted. Without knowledge and virtue there will be no harvest. The Devil plants evil in every heart. (We are not born with it!) Youth is the spring of life. The seeds planted then will determine the harvest later. Where is the only way that we can point our youth to God? It is not at social events, loud music, and loud drums, door prizes, push-ups, jogging, basketball, or other sports. It can only be done by teaching God's Word and then verify that the youth have learned the way and the price of salvation.

There is not a thought or action that does not strike a blow. Teachers of the youth when you are finished with them, and you soon will be, what has been your major blow? Has it been God's Word? There are no blocked doors to God's Word. I was a superintendent for a young people's Sunday School department for several years. I could get seventy-five of them in my yard for a "Cook- out Party" anytime on a Saturday. Only thirty to thirty-five would be in Sunday School the next day. They came to hear and learn God's Word. Teach them the Word and they **will** come. If you don't in college they will continue in campus sports, loud music with drums until midnight on Saturday and then sleep until noon on Sunday. Teachers of youth this is where you see your legacy. It is not at the goal line or goal post. A good teacher **always** produces teachers. How many teachers of God's Word have you produced? This is the sure way to judge your efforts. Is it goal lines or Bible classes? Every single day you are building, building, building forces either up or down. You will have your hour of testing and be seen just as you are not as you think you are. Are you building your own little world of, "Look what a good Christian I am!" Are you sowing for yourself or God? I have seen young people grow up in church and never go to church again before they died. Did God's Word fail or was the failure because we did not academically teach the Word?

In a church that I know I heard of a young person who for many years was a serious social and legal problem for his parents. The parents and an older preacher on many occasions pleaded with the judge to let the "good boy" off and the judge yielded. After years of this the now young man came to the pastor's office and beat his secretary of many years to a "bloody pulp". She survived and later retired to another town. I asked the old preacher if he had followed up on his many years of counseling.

Scriptures for Life

He said he had not. I asked him how did he know he had been doing it correctly? For many years we had "idiots" in the church counseling "idiots". **The law and lawsuits have gradually forced charitable organizations to be certified in anything they do**.

It has been said, " The liberal soul shall be made fat; and he that watereth shall be also be watered." (Proverbs 11:25) Many philosophers have said, "We cannot get more out of human life than we put into it." In my experience with many of the great men that I have known Christian or not Christian this is true. However, in my own life I have made the initial action or effort and God explodes it to be something bigger than I could ever do. I had the "thought" and dream of an international neurosciences center, but God made it happen. I made the effort and contribution to the Navy Reserve, but God made me an "Admiral". I made the extreme effort of removing a malignant brain tumor, but God made the patient live ten more years. Hang up good pictures everyday and you will reap a good destiny. **Sow the seeds of good habits and you will reap a good character**. Be persistent and persevere. **Adonia Judson** was five years in Burma before he had his first convert to Christ. **Morrison** waited seven years in China and **Newton Adams** was ten years in Port Natal. The London Missionary Society's efforts required ten years in Madagascar for the first convert, thirty years in Madras, and fifteen years in Tahiti. The Baptist worked twenty-one years for twenty converts among the Telugus, which grew to tens of thousands. **The persistent first days are the cornerstone of the days that follow**.

(12.) e. Your Harvest

"While the earth remaineth, seedtime and harvest, and cold and heat, and summer and winter, and day and night shall not cease."(Genesis 8:22) What have you left for the poor? "And thou shalt not glean thy vineyard, neither shalt thou gather every grape of thy vineyard; thou shalt leave them for the poor and stranger: I am the LORD your God."(Leviticus 19:10) "The harvest is past, the summer is ended, and we are not saved."(Jeremiah 8:20) They missed their last opportunity! Jesus said to His disciples a famous statement and plea for prayer for workers for the harvest. **"The harvest truly is plenteous, but the labourers are few." (Matthew 9:37, 38;Luke 10:2)** Jesus makes it clear the our harvest can be good or bad. **"The enemy that sowed them is the devil; the harvest is the end of the world; and the reapers are the angels. As therefore the tares are gathered and burned in the fire; so shall it be in the end of this world. The Son of man shall send forth his angels, and they shall gather out of his kingdom all things that offend, and them which do iniquity; And shall cast them into a furnace of fire: there shall be wailing and gnashing of teeth. Then shall the righteous shine forth as the sun in the kingdom of their Father. Who hath ears to hear, let him hear."** (Matthew 13:39-43) **"Lift up your eyes, and look on the fields; for they are white already to harvest."**(John 4:35)

Don't confuse religion and Christianity! Going to the altar in the front of the church having a verification prayer, being baptized, and living joyfully forever and doing nothing else is probably one of the most common ways to end up in Hell! That is religion, not Christianity.

Jesus said over and over as noted above, "Get to work!" "Faith without works is dead." (James 2:17) James goes on to say "One shows their faith by their works." (James 2:18) If you are one of 80% of church members that never does anything listen to what Jesus will say when He returns. **"I come quickly; and my reward is with me, to give every man according as his work shall be."**(Revelation 22:12) **<u>Do nothing</u>**. **<u>Get nothing</u>**. Modern society and modern man has revived on a larger scale the "**<u>ancient paganism</u>**." There has been the **<u>practical blending of man-made religion</u>** in the thousands of Protestant churches. This movement is known as rationalism. The rationalism (Guiding ones actions by what seems reasonable) is parallel to the syncretism (The combination of different forms of beliefs or practices) of Catholicism. The Protestants are last because they have no leaders that lead to a definite result. I have seen an illiterate man with a Bible in his hand take down trained theologians from their ignorant (Lacking intelligence) pedestal.

There are two religious diseases that are destroying Christianity.

One is Biblical Illiteracy, brought on by many years of leaders that "**don't care which Bible you use**" and have produced Biblically Illiterate children, young people, and their parents. If we had a king or emperor who with all human power wanted to correct the problem of Biblical Illiteracy it would take at least three generations to accomplish it. For fifty years I have watched this problem get worse. **After years some have accepted the fact that the word *"school"* when applied to Sunday School was a disgrace to the word "school"**. They are now being called "**Life Groups**". It's out in the open that the "Life Groups" are actually recruiting tools and not Biblical schools.

The second disease is in any large church one **sees untrained teachers teaching** from **many different Biblical translations**. The teacher picks the one that is the easiest for him or her to understand. Numerous religious leaders have written about the infectious Biblical Illiteracy. It is common knowledge to anyone who reads. The absolute amazing thing is that they are doing nothing about it. Their attachment to making the mighty dollar through the selling of Bibles and literature to captive hard-nosed denominational groups is obvious. The study of the history of religion, the psychology of religion, the philosophies of religion, and addictive religious books have **virtually wiped out the daily reading of the Bible**. Psychologically there is becoming no difference between Christianity and all the other religions. The number of "nones" (Those who profess no religion) is increasing each year. Most people recognize religion as indispensable. It matters little which religion one has to call his or her own.

Christianly is not the religion of most modern people. In this new ocean wave of religion everybody is an authority. The thought is, " I know all I want to know". If I believe it then that is my religion right or wrong. We would lose 99% of the teachers in Sunday School if they were required to take a test to prove their competence. The "**know nothings" about teaching are in control**. What they call teaching is actually their personal sermons. It has been repeatedly noted that **the tragedy of the religious unrest of our age is that modern man is so ignorant of what real Christianity is that he permits himself to be fooled into**

accepting almost any kind of mutation, imitation, and falsification of true Christianity.

The modern mix of religion involves layman and clergymen. The mixing of religions has been present for 5000 years. That is why God records in many places, "Thou shalt have no other gods but me." (Exodus 20:3; Deuteronomy 5:7) The worst sin is to put "something" before God. In this modern world people put many thing before God. This is idolatry! Paul listed idolatry together with murder and adultery and related, "They which do such things shall not inherit the kingdom of God." (Galatians 5:19-21) Our conscience will be our witness before God at our judgment. (Romans 2:15) One may know God and deny Him and there is no excuse. (Romans 1:19-20) His creation is His witness through "rain and fruitful seasons", "God made the world and all things therein", and He giveth to all life and breath, and all things," "And all nations one blood." (Acts 14:17; 17:24-26) **Many today have religion without God and thus are a pagan religiosity**. They are in a state of "self-deception". We have human ideas, human logic, human reason, human philosophy, human moral ideas, and all this leads religious ideas. From denominations and **religions of the world we develop ideology that clouds our soul**. It is realism important to human life, but the reality is, it comes from ones own human ideas. Man's consciousness of the divine has been developed by his own human mind. He experiences religion, but not God. His religion never gets beyond himself. As noted the Scriptures describe this religiosity as "sin". This filters to a personal, business, social, church, and home life of sin. Man's religiosity is not only the worst sin of the human race, but it is the greatest hindrance to him being saved. The Pharisees, etc., used their religion to oppose Jesus. Their long prayers, much alms to the poor, and fasting were walls of "devils" shielding their souls from the true God standing in their presence. This is clearly synonymous with many of the organized religions of this modern age. They stand like many devils **holding God's word away from the youth and even their own children**. I have heard several visiting preachers standing in the pulpit say, "I love your preacher, I love his wife, I love his children, etc." And in his whole sermon never says he loves God. (A politician par excellence, a Christian and spiritual preacher par zero.)

Scriptures for Life

True love (verb) loveliness (adjective), and love (noun) all lead to action. Show me a "lover" who does not talk about it and I will show you a person not to be trusted. **Personal religion is the strongest force against the Gospel of Jesus in the mission field and the entire world**. This is sorrowfully true in so-called "Christian lands." The situation is so bad that the main objective of some modern evangelists is to preach re-baptism to church people. The church is the best source available to them to preach to sinners, because the sinners not in the church are not available to them. Why travel the "Roman Road" when one can travel the "Christian Road"? A land that has been Christianized with a luxury religion of self-aggrandizement with all its intellectual religiosity is a tough "nut to crack". Christ is life and **without Christ one is no better that the "dirt" he was made from** is a point not preached without God's intervention. Street preachers are laughed at because God is not with them. They frequently find a few emotional people like themselves who love to talk. I know of an emotional person who admitted to being saved and baptized eight times. He was having emotional orgies, like one can have with alcohol, drugs, sex, or religion.

There is no cross or cross to bear, repentance, or re-birth (born again, a new life, a changed person, love for worship on Sunday, love for daily Bible reading, love for a planned prayer time, love to tell the story, etc.). Religiosity without Christ is immune to attack by true "religious armor". Religious people with a religiosity without Christ are the people most bitterly opposed to living Christianity with a daily walk with Christ. Christ is conscious of being "wholly unique". Christ is the only way to Heaven. Christianity is the only absolute religion. God's Word clearly places Christianity above and incompatible with all other religions. Other religions must be amputated from Christianity. All other religions are "sin" and Christianity is the only solution. Other religions are in tough with devils, Christianity is in touch with God. **"All things are delivered unto me of my Father: and no man knoweth the Son, but the Father; neither knoweth any man the Father, save the Son, and he to whomsoever the Son will reveal him."** (Matthew 11:27) **"Jesus saith unto him, I am the way, the truth, and the life: no man cometh unto the Father, but by me."** (John 14:6) "Neither is there salvation in any other: for there is none other name under heaven given among men, whereby we must be saved."(Acts 4:12) "Without Christ, Ye worship in ignorance!" (Acts 17:23) All worship outside of God, outside of Christianity is idolatry. Man made God and his Divine Image into a god of their own mind and religious consciousness. One of the best tests for a God oriented man is, "Can he quote the entire Lord's Prayer" without thinking of something else? They do not know the only true God. Sin stands between God and Us. God looks at the heart and if God is not there all worship ceremonies are empty. They are not only empty, but are an abomination before God. (Isaiah 1:13; Ezekiel 18:24; Amos 5:21)

<u>God relates to men only through Christ who is the only source for the forgiveness of sin.</u> God will not relate to sinners without the atonement provided only by Christ. A man cannot reach God thorough his religiosity where he experiences nothing but an image produced by him. Christ is the only doctrine where man and God can meet. Without Christ man cannot experience the idea of God. Man must communicate with God to achieve salvation. The self-cantered religiosity must be replaced by a humble human with recognition and sorrow for his sins asking God to save him from an eternal death and eternal separation from God. **<u>Christ stands alone as all other religions are against Christ</u>**. With Christ we read, speak, hear, and experience the love of Christ, which we feel in our soul. We have been freed from the sins of bondage and we, as God's children cry to God, "Father". Being "born again" makes you free from the eternal consequences of sin. We continue in times of weakness to sin, but we no longer love sin. The only way to escape sin is to have the love of our Savior in our hearts. We are constantly in the process of, with God's help, making ourselves better with efforts towards righteousness and holiness with the constant building of our sanctification as long as we are alive on this earth.

This chapter began with the question, **"What Can I Do"?** The answer is, **"Nothing Without God!"** To see results from the question, one must have God with them before they can do anything. With God ones life will show results or "fruits". Young man if you forget God when you are young God will probably forget you when you are old. Sins are very temporary and transient pleasures are followed by prolonged and constant mental sorrow. With repentance God will clearly forgive and "wash one white as snow", but there are sins that **we** may not forget. Young person, this is written primarily for you. God has forgiven me all my sins, which have been many. (He will continue to forgive us all when we ask for forgiveness.) I am happy as happy can be. I have learned from my sins and they have made me stronger. Even better they have given me an understanding that I do not believe I would have had unless I had walked in the footprints of a sinner. As I add all this up and look back I wish I could say to myself that I did not do many things that I did. **John B. Gough** said, "I would give my right hand if I could forget that which I learned of life in evil company." Young people I challenge you to study God's Word. It is the only Book that speaks. It can and will give you the desire or power to not do those superficial and transient pleasures. This includes everything a young person might do to include the "big" one of **PRIDE**. The closer to God we are the more evil we become in our personal image. It is said, "You are only young once and remember this when you are old". You are only young once, **but you are old many times**. You are old in the 50's when you get up at night only once for the bathroom, you are old when you get up twice in the 60's, and you are old when you get up three times in the70's. I'm still counting for the 80's. Only if you are old will you understand this! ☒

Having children is another age of growing old, having grandchildren is another age, and having great-grandchildren is yet another age. What are "signs" and "symptoms" that one loves? The answer is, "Grandchildren". The hugs and kisses far exceed that of any other age. It is the only process that makes one happy as their bank accounts go down. "Grandchildren are the crown of old men; and the glory of children are their fathers." **(Proverbs 17:6)**

What earthy thing does age have without esteem? The answer is, "Nothing". (Reference unknown) If one sows the seeds of family and waters them with love and fertilizes them with wisdom they will grow to trees larger than you. I have felt no burden of age except I cannot run as far or walk up as many steps as I would like to be able to do. I also have a problem picking up a straight pin off the floor.

A martyr may be burned at the stake, but his truth grows with a new luster. A patriot's head may fall from the block, but his triumph speeds to victory. A great that ends on earth never perishes, but lives on in the mind of others.

It is unlikely that when one is young that he will think of ever being old or that he will die or when he gets old he will remember when he was young and now knows that he will die. A young fighter pilot is great while he is young and acts by reflexes. When he gets about twenty eight he realizes that he can get killed and tries to decide every reaction. After that he flies transport planes or takes a desk job. A young woman's age (as compared to a fighter pilot), of physical beauty last from about 17 to 35 when she no longer wants her photograph to be taken with a twenty–one your old beauty. Time changes things.

Build your life on love and life only gets better. At age eighty-two I am living the best year of my life. My sixty-four year old wife is the most beautiful woman I have ever seen. The greatest miracle of this age is that every morning when I have finished shaving she tells me I am beautiful. I can only believe this because when my mother was in her eighties in a nursing home and was a skeleton with skin on it she was beautiful to me, but would be grotesque to anyone that didn't know her.

A man without God has no back-up strength when strong adversity and mean adversaries appear. Parents live, teach, and love your children so you will never have to ask, "Why did all or one turn out bad?"

What are the concerns of a non-Christian at old age?
- **A new beginning is impossible.**
- **There is not enough time.**
- **Previous hopes are a dream.**
- **The mind and body have been wounded.**

- The spirit is gone.
- **Sins are a big memory.**
- **A conscience that accuses us.**
- **Thinking we are too old and too bad to stand before an angry God.**

Remember at that last moment if you have the chance ask for forgiveness, accept Jesus as your savior, and acknowledge that God died for your sins, and they will be forgiven in a second simply for asking and you can meet God as one of His children. What a God we have that seeks us to the end.

(12.) f. Waste of Time
<u>A waste of time is synonymous with a youth without a plan and objective</u>. Many of our college students today finish college without a plan or objective. Over a hundred years ago **Carlyle** asked a student at Edinburgh University what he was studying for. His answer, "I have not made up my mind." A man without a purpose is like a canoe without a direction, or a blacksmith hammering a red-hot iron without knowing what he is making. The result will be nothing. <u>A man may sparkle with knowledge, but without purpose be an eternal failure</u>. When one turns their back on truth they face bad circumstances. It's like pouring water on a drowned mouse. They are sailing the sea in an eggshell. One cannot capture the end of a rainbow. **There must be a possible and known objective**. The weakest person by concentration on a simple object can accomplish something. With idleness the body and mind "rust out". The active mind needs a purpose and direction worthy of its activity.

(12.) g. Job Integrity
Be loyal in your occupational work. The greatest numbers of men fail due to moral failure. God smiles on those who do unto others, as they would have others do unto them. Do your job with eternity in your eyes. Hopefully clean hands earned the dollars you leave to your family.

(13.) Worldly Morality

The seeds of vice sown in the world or something at home are a powerful force in the young mind. A tainted thought by a father or mother may take possession of the soul and grow into shame.

Our true Christianity sustains Christian morals. The true Christian life plants an individual character that may lead to a national character and destiny. The Christian's heart's tastes and the minds decisions lead to the happiness of man and renews him to the highest form on earth. God sees the secrets of the heart. (Psalms 44:21)

(13.) a. Self-Centered or Self-Denial

True or false, good or evil. Your decisions for good or evil establishes the pathway of your life. Your trust can only be in God. Certain thoughts are prayers. "Moments spent with God are pearls strung for eternity." (**Charnock**) Choice is with God, a moral God created for us. Do everything with eternity in our eyes.

To be subdued before God is the beginning of life. Man frequently subconsciously refuses to meet God because he will not give up his self-centered life. This is ones self-confession that he does not love God and has not experienced God. One's thoughts, longings, and efforts, are for ones self. The demands of being a Christian frighten modern man so much that he runs like a rabbit over the slow turtles of his self-centered life. His mind blocks out reality so there is no mental distress. This irreconcilable contradiction of life fades into intellectual oblivion. **The rightful thinking of man should be mainly listening**. Another intellectual problem that many have with Christianity is that it is above criticism. One can criticize Christianity all one wants to but it does not change. Immature minds attempt to "out think" Christianity. These thought forms override past generations and mentally declare them "antiques". The psychology is, "I am not a man of ancient times. I am a modern man." **The modern man has become so modern that he really does not care where he comes from**. Things, fame, and bank accounts make him think he is pretty when he looks in the mirror even though his mother may admit that he is ugly. This becomes so absurd that a Christian scientist says he "**sees with his ears and hears with his nose**." He continues down the path until his morality is the morality of a real modern man. "He is big." This is the modern jungle of "take it and enjoy it." "It" is on "its" own. It belongs to itself and is an intensive possessive objective of itself. "It" has power and has mastered knowledge because "it" is a lifeless thing much like a fence post except it **sees with its ears through you while you are talking**. The impersonal verb of an "it" is personal only to itself.

When a man finds that there is something beyond this life **to live** and it gets into his now mature mind his actions start looking upward instead of inward. He frequently becomes a man of truth, a man of courage, and one with an earnest and energetic soul. The work of the self-denying action is transferred to his fellow man. He then realizes the worth of this own soul.

A holy association with God moves one away from self and increases his blessings from God. This mentality of looking up produces strength and a heart to get nearer to God and listen more to Him. Good does good. Those who are unlovable because of their new knowledge become lovable. We begin to see suffering humanity hand-to-hand, face-to-face, and heart to heart. As life becomes more unselfish there is blessedness that shines forth. The disregard of self reveals a true majestic self.

Here is the story of a rich man giving a basket full of loaves of bread to a group of poor girls. They charged and grabbed for their one loaf allowed. A small girl went slowly and picked the smallest loaf. She gave it to her mother who cut it open and silver coins fell out. The young girl thinking it was a mistake returned it to the rich man. He said, "My dear child, it was no mistake. I put the money in the bread as a reward to you. I have seen your actions. **Do not thank me**. Thank God who gave me the will to be useful to your needs."

(13.) b. Live Life With Accuracy
Accuracy in life means a controlled life.
- "It is better to have self-control than to conquer a city." (Solomon, Proverbs 16:32)
- "He that controls his tongue will have a long life." (Solomon, Proverbs 13:3)
- "Those who transform the world must be able to transform themselves." (Konrad Heiden)
- "Self-control is cool and is without waste." (Ralph Waldo Emerson)
- "There is no limit to self-restraint." (M. Gandhi)

Character must be learned and disciplined. A controlled life with honesty contributes more to success and includes a moral life and financial progress. Life is short, and minutes are precious. Any success demands that one learn to be brief. Long visits, stories, praises, and prayers rarely add to a life of success. Time cannot weigh what can be measured by eternity. Be productive here on earth. Actions are what they are and their results are what they will be. The loud noise of spinning wheels goes nowhere. Plan on your own in life and the target will get closer. Don't live day-to-day expecting something to show up.

Be alert for correct alternatives. Don't be like the man who drowned on top of his house and turned down a helicopter, ride because he was expecting a boat. Little things add up to big things. If you see something to do, do it as well as you can. A bad performance of a little thing becomes a big thing.

(13.) c. Be Smart
The kindest thing to do is to be done in the kindest way. Break the ice with kind words. Let the quiet, but heavy words seem to come by chance. A joker never gains an enemy, but may lose a friend.

"Never join with your friend when he abuses his horse or his wife, unless one is about to be sold and the other buried." (**Breese**) The world gives back to every man who smiles a smile and a frown to men who frown. Being smart adds to talent, but the most powerful force on earth is love. Being smart can bring out the good side of something bad. Be gracious to those you cannot refuse and work with those you cannot overcome. "The mind is the standard of the man, but we are measured by our soul." (**Isaac Watts**)

So our standard is that of our soul.
- "When God created us he gave us the rule of right and wrong". (*War and Peace*, XIV, 18) We all have that as a standard. Our standards from above reflect the stars of glory there.
- "A young man with something of the old and an old man with something of the young may grow old in body, but never grow old in mind." (Cicero, 106-43 B. C.)
- "The soul is captain and ruler of life of humans." (Gaius Sallustius Crispus, 86-34 B.C.)
- "Obedience is the rule of nature which we learn from the work of the honeybees who teach us the order of a peopled kingdom." (Shakespeare, *King Henry* V:1.2, 187)
- "Thoughts rule the world by great men who see that spiritual is stronger the any material force." (Emerson, Phi Beta Kappa Address, 1876)

<u>**The objective of education is the formation of character**</u>. Work is the foundation of progress. "The more that is given <u>**the less the people worked, and the less they worked**</u> their poverty increases." (**Tolstoy**, 1828-1910) I have asked the question, "What would be news today"? With modern communication everything becomes old news. The only thing I have heard that would be new news would be, "Man bites dog!"

Nothing is stronger than habit except man's God given "willpower". The habit of living must give way to dying, so prepare! <u>**True salvation is rare in adults and very rare over the age of 70**</u>. "Habit with him was all the test of truth. It must be right: I've done it from my youth." (The Borough) Habits form a second nature. Be careful of your habits. As streams make rivers, and rivers make ocean, habits gather by unsuspected degrees. "God does not play dice with the world." (**Albert Einstein**) God leaves the throwing of the dice or specific planning to us.

(13.) d. Do Not Live By the Power of Money!
Do not borrow more than you can repay. If you do borrow, plan each day to pay it back. Remember death is a debt where we are all alike. Death is a debt we all must pay. At death our debt has been paid or not paid. The results are obvious. In *"Vanity Fair"* everybody lives comfortable and are thoroughly in debt, and deny themselves nothing. This is the easy jolly of *"Vanity Fair"* in the minds. Our unpaid debts at our death are an embarrassment to our family and a loss to our debtors. The Bible is not clear how God will handle this, but He will probably list it under **integrity** or honesty. There is no beauty or freedom in a house that depends on borrowing and debt. It has been said. "Pay every debt as if God wrote the bill." Most of the problems of marriage are related to money. "Words pay no debts." (**Shakespeare**) A good mind possesses a kingdom on earth. The mind has a thousand eyes that die when life is done. The mind is like a wedding cake heavy with useless experience, which crumbles to pieces under the knife of facts. A little bit of Miller philosophy is to watch a pure and beautiful wedding cake be cut with its parts given to those with a taste for sweets and with a hand held out. All that is left of the cake is its crumbs. Get the facts and reality of life or crumble with it. The idle mind does not know what it wants. The free mind can look back, stand still, or look forward with or without the realities of life and death.

Inaction zaps the vigor of the mind. The mind of man is more beautiful than the earth in which he lives. The actions of a trained mind in danger will bring out the courage needed and leads others to nobility, temperance, sobriety, and the presence of mind to danger. If man's mind becomes torpid in old age from disuse it is his own fault. **Your mind is tossing on the ocean so be sure it is in a boat with a motor and a rudder.**

Spend less than you earn and pay as you go is a principle few people in this modern age have learned. When young men are destroyed by, "You must keep up appearances", we should not blame them, but we should blame the influences that had that effect on them, **us!** Borrowing for necessities is all right, but borrowing for unnecessary wants is wrong. This brings up the cutting edge of the knife to you and your family. I have seen families literally financially slaughtered by this process. I have seen men with big salaries "go under". God's Word says, "The borrower is servant to the lender." (Proverbs 22:7) Young men should be frightened to death of un-payable debts and not incur debt in the first place.

(13.) e. Financial Freedom

What is Financial Freedom? Is it being out of debt? No. Financial freedom is being out of debt and having a retirement where you will not need to work to live and pay your bills. Do you get it? Reach the time and age in life that your time is your own. You can do anything you want to do. It is a new life. Working at least 12 hours per day for 40 years caused me to fear retirement. I did not retire until age 70. It was my time to do it. When I arrived in Florida we paid cash for our retirement home on the water of Tampa Bay and a golf course. (I don't play golf.) We cruised in our boat for one year all around Florida, the Florida Keys, and northern Bahamas. There is much time to read a book. I read books I had always wanted to read and memorized Scriptures, including the Teachings on the Mount. I have written and published ten books including this one. We are free to enjoy all the blessings of life. We are more active in church than ever. I go to the neurosurgery conference each Friday morning, which is a wonderful deja-vu.

(14.) Wisdom

What is wisdom? It is said that in the world there is "**too much intelligence and too little wisdom**". **Einstein** said, "Before God, we are equally wise and equally foolish." I like, "Wisdom is common sense to an uncommon degree." My definition of wisdom is: "Get knowledge, study it until you understand it, then you have wisdom." **(Miller)** I believe **Solomon** may say it another way, "Retain my words. Get wisdom, then comes understanding." (Proverbs 4:4,5) (Understanding must be added between words and wisdom.)

An Arab philosopher is quoted as:
There are four kinds of people.

1. **The foolish.** These who know not and know not that they know not.
2. **The simple.** Those who know not, and know they know not.
3. **The instructed.** Those who know, and know not that they know.
4. **The wise.** Those who know, and know that they know. Pay attention to these.

Job had a lot to say about wisdom. "It will die with you."(Job12: 2), Wisdom will increase your days." (Job 12:12) Job says it best with this famous verse: "Behold, the fear of the Lord, that is wisdom; and to depart from evil is understanding. (Job 28: 28) David adds, "The fear of the LORD is the beginning of wisdom: a good understanding have all they that do his commandments: his praise endureth for ever." (Psalm 111:10)

Solomon adds something we have all seen. "Fools despise wisdom and instruction." (Proverbs 1:7) Solomon says it again. "Wisdom is the principal thing; therefore get wisdom: and with all thy getting get understanding." (Proverbs 4:7) The best of all is, "If any of you lack wisdom, let him ask of God, that giveth to **<u>all men liberally</u>**." (James 1:5)

(15.) Science
How important is science?
- **Where did the ant, a social insect and cousin to the bees come from? The bees have four wings and can make honey from nectar or pollen or can produce a painful sting. How do they relate to the butterfly with two wings, but only flies in the daytime?**

Scriptures for Life

- Where does the grasshopper fit in whose legs allow him to jump 20 feet and eat a leaf? Or the swift small, exceedingly fast bird with long wings that eat insects or its cousin the humming bird that can fly still or even backwards. How about the fish eating hawk with its cousins the eagle and the osprey?
- Where do the cousins of the weasels and their flesh-eating mammals the minks and the otters come from?
- Which came first the chicken or the egg? The mother hen said to the rooster, I laid three eggs and now I have three baby chickens so the eggs come first. The rooster told her no, I married you when you were a germ cell before you were an egg. (I thought you were going to be chick-a-de instead of an old hen.)
- A grain of sand will cover 500 pores in our skin. Look in the mirror, you are 86% water.
- How smart are you? We speak over 3000 languages. There are 100,000,000 stars. Their light travels to us at 186,000 miles each second.

What is science?
It is an area of knowledge. But, there are hundreds of areas of science. So, what is science? As a young researcher I described myself as a scientist. I was placing a microelectrode intra-cellular into the brain neuron of a cat.

Albert Einstein said, "Before God, we are all equally foolish." Paul said, "The wisdom of this world is foolishness with God, preaching to those that know God it is the power of God, to them that perish (do not know God) is foolishness." (I Corinthians 1:18; 3:19)

<u>**Nothing keeps man from knowledge and wisdom like thinking he has both.**</u> An hour meditating with God is worth a lifetime of discussions with man. To be humbled before God is the beginning of life. A paradox is a statement that seems contrary to common sense and yet it is true. Christianity is filled with paradoxes. Science repeatedly blasphemes God in the name of religious research and blots out 2000 years of Christianity.

Men who bring comparative religion up to God or God down to them with their unbelief will have the lowest spot in Hell. "Those who move God to that which is not **God burns in lowest Hell**." (Deuteronomy 32:21, 22) There are levels in Hell. Hell is never full as it is a bottomless pit. (Revelation 9:1,11; 11:17; 20:3)

In the name of historical religion there has been created a modern religious historical monstrosity. Historical research has not tried to do the same thing to other religions. In words they have constructed a religion that stands against true Christianity. Just as some of the newer Biblical translations have **changed words to produce a man's Bible instead of God's Words**. They have taken away the choice in Christianity and the choice is not determined by science. They even violate Apostolic, Nicene, and the Athanasian Creeds. They are indispensable to genuine and historical Christianity. It was a stumbling-block to the Jews (Romans 14:13); I Corinthians 1:23) and now to modern man. Young people today will not be young twenty-five years from now. Those young at that time will have been left behind by the young of today, my generation and the one before me. **"Blessed is he, whosoever shall not be offended in Me."** (Matthew 11:6)

If the intellectual modern man removes the cross from Christ he is committing "**intellectual suicide**". We do not find the real Christ by our intellect or thinking. We never find Christ without thinking, but **it is the experience with Christ that makes us Christians**. No one on earth can meet God without experiencing Christ first. We experience these things and think on these things. We read God's Word, the Bible, which is the book that speaks. Without the Cross one can be moral and religious, but in his life denies Christ Himself as his only Savior. **No choice is a choice**. Meeting and accepting Christ it is said that it "Undoes" your life. You continue to sin, but no longer do you love sin. God speaks and has taken the initiative by giving his Words to us in writing. Our doubts are gone and eternal security fills or souls. Our experience and our thinking put thinking in the correct place by replacing thinking with listening. "Take heed, and be quiet." (Isaiah 7:4) "In returning and rest shall ye be saved; in quietness and in confidence shall be your strength." (Isaiah 30:15)

"That ye study to be quiet." (I Thessalonians 4:11)

"The ornament of a meek and quiet spirit, which is in the sight of God of great price." (I Peter 3:4) "Be still, and know that I am God." (Psalms 46:10) Moses said, "Stand still, and see the salvation of the LORD, which he will shew to you to day:" (Exodus 14:13)

(16.) Know What Is Important

Know what is important and stand for it. Avoid standing for things of little importance. Standing for things that are not important is mocking the facts of importance. Work with men in the faith not with those who still need to drink milk in the faith. (I Corinthians 3:2; Hebrews 5:12) "Stand fast in the faith." (I Corinthians 16:13) "Stand fast in the liberty wherewith Christ hath made us free." (Galatians 5:1) "Stand fast in the Lord." (Philippians 4:1; I Thessalonians 3:8) "Stand perfect and complete in all the will of God." (Colossians 4:12) "Stand in the true grace of God." (I Peter 5:12) **Unimportant things are contingent and chance a weakness of mind that may alter ones destiny**. Avoid whining, sighing, and complaining people since they attract attention to themselves and away from what is important. **True Christianity makes people stand on faith**. They are the giants of Christianity. They have the courage to recognize and to acknowledge sin. They have the faith, courage and knowledge to go to God for reconciliation, which He offers. He gives the courage and desire to break with sin. We need to teach our youth the knowledge of truth, the courage of convictions to teach and stand fast before man and God. **This is the force of our lives** twenty-four hours a day and seven days a week. Faith and courage on Sunday's only is not courage or faith at all. There is nothing in God's creation so small that it cannot be great in the world. Some orchid seeds are the size of dust. The Indian lotus seeds are viable for 400 years. The seeds of the American artic lupine when frozen can last 10,000 years. Jesus said, **"The kingdom of heaven (Or God) is like a mustard seed that grows like a great tree and birds lodge on its branches."** (Matthew 13:31,32; Mark 4:31,332; Luke 13:18,19) and And Jesus said unto them, **"If ye have faith as a grain of mustard seed, ye shall say unto this mountain, Remove hence to yonder place; and it shall remove; and nothing shall be impossible** unto you."(Matthew 17:20) and "**If ye had faith as a grain of mustard seed, ye might say unto this sycamore tree, Be thou plucked up by the root, and be thou planted in the sea; and it should obey you.**" (Luke 17:6) In Jesus day the black mustard of Palestine grew wild along the roadsides and fields and it could grow to fifteen feet. <u>This was the smallest seed known in Jesus day</u>. Dust can be measured on balances or one can, with a three-inch piece of paper, make a two-inch mark on it and then weigh the mark. There is nothing so small that the Devil has not breathed his breath upon it. Little deeds and little words make up the Christian life. A wise man has focused eyes, good habits, and makes the best of everything. <u>A person's character is his most important action</u>. If one thinks money can do everything, they will do anything for money. Some feel that the world owes them a living. <u>They fake an illness or injury and find a crooked or dumb doctor and lawyer and finally get on disability</u>. They are proud to hang a disability sticker on their mirror and are proud to ride their big pick-up truck with a large machine tool chest on the back into a disabled parking space and then trot into a restaurant. Their mind has falsified to them that their check each month makes them a success. I have interviewed many of these people and finally even their families understand what they are. "<u>I'm tired of working while he fakes being disabled and gets paid for It</u>." Honesty, integrity, work, and productivity gives men honor on earth, glory in their graves, and immortality in Heaven. In some beggars pride is louder than their wants. Give all men love and you get respect for yourself.

(17.) Faint Ideas Explode

W.W. Breese (1883) notes: "A man in an insane asylum could read a newspaper upside down or sideways. A mental deficient could tell the time day or night even when waked from a sound sleep. Tom, a blind man from birth, had great musical powers. We have brief views, many more are hidden, that we will not know until we see the light in God's "eternal day."

I have met people who were so ignorant that they did not know how little they knew. I have met those that seemed un-teachable and they were advised to find another career. Since, I have revised my thinking to: There are those who are un-teachable in their current environment. I learned this one day when I received a call from a neurology department chairman. He was a person with a "nice" personality and it was his nature to not terminate anyone even though to him they seemed incompetent. He had heard of my **Teachings of Knowledge Relativity.** He asked if I would take a resident for one month and if I thought he was un-teachable he would "let him go". As a favor I accepted this unusual request as a challenge. After the first few minutes with this young man I knew his problem. **He felt he knew it all and could not listen**. When I began teaching him something I knew he did not know he was on edge waiting to tell me something. I established a "listening protocol" with him. I told him that he did not know anything I wanted to know or even hear about. I told him he was about to be fired and would be fired if he did not learn how to learn during his month with me. He was not to say anything that I did not say first and he was to immediately repeat everything I said. If I said, "good morning" he was to say "good morning", If I said "good-bye" he was to say "good bye". At the end of one month he had learned several of my "Learning Systems". He finished his neurology residency with pride and had the honor of learning a system of learning. Three years later after taking his Neurology Boards he called me immediately. At that time up to 50% of the neurologists were flunking their boards related to new knowledge in muscle disease. He first gave the examiner an extended outline as to how he would approach the problem and answer the question. The examiner said, "We will go to the next question." He had not said one thing about muscle disease. He related only how he planned to answer the question. He was very excited to tell me this story and that he had passed his boards.

There is probably no one un-teachable if one can develop the correct environment for learning. I had a resident that was so frightened at taking a "mock" board exam that this person could not speak. I noted this and asked a question that I knew they knew. They had previously answered the question to me, but under those conditions could not speak to give me the answers in their mind. That person went into another specialty. I met an uneducated man who said he read his Bible daily and

had been teaching Sunday School for several years. In a group I was in he gave an absolute wrong answer to a question. I corrected him and he reacted negatively. Later I asked if we could sit down and discuss the scripture? In a harsh manner he answered, "No, my mind is made up!" I went my own way **He was un-teachable in his current mental attitude** of "knowing it all". It is hard for me to imagine anyone thinking they know it all in Biblical theology. They can know all they need to know, but can never know it all. I met two seminary graduates who thought they knew enough and were not attuned to learn more. When I finished my training I was considering another year in a specific specialty. My professor told me I did not need another year, he said, "You never stop learning." I have learned that some people do stop learning. In medicine it is said the half-life of medical knowledge is five years. If one graduates and does not continue to learn by continued education he will be a doctor of obsolete knowledge in five years.

"The geologist digs deep but cannot strike bottom. He can go back many ages, but never to the beginning. He can tell you how deep he must dig to reach fire, but cannot tell you how come the fire there? Where did the sea come from? From vapor. Where did the vapor come from? He cannot tell you and that makes him a philosopher." **William Harvey** could not tell what started the heart. **Alexander Graham Bell** could not tell sound was transferred to the brain. We know and can show the ten layers of the retina, but cannot tell how the picture is transferred to the brain and to our mind. He who knows much is one who knows he knows little.

What is life? What is death? Can you understand the depths of the sea? You cannot understand the depths of God's Word, but "you can sail over it to heaven". God came to earth and told man what was in the world from whence He came and how we could get there. When the stones were hitting Stephen he cried, "I see the heavens opened." God's universe shows its life and its consciousness. The Arab proverb says life is in two parts, "The past a dream, and the future hope." They missed that we are under the shadow of the Throne. We hear the music of Heaven as the breeze through the trees, the waves or the shore, and the power in lightening. Man is a symbol of eternity held on earth by earthly time. Goodness and kindness communicate with themselves. The purest joy cannot be described and can only be felt. Right never dies! Words are leaves, but deeds are fruits. It matters not who we are. It matters what we are. He who knows Christ and the Cross is the Christian. There is no love to God without obedience to Him. (Calvin did not understand the love of God.) Innocence does no harm, wisdom is a right choice, and virtue loves the good of society above self. The formula of the skeptical scientist in "force, matter, nature, grind." The formula of the Christian is, "God, matter, love, growth". We dream of our life, but we see eternity ahead. Our lives are filled with a grand triumphal music and constant hymns of praise.

Are You A "Lighter Knot" Drifting in A River?
A *"Lighter Knot"* is a chunk of wood from the junction of a tree branch at the tree, etc. It is rich in resin and used to start wood fires. When floating down a river it is useless. When it is used to start of fire, fire must be applied to it. It readily burns and will start slow burning wood such as oak to burn. If you are a lighter knot in a river something must retrieve you from the river, use fire to get you lighted, and then you can light others who are slow to be lighted. The river is life flowing by the cities, farms, and industry that produces the physical world from products created by God for us. We take cotton to make clothes, rugs, etc., wood to make houses, barns, etc., Steel to make buildings, railroads, etc. Our deeds take what God supplies for us to make useful and beautiful things. God made animals and us to have dominion over them to be used for clothes, shoes, food, etc. When man and woman sinned they realized they were naked and made fig leaves to clothe themselves. God had mercy on them and made coats of skins for them to wear. (Apparently this was the first killing of animals for human use in the Bible. Genesis 3: 7, 21) Man and woman had to go to work as we do also. We can weave our lives, with good deeds, words, or with disobedience, meanness, and a bad character according to our choice. God lights the fire in all of us and makes it possible for us to light the same fire in others. We can contribute to a Christian civilization or to Satan's world. Either way our world is what we make it. An Indian of

the Oneida tribe of New York said in a sermon, "I am thankful that the Creator did not give the Indian enough language to allow him to be profane without first learning English." If your children are profane someone had to teach them. Empty houses get their windows broken as do empty heads, hearts, and idle hands.

(18.) The Nones

The "Nones" is one of the fastest growing groups. This has been defined as people with no religion. I am adding to this group another group, which I call those "Conscious of none". This is a large group. These people are not fit for anything productive that is good. They are not even satisfied with what they have. They are possessed with "What they have not." (In the beginning I called this group the "nots", but the "conscious of none" is more descriptive.) They desire for things unattainable to them. Certain groups because of past discrimination believe that they deserve what they don't have and think they can never earn. They ignore other members of their group who by working and planning have become highly successful and possess almost all things that they earned. This group is happy. We see represented the highest and lowest level of society. In many cases the lowest level resorts to crime to obtain things. Immorality also frequently manifests itself in this group by hurting each other or by lying or faking disability to get on welfare or disability. **They are further destroying themselves**.

I have seen family members turn against the fakes in their own family. A businessman friend of mine told me of a group of his employees who quit their farm job with him because they could move to the city and make more on disability and welfare than he was paying them. Egotism, self-assertion, and vulgarity replace that which is truth. Weakness replaces the strong, the larger the ego, the lesser the mind. This **ape-like man** is always rattling the bars of his cage. He holds out his paw for peanuts from society. The soldier who has not learned discipline, loyalty, or hard work visualizes himself as a general.

I remember very clearly a young man friend who was going to college without a clear pathway of a career. I advised him to take the pre-medical courses because later if he decided on medicine it would not cost him an extra year of college. At the end of two years of medium grades he came to me and said he was going into medicine. He literally punched me in the chest and said, " I am as good as you are!" I answered with the issue was not being as good as me, but was he willing to work as hard as I work. After five years of college he never qualified for medical school. He retired from an alternate job after many years as a teacher.

I finished my neurosurgical training and was serving two years of military service required at that time by the Doctor's Draft Law. I was doing research in a military facility. The research assistant and I spent many hours together in the lab. He was a part–time student at a local university. I asked him about his career pathway. His answer was amazing, "I have not decided yet, I am only 32." I have no follow-upon his career. I can duplicate similar stories of a lack of life preplanning many times.

A preacher described some church members "as high flying ignoramuses, very mighty about the doctrine of a sermon, and were as decisive as sledge hammers and as certain as death. They know nothing, but are confident in everything, bullheaded beyond belief, and certain as death." They are like a theologian who goes to a sandpit to look for sugar. They measure the grace of God and tie a knot in the length of His love. They are like boys in a peepshow and wiser than their teachers. They jump over Scriptures that do not suit their desires. Preachers who work to satisfy the cliques in their church are not men, but things being used by something other than God. The empty bubbles of our society have not learned that they cannot escape from God's drudgery.

The power of society is one of the strongest forces in some lives. People live beyond their means. Follow where God leads you and be proud of your position. If a woman marries a poor man or a man who becomes poor she should be proud to be poor and make his life the best life a poor man can have. This eliminates the concept of poverty. I heard of a wife whose husband lost his executive job who said, " I wish I could just disappear." She was concerned about what her friends would say.

In life we must be sincere in what we say, do, and feel. Being wealthy is an expensive thing, it costs more than its worth. I have asked men who were worth up to 200 million dollars what would one have to have be considered wealthy. It is always five million and another said if you have 100 million "you never have to worry." The difficulty with the answer seems to be, "there is never enough money for a person who has it whether they worked for it or inherited it.

The house that God built is the gate to Heaven. With a moral earnestness, weigh and study life, watch with a realistic eye, and know that all the acts and thoughts of life that make up our lives. Do not be a "conscious none" or one a stranger to the Divine, without courage to know right from wrong. Find something good and be faithful to it and it will grow and grow. Courage and convictions will lead to truthfulness and this leads to praise. Continue to find God, and be brave enough to become spiritual. I love to tell my preacher friends that, "I am a spiritual man." Their look and reaction is between shock and "This man is crazy". I then say, "I am also a man of this world." They relax and our conversation continues, as if I never said anything. I am a spiritual man and I know I am a man of this world.

One of our state religious papers gave the story of a "godly" man. Later, I heard a preacher in his sermon say that he had a problem with men being called "godly". I have known several men that I consider "godly", my father being number one. **Webster** defines *"godly"* as a word with one meaning as being *"devout."* If one has trouble with a man being called "godly" what would you call godly? How can you use Webster's word? In reality all men are "godly" since they are created in God's image. "Religious language has lost its original significance." Ones testimony must be true and not filled with sentimentality or exaggerations. You are a saint (All Christians are) so act like it! Enter to fellowship with fellow Christians. Do what you can, big or little including prayer, read and quote scripture, sing a hymn even if you can't sing and render some service to the other saints. Tell what the Lord has done for you. Jesus said, **"Howbeit Jesus suffered him not, but saith unto him, Go home to thy friends, and tell them how great things the Lord hath done for thee, and hath had compassion on thee."** (Mark 5:19) Most of us are at times cowards and ashamed of being true, whole-hearted Christians. "Yea, and all that will live godly in Christ Jesus shall suffer persecution."(II Timothy 3:12) "Having a form of godliness, but denying the power thereof: from such turn away."(II Timothy 3:5) According as his divine power hath given unto us all things that pertain unto life and godliness, through the knowledge of him that hath called us to glory and virtue: (II Peter 1:3,6) There is a strength of character and a magnanimity of soul. Remember prayer can resolve all of our problems.

The Desire to Investigate and Learn
The desire to learn is a blessing and a curse. The desire to learn can be toward good or bad. It frequently leads to sins. It is also the thirst of the soul. It has been said to be the **spiritual drunkenness of the soul** as the drunkard can never be satisfied. There may be a slow growing like leprosy of learning all the vast secrets of God until one finally becomes mentally numb and thinks he knows more than God. Eve's temptation to learn more than God and her ability to tempt Adam in the same way changed the world. Ones soul may be in one place and their heart in another. Our desires make us want to know how and why. The perseverance for a new generation of knowledge produces what has been called, "**a lust of the mind**." But, never miss a moment of learning because the desire may not return and the question remains a question in your mind forever.

The desire for knowledge produces one of the largest choices. We must learn to choose good or bad knowledge. There is an itch to see which is not to be seen. The forbidden fruit is always out there. Choose the direction for more knowledge and if the direction is good the circuits of the brain will grow to build the circuit network bigger and bigger. However, if the direction for knowledge is bad knowledge the circuits will also grow to be bigger and bigger. Remember all knowledge builds on itself. Leading scholars of the Middle Ages developed a mixture of Christianity and paganism, but in my opinion they were in kindergarten compared to the scholars of today. In the last 100 years there have been at least 250 Bible translations, but only three have been literal translations. Many of these had words missing or words added until they became man's words replacing God's Words. God gave us His Words. Only three translations are currently available that attempted to reproduce the original revelations of God. That should be our standard for teaching, but one can go into any church and learn that there are many non-scholastic teachers teaching from different translations all of them by their own choice. Nobody notices! Even worse since the methods of teaching are not proved or academic for100 years our church schools have produced parents and their children as Biblically Illiterate. We and all our leaders that I know of have violated God's commandment to teach our children and grandchildren His Word. (Deuteronomy 4:9 4:40, 5:29; 6:2, 7; 11:19, 21; Psalms 78:5, 103:17). Every one of us is charged, "As ye know how we exhorted and comforted and charged every one of you, as a father doth his children."(I Thessalonians 2:11) Paul learned when talking with the Hebrews "For when for the time ye ought to be teachers, ye have need that one teach you again which be the first principles of the oracles of God; and are become such as have need of milk, and not of strong meat." (Hebrews 5:12) There are thousands of such teachers teaching Scripture today who need teaching themselves. This is true of our entire public schools where many teachers need teaching as noted by their poor knowledge both in public schools and church schools.

(19.) Sevens of Character
(<u>The number "seven" has a prominent place in ethics</u>.)
There are seven scholastic gifts of the Holy Spirit, seven virtues, seven spiritual works of mercy, and seven corporal works of mercy, seven deadly sins, and seven penitential psalms.) (***Encyclopedia of Religion***, Vergilius Ferm, p. 705)

(19.) <u>a. Gifts of the Holy Spirit</u>
The **seven scholastic gifts of the Holy Spirit are:**

Scriptures for Life

Wisdom, understanding, counsel, might, knowledge, piety, and **the fear of the Lord**.
(Isaiah 11:2)

(19.) b. Spiritual Works

There are **seven spiritual** and **seven corporal** works of mercy from the scholastic theology of **Aquinas**.

The spiritual include:
To teach the ignorant, **to counsel** the doubtful, **to console** the sad, **to reprove** the sinner, **to forgive** the offender, **to bear with** the oppressive and troublesome, and **to pray** for all.

(19.) c. Corporal Works of Mercy
The corporal works of mercy are:
feed the hungry, **give drink** to the thirsty, **to clothe** the naked, **to shelter** the homeless, **to visit** the sick and prisoners, **to ransom** captives, and **to bury** the dead. (Matthew 25:35-44)

(19.) d. Deadly Sins
The **seven deadly sins** listed by **Gregory the Great** are:
Pride, envy, anger, dejection, avarice, gluttony, and **lust**.
Cassian listed eight:
gluttony, fornication, avarice, anger, dejection, sloth, vainglory, and **pride**.

(19.) e. Pentential Psalms
The **seven pentential psalms** are:
Pslam 6, 32, 38, 51, 102, 130, 143. These are listed as penitential exercises and to counteract the seven deadly sins. **Psalm 6 for wrath, Psalm**

32 for pride, **Psalm 38 for gluttony**, **Psalm 51 for lust**, **Palm 102 for avarice**, **Psalm 130 for envy** and **Psalm 143 for sloth**.

(19.) f. Virtues

The **seven virtues**, four of which are **Plato's** "cardinal virtues" of **prudence**, **temperance**, **fortitude**, and **justice** and three Christian theological virtues of **faith**, **hope**, and **love**.

(20) Character and Importance of Virtue

To be or not to be young man and young woman is the question you must answer to God and yourself and to the person you are immoral with. Young lady one slip and everyone knows what you are. Young man your many slips may be laughed at, but you and God and all your friends and girls know what you are. "A good name is rather to be chosen than great riches." (Proverbs 22:1) A man's name is the name he makes for himself. No man is rich enough to buy back his past. **Everyone should fear death until he has something that will live on after his death**. Whatever work you do, do well for in the grave where you are heading there is no more work. (Ecclesiastes 9:10) Courage to be moral leads to honor even to the girl you refused to lose your morality. Our soul and heart are free from the power of evil and its shackles on our flesh if we but control it for good. In this modern age more people than ever need courage. The conviction that no one cares is the modern barbarians who say there is no God. Young men do not be barbarians walking around with a proud face and a "know it all attitude". None of us knows it all. For those of us who are His, God counts our fears and raises up our moral courage. Living in this world is for the Lord's cause. Our words are the leaves, but our deeds are the fruit. Our diving energy gives action to our fruits and courage and honor to our souls.

Virtue
- "It is important, generosity of soul, sincerity, earnestness, and kindness." (Confucius)
- "The earth, sea, air, sky, and virtue are the dwelling places of God." (Lucan, the Civil War, IX, 1,578)

- "Virtue is its own reward." (Prior, *"Imitation of Horace"*, Silius Italicus, Diogenes Laertius, Thomas Brown, Religio Medici, John Barza, Washington Irving)
- "Love Virtue for she alone is free…or, if Virtue feeble were, Heaven itself would stoop to her." (John Milton's, *"Comus"*, 1.1019)
- "Peace is not an absence of war, it is a virtue, a state of mind, a disposition of benevolence, confidence, and justice," (Spinoza, *"Theological Political Treatise"*)
- "Ambition is the soldiers virtue" (Shakespeare, *"Antony and Cleopatra"* III, I, 22)
- "Uncommon Valor was a Common Virtue", (Chester Nimitz, "Marines at Iwo Jima", 1945)
- To die honorably is the greatest part of virtue. We lie here enjoying timeless fame. (Simonides, 556-468 B.C.)
- "The natural aristocracy among men is virtue and talents." (Thomas Jefferson in a letter to John Adams, 1813)
- "Virtue extends our days". (Marcus Martialis, 40-104 A.D.)
- "Ours is a world of nuclear giants and ethical infants." (No virtue) (Omar Bradley, 1948)

Human virtues make other human virtues stronger and add to their number. Our virtue speaks as we think and performs as we do which produces good that adds to good, and so on and so on. Virtues build up in our soul. **The test of our love to God is our obedience**. To help heal the evils we must be free from them. We cannot show the way we must walk the way. We cannot pray, as we should unless we live, as we should. A man who is variable in his character is inconsistent in his luxuries. Charity itself is a luxury.

(21.) Nine Charismatic Gifts

There are nine charismatic gifts described as fruit of the Spirit by Paul and they are:
- Love
- Joy
- Peace

- **Longsuffering**
- **Gentleness**
- **Goodness**
- **Faith**
- **Meekness**
- **Temperance**

(Galatians 5:22,23)

67 Criteria Noted

Final Note:

When one thinks of one's character, remember the Holy Spirit dwells in us (Romans 8:11; Ephesians 4:6) and guides us. (John 16:13) and the Kingdom of Heaven is within us. (Luke 17:21)

"Even so, come Lord Jesus. (Revelation 22:20)

About the Author

Rear Admiral Joseph H. Miller (MC) USNR retired from the Navy Reserve in 1986 after 34 years. Since retirement with annual Permissive Orders he has had consecutive Navy Orders since 1952 or for 60 years. The Permissive Orders included lectures, consultations, and informal visits to Navy hospitals. At retirement RADM Miller had completed three years as the first reservist to serve as a Deputy Surgeon General for Reserve Affairs (OP093R), Pentagon, and concurrently as Commander Naval Reserve Force, Force Medical Officer (006), New Orleans, 1983-1986. On active duty he served as Chief of Neurosurgery, National Naval Medical Center, Bethesda, Maryland, and subsequently as Chief of Neurosurgery, US Naval Hospital, Da Nang, Vietnam. As a consultant to the Surgeon General RADM Miller chaired a committee of five prominent civilian leaders of neurosurgery to develop a Navy neurosurgical residency. In the Pentagon with Dr. Barry he wrote and staffed the directive for the establishment of Physician Reservists in Medical Universities and Schools. (PRIMUS). RADM Miller has been to Bethesda over 100 times, Yokosuka, Japan 40 times and every other Navy hospital in the world and several of the large Air Force and Army hospitals. (For 2 months he provided neurosurgery coverage at the Tripler Army Medical Center.) He served in the Joint Chiefs of Staff (J4) war planning section as the only Flag officer. Later a Flag officer billet was established in J4. The first assignment was a Navy Reserve Flag Officer.

He had duty with the Commander in Chief Central Command, MacDill Air Force Base, December 1982, February 1983, and February 1984.

RADM Miller's Military decorations include: Legion of Merit, National Defense Service Medal, Armed Forces Reserve Medal, Navy Unit Commendations, Republic of Vietnam Civil Action Unit Citation, Vietnam Service Medal, Republic of Vietnam Gallantry Cross Unit Citation, Navy Pistol Marksmanship, Meritorious Unit Commendation, Combat Action Ribbon, and Navy Commendation Medal with Combat V.

In civilian life RADM Miller practiced Neurosurgery from 1960 through December 2000 (40 years) and served as Chief of Neurosurgery at Methodist University Hospital, Memphis, and Vice-Chairman of the Department of Neurosurgery University of Tennessee and University of Tennessee Training Director in Neurosurgery at the Methodist University Hospital. (1983-2000)

RADM Miller was Founder and Director of the Memphis Neurosciences Center at Methodist Hospital and the University of Tennessee. He developed an international academic interchange in Neurosurgery with 27 countries. (1985-2000) He is on the Voluntary Faculty of USF Medical School.

He developed 24 Clinical Teaching Systems, was an invited medical lecturer 56 times and had numerous Medical Journal publications.

He is certified by the American Board of Neurosurgery and his memberships include: The American Association of Neurological Surgeons, The Society of Neurological Surgeons, The American College of Surgeons, The Society of Medical Consultants to the Armed Forces and The Association of Military Surgeons of the United States. Civilian activities include: Mission Service Corps, The White House, May 1978. Served on the Boards of Union University, Mars Hill College, Samford University, and Regions Bank. He has researched and lectured on the *Philosophy of War* more than ninety times.

RADM Miller has been a Southern Baptist Deacon for 59 years, and taught Sunday School for 58 years. He is currently a member of First Baptist Church, Brandon, Florida. He is a 5,258-hour pilot and recently passed the course to be a Coast Guard Captain. He is married to Cathy Miller and they live in Apollo Beach, Florida.

His books with AuthorHouse:

1. *Mysteries of the Southern Baptist Beliefs Revealed*
2. *You live! You Die! Who Decides*
3. *Faked Disability: A Shame of America*
4. *Explore the Brain for the Soul*
5. *Calvin, The Psychopath*
6. *The One Love*
7. *Eighty Years Behind the Masts*
8. *After 400 Years of the King James Bible*
9. *The Few*
10. *Scriptures for Life*

CPSIA information can be obtained at www.ICGtesting.com
Printed in the USA
LVOW120816021012

301095LV00001B/5/P

9 781477 271247